CHINA

A
Multimedia
Guide

Mary
Robinson
Sive

D1367481

Neal-Schuman Publishers, Inc.

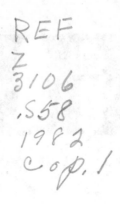
Published by Neal-Schuman Publishers, Inc.
23 Cornelia Street
New York, New York 10014

Printed and bound in the United States of America

Library of Congress Cataloging in Publication Data

Sive, Mary Robinson, 1928-
    China, a multimedia guide.

    Includes indexes.
    1. China--Bibliography.   I. Title.
Z3106.S58 [DS706]   016.951   81-22390
ISBN 0-918212-53-7   AACR2

China offers us the example of the most people
living together over the longest period of time.
How they worked things out is the most
fascinating and least known segment of the
human story.

—John King Fairbank

Contents

Foreword

During the last five years, first and third grade students participating in an ongoing research project, initiated by the staff of the Information Center on Children's Cultures, were asked to comment on their knowledge of and attitudes towards the world's peoples. The Chinese were one of the specific cultures included in the questionnaire. Most students had a positive impression of the Chinese people, but when asked questions that related to cognitive knowledge, many children gave some variation of the following: they use chopsticks; they look different; they eat good food; they celebrate Chinese New Year; they speak a different language. If one were to survey students at higher grade levels throughout the United States today, I am confident that the answers would not differ greatly. Although the People's Republic of China is constantly in the news, most Americans have little real knowledge of this nation.

For many years, China was not open to visitors from Western countries. It was difficult for writers to produce informative, current materials. Since 1976, with the liberalization of Chinese policies concerning tourism and the great changes which have taken place in Chinese society, a flood of publications and audiovisual productions has appeared. Ms. Sive's *China: A Multimedia Guide* is the first extensive listing of recent materials in all formats for grades K–12. This selective guide also includes earlier works that can still be recommended.

In my daily work as Director of the Information Center on Children's Cultures, I have noticed a great increase in the number of questions about China. Some of these information requests come from growing Chinese–American communities and from educational systems whose teachers and librarians recognize their responsibility to present materials about the various ethnic groups living in their districts. Other requests are coming from areas in which the study of China is being emphasized in the Asian or global studies curriculum due to China's size, population, and distinctive political and social system.

As the reviewer of Asian materials for the Center's bibliographies, I am able to examine the majority of educational resources on China for elementary and junior high students. However, most teachers and librarians do not have the opportunity nor the time to review such a wide range of materials. This *Multimedia Guide*, with its descriptive as well as critical statements about each book, film, filmstrip, record or other item, will be most helpful to the teacher or librarian wishing to expand a limited collection. Ms. Sive's comparative assessments, which cross-reference items in different formats, will further assist the user. In addition to its coverage of print and nonprint materials, the *Guide* also notes outreach centers, museums, and special libraries, all sources of additional information. The inclusion of materials on the People's Republic of China, Taiwan, Hong Kong, and the Chinese population in North America, and the listing of some foreign imprints, increase the usefulness of this volume.

No longer can a single textbook provide the knowledge and insight that today's students require. A wide variety of resources in many formats is necessary for an enriching educational experience that will allow students to immerse themselves in the study of another culture. Ms. Sive's *Guide* will facilitate the expansion of students' knowledge beyond the "chopstick and Chinese New Year" syndrome.

Melinda Greenblatt
Director-Librarian
Information Center on Children's Cultures
January 1982

Preface

In February 1976, while visiting San Francisco for a conference, I took an early morning stroll through Chinatown. In a small park a group of people were engaged in dance movements that riveted my attention. I inquired of a bystander, and was told the group was performing Tai Ji Quan. Hooked, I myself began the study of Tai Ji Quan approximately one year thereafter.

It may be my acquaintance with this one aspect of things Chinese that predisposed me to note the flood of China materials on the educational market. As editor of *Media Monitor*, a periodical guide to learning resources, author of *Selecting Instructional Media*, a standard media selection reference, and author of the "Media Notes" column in *Curriculum Review*, I routinely scan catalogs, reviews, and announcements of books, films, and audiovisual releases. The China emphasis could not be missed. It occurred, of course, in response to political developments—the continuing improvement of relations between the United States and the People's Republic of China, culminating in the exchange of diplomatic representatives on January 1, 1979. As this is written, a Chinese trade exhibit is touring the United States.

The 1971–72 rapprochement between the two countries had signaled an earlier outpouring of instructional materials, assessed, along with books and films from the 1960s and earlier, in Posner and deKeijzer's *China: A Resource and Curriculum Guide* (entry 555, first edition, 1972). That authoritative and indispensable work cannot help with the output of the five years since the publication of its most recent edition (1976). The deaths of Zhou Enlai and Mao Zedong in 1976 triggered vast changes in Chinese politics and society, making some works from the early 1970s obsolete.

It appeared that a comprehensive survey of all media offered to schools or likely to be of use to them could perform a service. Such a survey would result in a guide to resources that could be recommended for instructional and reference use by students in grades kindergarten through junior college, and their teachers.

That this work hopes to do.

This guide is comprehensive in scope, encompassing

1. the Chinese populations of Hong Kong and Taiwan and persons of Chinese descent in North America, in addition to the People's Republic
2. fiction and folklore, in additon to nonfiction
3. information carriers in all formats—books, pamphlets, government

documents, films, filmstrips, slides, recordings, maps, pictures, posters, and study prints

It is selective, seeking out materials meeting stated criteria only. Those criteria are detailed in the Introduction.

It is up-to-date, encompassing materials released through December 1980 (and a few for 1981). Several titles released in 1981 would have deserved a place here had there been the opportunity to add them during the process of publication. One must be singled out: a new edition of *Through Chinese Eyes* (ed. by Peter J. Seybolt. Dist. by Center for Teaching About China, entry 568. 2 vols., 160 pp. ea., $5.95 ea. pap.) which compiles excerpts from periodicals published in China.

While primarily intended for elementary and secondary schools, this work may be applicable also in two-year colleges. It is designed to aid media specialists and librarians who need to improve their collections dealing with China; teachers and students who need resources for specific classroom needs; and curriculum developers who want to know the full range of available resources.

The need for a bibliographic guide to instructional materials about China may not be apparent when one considers that United States schools spend little time on the study of Asian cultures and history. But the opening of the United States diplomatic relations with the People's Republic in 1978 brought back into the nation's consciousness what had been a forbidden subject for three decades. Now that the Chinese mainland is once again an accepted trade partner and travel destination for United States citizens, the need for accurate information becomes imperative.

Too, over a half-million persons of Chinese birth or ancestry live in the United States, about 120,000 in Canada. They have both emotional ties to and a "need to know" about their ancestral homeland.

The selection of instructional materials is not an exact science and any particular exercise thereof is bound to be subjective. Another selector's choices of materials for the study of China would undoubtedly differ from this particular one, but it probably would not differ substantially.

It is hoped that the array presented here is sufficiently broad to offer something for most, and a variety of materials for many instructional purposes. Educators can make their own initial selections here, preview them, preview other, perhaps newer materials, and compare. I ask them to bring errors of omission or commission to my attention.

This work could not have been accomplished without the help of experts. The manuscript benefited enormously from close readings given it by Terry Lautz of the China Council of the Asia Society and Carrie Waara of the University of Michigan–PEASE, and I am extremely grateful for their interest. I was fortunate in having access to the extensive library of the Information Center on Children's Cultures in New York City and to the friendly help and advice of its staff, headed by Melinda Greenblatt, Director. Rosalind Daly of the National Committee on United States–China Relations and Susan L. Rhodes of the Asia Society, New York office, steered a newcomer to the subject in the right direction. Outreach directors at university Asian studies centers proved unfailingly resourceful and interested in the project. Finally, I would like to thank Hon. Benjamin Gilman, Member of Congress, for help with obtaining government documents; Larry Lazar, Principal, Franklin Avenue Elementary School, Pearl River, New York, for providing screening facilities; Michael Miller, Donnell Film Library, New York City, for many hours of China films; my patient editor, Maureen Crowley; and the dozens of publishers and audiovisual distributors who provided examination copies. I alone am of course responsible for any errors.

Mary Robinson Sive

Introduction

China: A Multimedia Guide brings books, pamphlets, and periodicals (including government publications and ERIC documents), audiovisual products, maps and atlases, and sources for further information to the attention of teachers and students. Each is described in sufficient detail to enable readers to make informed decisions about its potential uses. Brief references to additional materials within the text of the numbered entries, and listings of art and historical museums, and of China Council affiliates bring the total sources to over 650.

Most of the numbered entries were examined by the compiler and can be recommended, if only to illustrate varying points of view. Those that could not be seen but are included on the basis of what could be learned about them from reviews in professional journals and other secondhand information, including publishers' announcements, are marked with an asterisk (*).

In choosing from a total of well over twice the numbered entries, the compiler was guided by the overall purpose of this guide. That purpose is to seek out not the "best" materials on China, but those deemed best for instructional uses in North American elementary and secondary schools. This intention in turn required a definition of the objectives likely to be common to such instructional purposes.

"A Curriculum for International Education," a statement by the Asia Society (see entries 566 and 579), eloquently expresses goals that, it was assumed, would apply to most China curricula. It is reprinted in the Appendix (pp. 169–173).

There is more to learning about China than reciting its dynasties, or eating with chopsticks. Suitable objectives are exhaustively articulated in *Studying China* (entry 552) by Professor Leonard S. Kenworthy, a longtime champion of international education.

The premise was that an essential aspect of almost any China study, even a brief one, would seek to convey some of the following understandings at appropriate maturity levels:

1. acquaintance with a culture not one's own. Where China study is undertaken in connection with a bilingual, bicultural, or ethnic heritage program, this objective would read "greater knowledge of one's ancestral heritage."

2. respect for cultural differences. Programs designed to demonstrate the power of stereotypical thinking are annotated below (see entries 497, 498, 501). Breaking down cultural barriers in students' thinking can be initiated with games such as *Bafa-Bafa*[1] where

players learn to play by seemingly arbitrary cultural rules. *Global Studies for American Schools*[2] has many specific ideas and lesson plans, and suggestions for program and student evaluation.

3. comparative distances in time in Chinese, European, and American and Canadian history, and China's discovery of Europe long before Europe's of China. Genevieve Foster's many children's books with such titles as *The Year of Columbus, The World of William Penn, George Washington's World, The Year of the Flying Machine*,[3] and others, can help correlate events in China to simultaneous ones from about 1500 on, but that period represents only a little over one-tenth of recorded Chinese history.

4. Chinese ethnocentrism as a factor of the country's three-thousand year self-sufficiency

5. Chinese adaptation of a Western idea, Marxism, to its peculiar situation. Additional sources on Socialism and Communism such as Michael Harrington's *Socialism*[4] may be required.

6. hard work and frugal living are not new to most Chinese

7. differences and similarities among the three Chinese countries —The People's Republic of China, The Republic of China (Taiwan), the Crown Colony of Hong Kong

8. the place of the individual in Eastern versus Western thought and social structures

9. ideographic versus alphabetic writing

10. the manipulation of public opinion in China and the West. It is almost impossible to enter on a study of China without also embarking on one of propaganda. For that reason a deliberate effort was made to include materials promoting varying points of view.

Materials included in this guide had to be pertinent to the achievement of such goals and objectives. They were also judged on content, authority, format, technical quality, cost, and availability.

Content

Subject coverage of this work, as noted in the Preface, extends to all aspects of Chinese life now and in the past. It strives, particularly, to alert the reader to works that correctly present the China that is evolving since Chairman Mao's death in September 1976. A post–1976 publication or release date does not necessarily guarantee that that will be the case, and annotations point out instances where coverage of recent changes in leadership and direction is lacking.

Fiction can convey powerful understandings and has an important place in learning about other times and places. Both Chinese and non–Chinese writers are represented. The children's and adult stories coming out of the People's Republic in translation give insight more into what its residents are taught than into actual conditions—but that is significant in itself. As was said above, China offers a superb field for a case study of propaganda.

Folktales are an effective way of bringing another culture to young children. The selection presented here can serve both for reading aloud and for independent reading.

A word must be said about the titles that have passed for books about China in standard children's literature collections. *The Five Chinese Brothers, Fish in the Air*, the *Little Pear* books, *Tikki Tikki Tembo, The Story About Ping, Young Fu of the Upper Yangtze* are all fine, and the books and their film and filmstrip versions can be enjoyed for their own sake. But the child who knows China only from books such as these knows little about its past and nothing about its present. Regrettably, a search of many standard selection tools for children's media will turn up little besides these.

Biography offers a human interest approach to the study of a foreign milieu that has great appeal to young people. It is for that reason than an effort was made to list a maximum number of biographies, a number of them unfortunately out-of-print.

The target audience specified dictated the omission, with few exceptions, of university press books, and of others of interest primarily to the scholar or the specialist. Only some that lend themselves to reference use by teachers or advanced high school students were included, particularly where subject coverage would otherwise be meager.

Other categories deliberately omitted are books catering to the specialized interests of business people, those of fleeting popular attention, and reminiscences by Westerners of the "good old days" in China before World War II.

Authority

Most of the materials included present objective or balanced points of view. Others, for reasons stated, are quite partisan. Students can learn to discriminate by comparing differing points of view. They need to understand, for example, the political climate of the Korean War and Cold War periods. They will learn that it is not easy to know the truth, particularly about a subject long shrouded in mystery, as China was.

Negative views of the People's Republic of China undoubtedly are well exemplified in materials that remain on library and media center shelves from the 1950s and 1960s. To achieve fuller representation of more recent expressions of that nature, this guide makes room for one or two titles that might otherwise have been excluded.

The thrust throughout was to inject a healthy dose of realism into the quaintness with which China and the Chinese have traditionally been pictured. Titles that in any way depict Chinese as inferior or peculiar, or express other forms of condescension, were omitted. The Asia Society in a 1976 study found that textbooks on Asia published for use in United States schools were frequently characterized by

- superficial treatment of Taoism and Confucianism;
- overemphasis on 'stagnation' before the 20th century;
- inaccurate emphasis on economic poverty and problems;
- preoccupation with political and social restrictions, without examining alternative interpretations such as the "serve the people" spirit;
- outdated treatment of United States relations with the People's Republic of China.[5]

With the new enthusiasm in the United States for detente and intensive trade with the People's Republic, a certain amount of naiveté is becoming noticeable in some materials, and could be added to the list.

The Society's warnings in "Approaching Materials on Asia" are available from the Society, and a more pointed evaluation form, derived in part from the textbook project and formulated by the University of Michigan Project on Asian Studies in Education (entry 575) is reprinted on pages 173–175. Both entered into the selection process for the present work.

Recognized China scholars are represented by those of their books that most nearly fit the intended audience of this work, and an effort was made to include most of them while avoiding works of an entirely academic nature.

Another group of authors is also represented: those who wrote favorably about the Chinese Communists before it became fashionable to do so. Edgar Snow, Agnes Smedley, Anna Louise Strong suffered in the Cold War period. Today their works are again in print.

Format

As noted in the Preface, print and nonprint media in all formats were within the purview of this guide. This scope includes periodicals concerned solely with China, and special issues of others where such issues are devoted entirely to China, but not separate periodical articles, with one or two exceptions.

The emphasis is on monographs, but chapters within larger works are cited when necessary for effective subject coverage (e.g., religion, science). There the preference went to books, including textbooks, of regional or continental rather than worldwide scope (e.g., *East Asia*,

Asian Folktales). It goes without saying that relevant information may be found in general encyclopedias, historical dictionaries, geographic handbooks, and other common reference works and that, in fact, these may offer an excellent starting point (but note the comment about bibliographies below, p. xxi). It should also be noted that for highly current data, reference to such sources as *Current Biography*,[6] *Facts on File*,[7] and *Statesman's Yearbook*[8] is a must. The names and data are changing frequently.

Filmstrip sets devoted entirely to China or the Chinese were given preference, but in one or two cases a portion of a set is singled out, particularly where such portion may be purchased separately. Again, many other sets contain one or two strips in point. Teachers are advised to search the collections of their school or district for such titles, comparing them to those recommended here.

Though an effort was made to achieve subject coverage in a variety of media for each age level, selection did involve some choices between formats. Operative factors for such choices were suitability of presentation to subject matter, expected instructional usage, and—other factors being equal—cost. The study of China and the Chinese is not a standard curriculum component, certainly not at elementary and middle school levels, but may be a good choice for enrichment work by especially interested, or gifted and talented, students. Small "building level" media are quite appropriate for such independent or small group study and for cognitive skill development, and were given preference over the more costly film medium. But a book could be an even better choice, as when the choice is between a $35 beautifully produced art book and a $75 filmstrip set with inferior narration.

Cost

Its availability in a paperback edition was an important factor for choosing a book for annotation, as was the cost in relation to subject coverage for all media. Schools and libraries cannot afford—and should not be asked to pay for—padding, whether it is pages in books or frames in filmstrips that are essentially void of content. They must choose the most cost-effective presentation that will achieve the intended purpose—possibly choosing a heavily illustrated book over a set of slides, slides over a film, or a book over a multimedia kit in which the printed materials are the most valuable part. The cost of purchase must be weighed against the expected usage.

In making choices for this guide, filmstrips were sought out whose parts can be purchased separately and which sell for $100 or less. It was also recognized that films over thirty minutes in length may become tedious and do not permit class discussion after showing. Shorter films, besides being less expensive, may make their points more effectively. They were selected whenever possible. The availability of 16mm films in less expensive videocassette format is noted in many cases; in others, inquiry should be made of distributors.

All annotations are written so as to give readers clues for making their own cost/benefit analyses knowing their own classroom needs.

Technical Quality

Superb execution was expected of a book selling for $25–$30 or more, or of a film costing several hundred dollars, particularly where the topic was art. The same pictorial quality cannot be expected in a paperback or an inexpensive study print. Some of the Foreign Languages Press paperbacks indeed are produced in a manner not considered acceptable in the United States, but the price is right and they offer unique primary source material.

Other considerations were comprehensible organization, pleasing layout, proper correlation of text and visuals, clear soundtrack, well-captioned illustrations—the bare essentials for bringing content effectively to the user.

In the case of children's books it was expected that the reading level would be appropriate to the interest level and to the book's appearance.

The quality of a teacher's guide counted in evaluating audiovisual productions, and is generally described in the respective annotation. Films and other media unaccompanied by teacher's guides were included where little or nothing else was available, or where it was deemed a guide was not essential.

Free booklets from the official Taiwan Chinese Information Service (entry 580) are enumerated to provide balance to the preponderance of resources favorable to the People's Republic.

Availability

Annotated books were ascertained, whenever possible, to be in print as of 1980/81 or, if out of print (o.p.), are titles that readers can reasonably expect to find in school or public libraries. The availability status of books changes rapidly and it would be impossible to arrive at a listing that excluded out-of-print or out-of-stock titles. In any case, this work is intended not only as a purchasing but also as a library guide. China Books & Periodicals (entry 562) distributes some books that publishers have declared out-of-print, and others may be obtained from wholesalers or remainder houses.

Anyone planning to teach about China will need Posner and deKeijzer's *China: A Resource and Curriculum Guide* (entry 555) for its essays and its evaluations of adult and high school books and films released to 1974. For that reason there was no need to include many titles mentioned in that source. Those that are mentioned are here because of their unique merits, or for the sake of complete subject coverage—but only if they are in print.

Audiovisual items are included only if they are offered for sale in vendors' 1980/81 catalogs, except in the case of films. Withdrawn films are noted as "available from rental libraries."

With few exceptions, annotated items are the output of United States publishers and audiovisual producers, or, if published elsewhere, are available through United States distributors.

Final Selections

Further choices had to be made, within the confines of the criteria stated above, to achieve some degree of balance of topics, age levels, and media.

Certain topics are widely covered in a variety of media, offering considerable latitude for selection. Others have to be searched for, and it may be necessary to settle for a less suitable presentation.

Fewer materials are available for elementary grades on almost all topics, with the exception of folklore. Thus, the choices there were less selective and some titles are included simply because they are the only ones to be had.

An occasional book or filmstrip set includes one or several chapters or segments that seemed valuable enough to compensate for lack or merit of other portions, and were selected for that reason. The determining factor was reasonable cost in relation to potential benefit, and the need for subject coverage.

Annotations for titles that may not be first-choice generally state, directly or by implication, the rationale for their inclusion, or issue the necessary caveats.

Looking within a brief period of time at the whole universe of media on a given subject enables one to evaluate each title in context far more readily than can be done when reviewing one at a time. Reviewers for library-oriented publications such as *American Reference Books Annual, Booklist, Choice, Library Journal*, or *School Library Journal* are expected to assess each title they review in relation to comparable ones already in existence. Even they are not expected to make cross-media comparisons, i.e., comparing filmstrip X on a given topic with multimedia kit Y, charts or study prints with an illustrated book or booklet.

This guide makes a deliberate effort at such comparisons, stressing presentation in the most appropriate medium and alerting the reader to alternatives.

Publishers and audiovisual distributors vary widely in their policies regarding requests for review and preview copies. Some omissions may have resulted from an item's remaining elusive despite searches in a half-dozen libraries and repeated requests. These, though unavoidable, are regretted.

Organization

The five main parts of this work annotate resources for, respectively, primary and elementary grades, middle school and junior high schools, senior high schools and adults; maps and atlases; and professional resources for teachers. Parts 1 through 3 are in turn subdivided into non-fiction and fiction, and books and audiovisual media. Part 5 consists of two sections—books, and sources of further information such as outreach centers and organizations. Sundry directories and media evaluation guidelines, a chronology, and a table of variant spellings complete the contents. Author and name, title, and subject indexes give access to all numbered entries and to additional materials mentioned in annotations and in the Introduction.

The bibliographical citation for each numbered entry supplies all data needed to find the item in a library or to order it. These include, for print: author or editor's name, title, series information, edition, place of publication, publisher, year of publication, whether illustrated, number of pages, price, paperback publisher if different, price of paperback, grade level. The reading level, as stated by the publisher, is added in a few cases, and ED numbers are noted for ERIC documents, as are SuDoc numbers and S/N numbers for government publications.

Nonprint entries include the title; series, set, or kit information, if appropriate; a description, including running time, color, black and white, frames, etc.; producer's name; date of production; distributor if different; price; rental price; grade level. Parts of filmstrip sets are entered under the discrete title, with the title of the set in parenthesis, if the part can be purchased separately. Both individual and set titles are entered in the Title Index.

The prices are those noted in the 1980–81 edition of *Books in Print* or in publishers' or distributors' 1980–81 catalogs.

The annotations for items not examined by the compiler are restricted to objective data. When the latest edition of an annual publication was not available for examination, the review makes reference to the one seen, while the bibliographical citation describes the current edition.

The annotations seek to convey the subject coverage of each title selected for entry, note its special features, and make occasional suggestions with reference to usage or mention comparable or related titles in the same or other formats. When a nonfiction book does not have an index this fact is noted. Only bibliographies of unusual merit receive mention.

Additional Guides

To supplement the present work educators will want to turn to the books noted in Part 5, Professional Resources. They will likewise want to extend this guide with regional directories annotated in that section to learn about resources within their own regions, or to seek the help of regional outreach centers.

Students are not well served by the bibliographies appearing in the reference books they are likely to find in their school and public libraries. The listings in the *Encyclopedia of China Today* (entry 312), in the Reference Shelf volumes (entries 304, 343), and in even the *Worldmark Encyclopedia of the Nations*,[9] a reference work in common use by upper elementary students, consist almost entirely of books suitable for the college level and up. As the present work demonstrates, there are many, many titles more appropriate to younger age groups.

A Note on Spelling

Pinyin romanization is the transliteration system officially adopted by the People's Republic of China, and for that reason is employed in this volume. The Table of Variant Spellings in the Appendixes (p. 188) supplies equivalents in the more familiar Wade–Giles transcription.

Chinese names commonly state the family name first, followed by the given name without an intervening comma (Doe John). In this work a comma is added in the case of author entries (Doe, John). This may be a usage abhorrent to purists, but it does avoid confusion and clearly identifies the last name for those accustomed to the practice of European languages.

How to Order

Titles should be ordered directly from their publishers or distributors (see the Directory, pp. 189–202), or from wholesalers. Government documents should be ordered from the Superintendent of Documents, using S/N numbers and enclosing payment. Some may be available free on request to the issuing agency, or through members of Congress. ERIC documents may be ordered on microfiche from ERIC Document Reproduction Service at $.91 for up to five fiche of ninety-eight pages each. The ED number and payment, including postage, must be included.

Notes

1. simulation game. Del Mar, Calif.: Simile II, 1973.
2. Washington, D.C.: National Education Assn., 1979. 88pp. $5.95 pap.
3. Foster, Genevieve. *George Washington's World.* New York: Scribner, 1977. *The World of William Penn.* New York: Scribner, 1973. *The Year of Columbus.* New York: Scribner, 1969. *The Year of the Flying Machine.* New York: Scribner, 1977.
4. New York: Bantam, 1973.
5. Asia Society. *Asia in American Textbooks: An Evaluation.* 1976. 342pp. ED 124 439
6. New York: H.W. Wilson. monthly.
7. New York: Facts on File. weekly.
8. New York: Macmillan. annual.
9. 5th ed. New York: Worldmark Press, 1976.

Part 1
Materials for the
Primary–Elementary Grades

Books

Nonfiction

Most of the titles annotated in this section are trade books, with the exception of two especially structured for classroom use (entries 18 and 25). Books and one periodical from Part 2, Materials for the Middle School–Junior High, are cross-referenced as also appropriate for intermediate grades.

The Chinese imports (entries 20, 24, 47, 53, 71, 79, 81) are representative of, though superior to, the run of the Foreign Languages Press picture books, which are often full of unsubtle moralizing and tedious illustrations with little appeal. Check the catalog of China Books and Periodicals (entry 562) for titles available at any given time.

1. Balen, Carol Ann. *Chinatown Sunday: The Story of Lillian Der.* Chicago, Ill.: Contemporary Books, 1973. o.p. illus. unp. Gr. 4–6.

This black-and-white photo-essay with first-person narrative follows the life of a spirited Chinese-American fifth-grade girl living in a Chicago suburb. Lillian has a Chinese name as well, but when asked whether she is from China or Japan, she answers that she is from Chicago.

2. Barker, Felix. *The Glorious Age of Exploration.* New York: Doubleday, 1973. illus. 488pp. o.p. Gr. 5 up.

Chapters on the Silk Road, Genghis Kahn, Kubla Khan, and the Polos are accompanied by numerous reproductions of contemporary representations.

Beers. *Chiliying.* See entry 151.

3. *The Bellerophon Book of Ancient China.* Santa Barbara, Calif.: Bellerophon, n.d. Dist. by China Books & Periodicals. unp. $2.95 pap. Gr. K–4.

A large-size coloring book with good bits of Chinese history and culture, though suffering from some inaccuracies and careless spellings of Chinese words.

Bonavia. *Peking.* See entry 154.

4. Borja, Robert and Corinne. *Making Chinese Papercuts.* Chicago, Ill.: Whitman, 1980. illus. map. 40pp. $8.25. Gr. 4 up.

Examples of scissor-cut and knife-cut designs from China's various regions are illustrated, and there are also directions for making papercuts from patterns provided and from one's own designs.

5. Boyd, Mildred. *Rulers in Petticoats.* New York: Criterion, 1966. illus. 224pp. o.p. Gr. 5–9.

Empress Zi Xi (Tzu Hsi), the last Manchu ruler, is given about ten pages, but they touch only slightly on the corrupt and shaky nature of her regime.

6. Buck, Pearl S. *The Man Who Changed China: The Story of Sun Yat-sen.* Landmark Series. New York: Random, 1953. illus. 185pp. $4.39. Gr. 4–6.

A sympathetic presentation by the compassionate American woman who grew up in China and was the prolific author of books on matters Chinese for both adults and children. Dr. Sun (1866–1925) devoted his life to the overthrow of the Manchu dynasty and the achievement of national unity under a republican government. He served briefly as the first president of the Chinese Republic. See also the biography by Spencer (entry 211) for an older age group.

7. Buell, Hal. *The World of Red China.* New York: Dodd, 1967. illus. 79pp. $5.95. Gr. 5–9.

Considering the date of its publication, Buell's book is an astoundingly objective treatment of life in the People's Republic, though the "Red" in the title is unfortunate. Introductory material covers history and geography. The black-and-white photographs, mostly from Japanese sources, emphasize children and young people.

Carpenter. *The Old China Trade.* See entry 162.

8. Cheng, Hou-Tien. *The Chinese New Year.* New York: Holt, 1976. illus. unp. $5.50. Gr. K–4.

Scissor cuts by the author with minimal text illustrate customs associated with the New Year, from preparations through the Lantern Festival.

Family observances and visiting of friends and relations are emphasized, and the signs of the Chinese zodiac and methods for calculating the animal symbol for each year are explained.

China: All Provinces and Autonomous Regions. See entry 166.

China Pictorial. See entry 167.

9. Cooke, David C. *Taiwan, Island China.* New York: Dodd, 1975. illus. 158pp. $5.95. Gr. 5–9.

Cooke, the author of numerous nonfiction books for young people, writes clearly and understandably about the land and people, the capital, philosophy and religion, food, language, family life, festivals and celebrations, marriage customs, and other topics. The many photographs, mostly from official sources, show a more motorized and Westernized society than that of the People's Republic. The book is objective, with much information that is applicable to Chinese culture in general, and only slightly dated.

Crook. *Abacus Arithmetic.* See entry 173.

10. Dietz, Betty, and Park, Thomas C. *Folksongs of China, Japan and Korea.* New York: Day, 1964. illus. 47pp. o.p. Gr. 5 up.

Includes nine traditional songs from various Chinese provinces, with music (in key of C or G), Chinese text in phonetic transcription and English words. (The floppy disc that comes with the book has Japanese and Korean songs only.)

Doeringer. *People of East Asia.* See entry 175.

Dupuy. *Military History of the Chinese Civil War.* See entry 176.

11. Fawdry, Marguerite. *Chinese Childhood.* New York: Barron's, 1977. illus. 192pp. $14.95. Gr. 3 up.

An eighteenth-century Chinese scroll depicting boys at play is the loose frame for this miscellany of games, puzzles, puppets, sweets, dolls, embroidery, toys, dragons, and other artifacts of childhood. Some photographs of contemporary children and modern toys are included. The author is director of the Toy Museum in London.

12. *Festivals in Asia.* New York: Kodansha, 1975. illus. 66pp. $6.95. Gr. K–4.

"New Year with Hsiao Ming" tells of a New Year celebration by Chinese living in Singapore, with watercolor illustrations that convey the multiracial character of that city. It is useful for conveying the concept of "Overseas Chinese" to very young students.

Fitch. *Their Search for God.* See entry 180.

13. Glubok, Shirley. *The Art of China.* New York: Macmillan, 1973. illus. 48pp. $6.95. Gr. 4 up.

Glubok, on the staff of the Metropolitan Museum of Art, has written many similar works, each serving as a superior introduction to the art of a specific people or culture. The scope of this work extends through the nineteenth century, and historical contexts are usually supplied.

14. Goldston, Robert. *Long March, Nineteen Thirty-Four to Thirty-Five: A Red Army Survives to Bring Communism to China.* New York: Watts, 1971. illus. 66pp. $4.47. Gr. 6 up.

The title is a misnomer, as this is a straightforward history of China from 2000 B.C. to 1949, with only a few pages about the Long March. The use of the pejorative "Red" is regrettable.

15. *Graves, Charles P. *Marco Polo.* Champaign, Ill.: Garrard, 1963. 96pp. o.p. Gr. 3–6.

A large-print simplified biography for beginning readers.

16. Gray, Noel. *Looking at China.* New York: Lippincott, 1974. illus. maps. 64pp. $8.95. Gr. 3–6.

Clear, unbusy black-and-white and color photographs and the text shed light on life in a commune, school and work life of young people, history, land and waterways, food, clothing, health, science, industry, sports, performing arts, and the cities of Hangzhou (Hangchow), Nanjing (Nanking), Shanghai, Suzhou (Soochow), and Xian (Sian). The coverage reflects educational practices of the early 1970s.

17. Gross, Ruth B. *A Book about Pandas.* New York: Dial, 1974. illus. unp. $4.95. Scholastic, $1.25 pap. Gr. K–3.

Covers the habitat of pandas and their relation to raccoons, and includes delightful black-and-white shots of playful pandas in zoos.

18. Hammond, Jonathan. *China: The Land and Its People.* Morristown, N.J.: Silver-Burdett, 1976. illus. maps. tables. 61pp. $6.99. Gr. 4–9.

A good introductory text with excellent art work, many color photographs, and political and physical maps, but also some textbook-type pictures. A charming captionless "daily timetable for commune family" illustrates the round of farm chores, family and communal meals, and the roles of father and mother, and could serve as a springboard for crosscultural studies even for primary students. Other visuals include the layout of a typical commune, a schematic representation of China's government, and a historical timetable. There is also a brief gazetteer and statistical data (as of 1974). The text touches on the land and people (including ethnic diversity), early history, old and new art, present-day family life, food, sports, education, writing, wall newspapers, the army, medicine, communist ideology, inventions, and the Cultural Revolution, and includes biographical sketches of Sun and Mao.

19. Hawley, E.M. *Chinese Folk Designs.* New York: Dover, 1949. illus. 315pp. $6.50 pap. Gr. 4 up.

Several hundred papercut designs in white on colored backgrounds.

20. He, Yanrong. *The Little Athletes.* Beijing: Foreign Languages Press, 1979. Dist. by China Books & Periodicals. illus. 20pp. $1 pap. Gr. K–4.

Only captions accompany the bright pictures of Chinese youngsters engaged in high jumping, tug-of-war, ping-pong, jump rope, and other games and sports similar to those played in North America.

21. Hitz, Demi. *Lu Pan, The Carpenter's Apprentice.* Englewood Cliffs, N.J.: Prentice-Hall, 1978. illus. 48pp. $5.95. Gr. 3–5.

Delicate line drawings by the author illustrate the believably told biography of the builder and inventor who lived in the fifth century B.C., and whose carpenter's manual is still in use. One of the few realistic books about China for the very young.

22. Hsiao, Ellen. *A Chinese Year.* New York: Lippincott, 1970. illus. 64pp. $3.95. Gr. 4–6.

The Chinese-born author–illustrator describes the customs, legends, and events experienced by herself and her brother when they spent a year with their grandfather in a small town, in pre-World War II days. The book is illustrated with papercuts and pen-and-ink sketches.

23. Hughes-Stanton, Penelope. *See Inside an Ancient Chinese Town.* New York: Watts, 1979. illus. map. 29pp. $6.90. Gr. 5 up.

Text and better-than-average textbook illustrations in this British import extensively describe the life of the people in Loyang, capital of the Han empire in the first century A.D., without attention to political events. Coverage extends to topics such as the Great Wall, papermaking (well illustrated), farm work, burial customs, leisure activities, marketplaces, food preparation, and the life of the upper classes.

24. *I Am On Duty Today.* Beijing: Foreign Languages Press, n.d. Dist. by China Books & Periodicals. illus. 13pp. $1.50 pap. Gr. K–3.

A delightful picturebook of "helpers" (identified by red armbands) in a Chinese kindergarten.

25. Jennings, Jerry E., and Hertel, Margaret Fisher. *China.* Grand Rapids, Mich.: Fideler, 1979. illus. maps. tables. 224pp. $9.95. Gr. 5 up. R.L. 6.0–7.4.

The well-illustrated, easy-to-read text presents a fair picture of the land and climate, history (brief), government (present), communes, cities, education, sports and recreation, arts and crafts, economy, agriculture, natural resources, industry, transportation, and communication. There are three pages on Taiwan, and chapters of similar length on the changing role of women, the shaping of public opinion, and communism. It is geared for conceptual teaching emphasizing basic human needs and the development of thinking and problem-solving skills. Sample lesson plans, discovery materials for students, and unit tests are available. The text and data vary hardly at all from the 1977 edition, and the index has no entries for "Gang of Four" or "modernization."

26. Johnston, Susan. *The Fun with Tangrams Kit.* New York: Dover, 1977. illus. 32pp. $1.75 pap. Gr. 3 up.

Tangrams are Chinese puzzles made by cutting a square into seven prescribed shapes that are then recombined into many different figures.

This work supplies 120 tangram designs and their solutions and two sets of tangram pieces.

27. Jue, David F. *Chinese Kites: How to Make and Fly Them.* Rutland, Vt.: Tuttle, 1967. illus. 51pp. $6.50 pap. Gr. 5 up.

History and uses of kites, materials needed, and instructions for ten designs.

28. Kan, Bettie S.L. *Jing Ho Hauk Ho.* 1976. Dist. by Childrens Book and Music Center. 2 vols. $5.25 ea. pap. Gr. 3–6.

Designs for tracing and directions for constructing an abacus, papercuts, tangrams, kites, lanterns, noisemakers, and other objects will be excellent for craft projects.

29. Knox, Robert. *Ancient China.* New York: Watts, 1979. illus. 44pp. $6.90. Gr. 5–9.

Encyclopedic coverage of the role of rivers, life on farms and in towns, gods and thinkers (Confucius, Lao-Tzu, Buddha), war and weapons, clothes, life at court, arts and crafts, technology, writing and painting, death and burial, music, gardens, hunting, trade and travel (the Silk Road). Text is set in two columns and is well broken up with plentiful illustrations and boxes highlighting various topics. Color photos of art works make up most of the visuals; others are undistinguished. Parallel chronology of events in China, Asia, the Mediterranean world, and Northern Europe from 1500 B.C. to A.D. 907 is given, and a glossary is included.

30. Lamb, Harold. *Genghis Khan and the Mongol Horde.* Landmark Series. New York: Random, 1953. 182pp. o.p. Gr. 4–8.

Aside from the title's "horde" and the jacket picture showing objectionable stereotypes, this is an acceptable account of the thirteenth-century Mongol leader and ruler. No children's biographies of him are in print.

31. Leckie, Robert. *The War in Korea, 1950–1953.* Landmark Series. New York: Random, 1963. 173p. illus. o.p. Gr. 4–8.

Good coverage of the China aspect of the Korean war.

32. Lewis, John. *The Chinese Word for Horse and Other Stories*. New York: Schocken, 1980. illus. 96pp. $7.95 pap. Gr. 3 up.

The title story, a cautionary tale of a farmer who wants to be a man of leisure, introduces the Chinese characters for man, horse, tree, forest, rain, stream, and others with clear and bold graphics that take some liberties with accepted Chinese brush strokes but are quite appealing. Two additional stories employing similar techniques are "The Chinese Word for Thief" and "The Chinese Man and the Chinese Woman." Each of the stories is also published separately by Two Continents Press (New York: 1977. $3.95 ea. pap.).

33. Lim, Sing. *West Coast Chinese Boy*. New York: Scribner, 1979. illus. 64pp. $12.95. Gr. 3–5.

The author grew up in Vancouver and writes most informatively of the tasks and incidents of childhood. The first-person text is suitable for young people older than the grade range indicated but they—though not adults—may be turned off by the author's childlike illustrations, particularly those in color. Wong's *Fifth Chinese Daughter* (entry 218) is the classic Chinese-American biography for young people.

MacFarquhar. *The Forbidden City*. See entry 186.

Meltzer. *The Chinese Americans*. See entry 191.

34. Moore, Joanna. *China in Pictures*. New York: Sterling, 1979. illus. 64pp. $4.99; $2.50 pap. Gr. 5 up.

Topics include geographical features, resources, history (mostly pre-1949), government structure, the Communist Party, the People's Liberation Army, family life, education, sports, music, arts and crafts, food, health, religion, agriculture (by region), industry, fishing, and mining. There are black-and-white photographs.

Moskin. *In Search of God*. See entry 193.

35. Nach, James. *Hong Kong in Pictures*. New York: Sterling, 1977. illus. 64pp. $4.99; $2.95 pap. Gr. 5 up.

After a brief historical sketch, over one hundred black-and-white photos from British Information Services and official Hong Kong sources, their informative captions, and the brief text deliver information on all aspects of life in Hong Kong today. The book covers the land, climate, resources, government, life of the people (housing, medical care, customs), the arts, economy, tourism, agriculture, trade, fishing, industry—and smuggling.

36. Nancarrow, Peter. *Early China and the Wall.* Cambridge Topic Book. Minneapolis, Minn.: Lerner Publications Company, 1980. (first published by Cambridge University Press, 1978). illus. 51pp. $5.95. Gr. 4–9.

Some of the black-and-white illustrations are highly informative, showing the method of molding bronze objects, a schematic representation of the period of the warring states (480 to 220 B.C.), ancient city plans, and the method of constructing the Great Wall by means of forms made of bamboo poles lashed together (scaffolding made of lashed bamboo poles is still used today for high-rise buildings). The focus is on the period to about 200 B.C.

37. Newton, Douglas. *The First Book of Kings.* New York: Watts, 1961. illus. 66pp. o.p. Gr. 5 up.

Included are one-page sketches of Emperors Kang Xi (K'ang-Hsi, 1654–1722) and Qin Shi Huang Di (Ch'in Shih Huang Ti, 259–210 B.C.) and of Genghis Khan.

38. Pine, Tillie S., and Levine, Joseph. *The Chinese Knew.* illus. by Ezra Jack Keats. New York: McGraw-Hill, 1958. illus. 32pp. o.p. Gr. 3–5.

Simple text and colorful pictures show basic science concepts involved in various Chinese inventions—kites, shadow pictures, pottery and porcelain, stringed instruments, the abacus, papermaking, ink, block printing, the compass, the wheel, waterproofing of cloth, and watertight sections in ships. Traditional Chinese practice is contrasted with today's technology, followed by directions for simple experiments applying the principles entailed. Text and illustrations relating to the abacus make references to computers that are seriously dated, but the rest remains topical.

39. Rau, Margaret. *The Giant Panda at Home.* New York: Knopf, 1977. illus. 80pp. $6.99. Gr. 3–6.

Detailed pencil drawings and text describe the panda's natural habitat and other birds and animals of its mountain environment.

40. Rau, Margaret. *Our World: The People's Republic of China.* New York: Messner, 1978. illus. 128pp. $7.79. Gr. 4–8.

An account of the admission of the People's Republic to the United Nations in 1971 introduces a brief overview of traditional China—seen as built on the suppression of peasants and women—and of the political events of the 1920s and 1930s culminating in the Communist triumph of 1949. The bulk of the volume portrays life in the People's Republic, emphasizing school and sports, Beijing (Peking) and other cities, communes, doctors and medicine, the army, natural resources, the Great Leap Forward, and the Cultural Revolution. The discussion of foreign relations notes the takeover of Tibet and war with India in the 1950s. The author was born in China of missionary parents.

41. Rau, Margaret. *The People of New China.* New York: Messner. 1978. illus. 128pp. $7.79. Gr. 4–6.

Eight vignettes of contemporary life in a village, a town, a river port, and five cities portray three-generation families engaged in various occupations and stress the contrast between the old and the new China. Black-and-white photographs are by the author, who was born and reared in China. A pronunciation guide is included.

42. Rau, Margaret. *The Yangtze River.* New York: Messner, 1970. illus. 96pp. $3.64. Gr. 4–6.

43. ———. *The Yellow River.* New York: Messner, 1969. illus. 95pp. $3.64. Gr. 4–6.

Black-and-white photographs and large-print text supply essential geographical information, and some on history, culture, and industry.

Romualdez. *China: A Personal Encounter.* See entry 202.

Rugoff. *Marco Polo's Adventures.* See entry 203.

44. Sasek, Miroslav. *This Is Hong Kong.* New York: Macmillan, 1965. illus. 60pp. $5.95. Gr. 3–5.

A colorful, picturebook introduction to farmers, city dwellers, and boat people of Hong Kong, with no mention of the influx of refugees from the People's Republic after 1949.

Schafer. *Ancient China.* See entry 204.

Schell. *Modern China.* See entry 205.

45. Schloat, G. Warren, Jr. *Fay Gow: A Boy of Hong Kong.* New York: Knopf, 1964. illus. unp. o.p. Gr. K–5.

The black-and-white photographs tell the story here, with a little text to help. They depict the daily life of a family of fishermen living on a junk, even showing such details as how to hold chopsticks when eating rice or soup.

46. Seabolm, Seth H. *China Coloring Guide.* 1979. Dist. by China Books & Periodicals. 32pp. $2.50 pap. Gr. K–3.

Outline pictures of the Great Wall, ping pong, and Chinese people, activities and objects.

Seeger. *Eastern Religions.* See entry 206.

47. *Selected Drawings by Chinese Children.* Beijing: Foreign Languages Press, 1979. Dist. by China Books & Periodicals. illus. 80pp. $3.95 pap. Gr. K–5.

Seventy pictures, in color, by Chinese children from three to fourteen show school scenes, home and farm activities, the zoo, and other familiar—and unfamiliar—doings. The same publisher's *Pictures by Chinese Children* (1976, 72pp., $3.95) can serve the same purpose.

48. Shannon, Terry. *Children of Hong Kong.* Golden Gate Junior Book. Chicago, Ill.: Childrens Pr., 1975. illus. maps. 61pp. o.p. Gr. 4–6.

Many black-and-white color photos, plus brief text, tell about the lives of children from various social classes, their families' customs, and their festivals.

Sidel. *Revolutionary China.* See entry 207.

49. Soong, Maying. *The Art of Chinese Paper Folding: For Young and Old.* New York: Harcourt, 1948. illus. 132pp. $6.50. Gr. 1–5.

Students can follow the directions in over two hundred diagrams without adult help.

50. Sung, Betty L. *An Album of Chinese Americans.* New York: Watts, 1977. illus. 65pp. $5.90. Gr. 5–9.

Black-and-white photographs and text illustrate present-day Chinese-American life, personalities, customs, and problems, as well as Chinese-American history.

51. Sung, Betty L. *The Chinese in America.* New York: Macmillan, 1972. illus. 120pp. $6.95. Gr. 4–7.

This upbeat history of Chinese immigration from the early days of discrimination to, as the author sees it, the present climate of opportunity includes black-and-white photographs.

Tamarin. *Voyaging to Cathay.* See entry 213.

52. Thompson, Brenda, and Overbeck, Cynthia. *The Great Wall of China.* First Fact Books. Minneapolis, Minn.: Lerner, 1977. illus. maps. unp. $4.95. Gr. 2–3.

Nice outline maps clearly show the extent of China at various times in its early history, the location of the Wall, and the route of Marco Polo. Other illustrations are of no more than comic-book quality, but the total adequately presents the story of China's unification, its invasion by the Huns, the building of the Wall, and Mongol rule.

53. Tian, Yuan. *Chinese Folk Toys and Ornaments.* Beijing: Foreign Languages Press, 1980. Dist. by China Books & Periodicals. illus. 77pp. $4.95 pap. Gr. K up.

Artists' interpretations of traditional toys used in the celebration of festivals show clay figurines and others made of wood, bamboo, and porcelain.

54. Van Note, Peter. *Tangrams, Picture-making Puzzle Game.* Rutland, Vt.: Tuttle, 1966. illus. 55pp. $1.95 pap. Gr. 3 up.

Tangrams, the Chinese puzzles made by cutting a square into seven prescribed shapes that can then be recombined into hundreds of different figures, offer a unique outlet for creativity and an avenue for enrichment. Here we are shown some two dozen figures and are given a set cut from construction paper with which to copy them. Solutions are in the second half of the book. See also the film *Tangram* (entry 139).

55. Van Woerkom, Dorothy. *The Rat, the Ox, and the Zodiac*. New York: Crown, 1976. illus. by Errol Le Cain. unp. o.p. Gr. K–3.

The Chinese system for naming the years is explained through a legend. The attractive large pictures can easily be seen by those listening to the stories.

56. Walsh, Richard. *Adventures and Discoveries of Marco Polo*. Landmark Books. New York: Random, 1953. illus. 183pp. o.p. Gr. 4–6.

Rugoff's *Marco Polo's Adventures in China* (entry 203) may be used to supplement the quite meager illustrations here.

57. Watson, Jane Werner. *The People's Republic of China: Red Star of the East*. Champaign, Ill.: Garrard, 1976. illus. 112pp. $6.57. Gr. 3–6.

Easy-to-read text in good-sized print and black-and-white photos survey the history, geography, and past and current social conditions, including life at home and in school.

58. Wolff, Diane. *Chinese Writing: An Introduction*. New York: Holt, 1975. illus. 46pp. $5.95; $2.50 pap. Gr. 4–9.

This should be the first choice for introducing the notion of a written language whose characters may be read in any one of several spoken languages (the same ideographs serve both various Chinese dialects and also Japanese). The author explains the function of tone in spoken Chinese, the construction of written sentences, and finally instructs the reader in the materials needed, how to hold the brush, how to form strokes, and in the stroke order. Her overemphasis on "pictures" in Chinese characters causes some confusion. Black-and-white photos and drawings amply illustrate the text, which also includes a dictionary for practice.

59. *The World's Great Religions*. New York: Golden Pr., 1958. illus. 192pp. o.p. Gr. 5 up.

Relevant chapters are "The Path of Buddhism," with a map showing its spread from India, and "The Philosophy of China." The latter comments on the decline of religious practice under Communism, after explaining the concepts of Yin and Yang, the practice of ancestor worship, and the teachings of Lao Tzu and Confucius. Pictures showing religious observances predominate over text.

Zetterholm. *China: Dream of Many.* See entry 220.

Fiction, Folklore, Poetry

The reader who misses familiar titles à la The Five Chinese Brothers *here should refer to the discussion in the Introduction, page xv. In choosing folktales for this section, preference went to the relatively few interpretations by writers and artists of Chinese extraction and to anthologies, particularly those published in paperback. Besides folktales, this section cites representative children's literature from the People's Republic, in translation, and the few English-language children's books that deal with Chinese and Tibetan themes, present and past, in a fairly realistic manner. Advanced students may wish to try some listed in Part 2, Materials for Middle School-Junior High Grades.*

Many of the children's books put out by Foreign Languages Press are quite heavy-handed in their moralizing, and the illustrations also are generally unsubtle. Check the catalog of China Books & Periodicals (entry 562) for titles available at any given time.

60. *Belting, Natalia. *The Land of the Taffeta Dawn.* New York: Dutton, 1973. illus. o.p. Gr. 1–4.

Highly imaginative text and illustrations of Tang China as seen by Viking Traders.

61. Carpenter, Frances. *Tales of a Chinese Grandmother.* Rutland, Vt.: Tuttle, 1972. illus. 261pp. $5.95 pap. Gr. 3–5.

This collection of thirty tales from authoritative sources was originally published in 1937.

62. Chang, Isabelle C. *Chinese Fairy Tales.* New York: Schocken, 1968. illus. 74pp. o.p. Gr. 2–5.

A handsomely illustrated collection of twenty-six tales, good for independent reading. Some have been recorded (entry 109).

63. Cheney, Cora. *Tales from a Taiwan Kitchen.* New York: Dodd, 1976. illus. 160pp. $5.95. Gr. 4-6.

Twenty-one stories representing the Chinese, aboriginal, and Japanese cultures on the island, authentically illustrated with paper cuttings by a Taiwan artist and by reproductions of paintings. The editor collected the stories while stationed in Taiwan with the U.S. Navy.

64. Cheng, Hou-tien. *Six Chinese Brothers.* New York: Holt, 1979. illus. unp. $5.95. Gr. K-4.

This variation of the familiar folktale tells how the boys outwit the king. It is illustrated with the author's red-and-black scissor cuts.

65. *Chinese Fairy Tales.* New York: Peter Pauper Press, 1961. illus. 60pp. $2.95. Gr. 4-6.

Woodcuts in red, gold, and black accompany twelve traditional tales.

66. Crofts, Trudy, ed. *The Hunter and the Quail.* Emeryville, Calif.: Dharma Publishing, 1976. illus. unp. $3.75 pap. Gr. 2-6.

A legend told by the Buddha about one of his former lives, from the Jataka Tales. See also *Jataka Tales* (entry 68).

De Jong. *House of Sixty Fathers.* See entry 223.

67. *Demi. *Liang and the Magic Paintbrush.* New York: Holt, 1980. illus. unp. $9.95. Gr. 1-4.

The magic brush makes everything Liang paints come to life. For other versions see entries 75, 82, and (in a filmstrip) 114.

68. DeRoin, Nancy, ed. *Jataka Tales.* Boston: Houghton, 1975. illus. 82pp. $5.95. New York: Dell, $.95 pap. Gr. 3-6.

A readable retelling of thirty tales attributed to the Buddha. See also Crofts' *The Hunter and the Quail.* (entry 66).

69. Dolch, Edward W. *Stories from Old China.* Champaign, Ill.: Garrard, 1964. illus. 166pp. $6.57. Gr. 2–5. R.L. 3.

The only in-print collection for beginning readers, this contains twenty stories and is enhanced by a pronunciation glossary.

70. *Harris, Peter. *Monkey and the Three Wizards.* Scarsdale, N.Y.: Bradbury, 1977. illus. unp. $7.95. Gr. 3–5.

Monkey outwits three evil wizards in this episode from *Journey to the West.* Other adaptations are found in entries 73 and 81.

71. *Havoc in Heaven.* Beijing: Foreign Languages Press, 1979. Dist. by China Books & Periodicals. illus. 84pp. $3.95 pap. Gr. K–3.

Stills from a cartoon film adaptation of the Chinese classic *Journey to the West,* with brief captions, telling some of the adventures of the Monkey King. See also entries 81 and 89; for a filmstrip version see entry 141; and for an opera based on the same legend, see entry 134.

72. Hume, Lotta C. *Favorite Children's Stories from China and Tibet.* Rutland, Vt.: Tuttle, 1962. illus. 119pp. $7.50. Gr. 2–5.

The nineteen stories are brief and the illustrations old-fashioned.

73. Jagendorf, M.A., and Weng, Virginia. *The Magic Boat and Other Chinese Folk Stories.* New York: Vanguard, 1980. illus. 236pp. $8.95. Gr. 3–6.

One of the few anthologies that assembles folktales from both the Han Chinese and minority cultures, this handsome collection of thirty-three tales from twenty-one ethnic groups also features notes about the stories and the different nationalities. Sensitive black-and-white line drawings by Wan-go Weng lend grace.

74. Kendall, Carol, and Li, Yaowen. *Sweet and Sour: Tales from China.* Greenwich, Ct.: Seabury, 1978. illus. 112pp. $7.95. Gr. 3–6.

Twenty-four tales, whose themes include Taoist beliefs about nature, humor, and hero tales, are illustrated with line drawings. Their dates, from the third century B.C. to 1911, are indicated.

75. Kimishima, Hisako. *Ma Lien and the Magic Brush.* New York: Four

Winds, 1968. Dist. by Childrens Book and Music Center. illus. unp. $5.95. Gr. 1–4.

The story of the boy who learns to paint with a magic paintbrush and outwits the greedy mandarin is here translated from Japanese and interpreted by a Japanese illustrator. Other interpretations are Demi's *Liang and the Magic Paintbrush* (entry 67) and Mui's *The Magic Brush* (entry 82). *Chinese Tales* (entry 114) contains a filmstrip version which lacks the sensitivity of these books.

76. Kuo, Louise and Yuan-Hsi. *Chinese Folktales*. Millbrae, Calif.: Celestial Arts, 1976. illus. map. 175pp. $5.95 pap. Gr. 4 up.

A map of China, a chronology of Chinese history, and a glossary extend the usefulness of this collection of thirty-five stories from both the Han Chinese and other ethnic traditions.

77. Lewis, Richard, ed. *The Moment of Wonder*. New York: Dial, 1964. illus. 138pp. o.p. Gr. 3–7.

Chinese and Japanese nature poetry with fine black-and-white illustrations. Authors and their approximate dates are indicated. Poems by Chinese authors, most of them written prior to 1000 A.D., may be found by noting Chinese names in the index.

78. *Lewis, Thomas. *The Dragon Kite*. New York: Holt, 1974. illus. unp. o.p. Gr. K–4.

An easy-to-read story set in a Buddhist lamasery.

79. *Little Sisters of the Grassland*. Beijing: Foreign Languages Press, 1973. Dist. by China Books & Periodicals. illus. 89pp. $3.95; $1.95 pap. Gr. 2–5.

The exciting true story of two sisters who save a herd of sheep in a blizzard has become a modern classic, available in the United States also in filmstrip (see *Treasury of Chinese Folk Tales*, entry 141) and film versions like *Two Heroic Sisters of the Grasslands* (16mm, 42 min, color, available from film rental libraries). Related slides may be borrowed from several outreach programs (for example, entries 565 and 583).

80. Mandel, Oscar. *Chi Po and the Sorcerer: A Chinese Tale for*

Children and Philosophers. Rutland, Vt.: Tuttle, 1964. illus. 85pp. o.p. Gr. 3–5.

Chi Po makes friends with the sorcerer Bu Fu and becomes a great painter.

81. *Monkey Subdues the White-Bone Demon.* Beijing: Foreign Languages Press, 1975. Dist. by China Books & Periodicals. illus. 110pp. $2.95. Gr. 4–6.

Episodes from *Journey to the West* are illustrated with full-page line-drawings. See also *Havoc in Heaven* (entry 71) and Wriggins's *White Monkey King* (entry 89), an American adaptation. For a filmstrip version see *Treasury of Chinese Folk Tales* (entry 141); for a traditional opera based on the same legend, see *A Night at the Peking Opera* (entry 134).

82. Mui, Y.T. *The Magic Brush.* Honolulu, Hawaii: Island Heritage, 1974. illus. unp. $5.95. Gr. 1–4.

Earth tones and strong colors predominate in the illustrations for this version of the story of the boy who learns to paint with a magic brush and outwits the greedy emperor. See also *Liang and the Magic Paintbrush* (entry 67), *Ma Lien and the Magic Brush* (entry 75) and the less successful filmstrip version in *Chinese Tales* (entry 114).

83. Phelps, Ethel J., ed. *Tatterhood and other Tales.* Westbury, N.Y.: Feminist Press, 1978. illus. 165pp. $11.95; $5.95 pap. Gr. 3–6.

This collection of folktales from many countries revolves around women as heroines. It includes two from China, one traditional ("The Young Head of the Family"), and one from the post-1949 period ("Wild Goose Lake").

84. Pinkwater, Manus. *Wingman.* New York: Dodd, 1975. illus. 63pp. $5.95. Dell, $.95 pap. Gr. 2–5.

A sensitive, easy-to-read story of Donald, a boy who, as the only Chinese American in his uptown Manhattan school, prefers to play hooky and daydream. In a dream Wingman carries Donald to China. His paintings of what he saw there finally gain him acceptance with his peers.

85. Shah, Idries, ed. *World Tales.* New York: Harcourt, 1979. illus. 258pp. $19.95. Gr. 4 up.

Two tales from China and the editor's comments on parallel tales from other countries and other continents are included in this collection. The full-page illustrations are striking.

86. Thomas, Leslie. *The Story of the Willow Plate*. New York: Schocken, 1969(c1940). illus. 47pp. o.p. Gr. 4–7.

Bright blue-and-white illustrations by the author make this an attractive edition of the folktale depicted on Blue Willow china, which was first made popular in America by eighteenth-century chinoiserie.

87. Tung, S.T. *One Small Dog*. New York: Dodd, 1975. illus. 160pp. $4.95. Gr. 4–8.

Dogs and other pets consume food supplies the Chinese government would rather see used to feed hungry people. This story takes place during the extermination campaigns of the Great Leap Forward, and dramatizes a boy's attempt to save his dog. The author is a refugee from Communist China, now living in the United States.

88. Wolkstein, Diane. *White Wave: A Chinese Tale*. New York: Crowell, 1979. illus. by Ed Young. unp. $7.95. Gr. 1–4.

A folktale in the Taoist tradition, here presented by a professional storyteller with sophisticated drawings by a Chinese-born artist.

89. Wriggins, Sally. *White Monkey King*. New York: Random, 1977. illus. 128pp. $5.95. Gr. 3–6.

This is a retelling of a portion of *Journey to the West*, a collection of legends of the travels of a seventh-century monk to India. Here he is accompanied by a mischievous monkey, another fixture of Chinese folklore. See also entries 71, 81, 134, and 141.

90. Wyndham, Lee. *Folktales of China*. Indianapolis, Ind.: Bobbs-Merrill, 1963. illus. 126pp. o.p. Gr. 3–6.

These sixteen stories are retold in controlled vocabulary and presented in a format suitable to uncertain readers in upper elementary grades. The illustrations are undistinguished.

91. Wyndham, Robert. *Chinese Mother Goose Rhymes*. Cleveland, Ohio: World, 1968. illus. by Ed Young. unp. o.p. Gr. K–3.

Forty-one traditional rhymes in English and Chinese are accompanied by appealing watercolor illustrations.

92. Wyndham, Robert. *Tales the People Tell in China.* New York: Messner, 1971. illus. 92pp. $7.29. Gr. 3–5.

These fourteen legends, myths, and folktales in a pleasing presentation are suitable for both independent reading and reading out loud.

93. Young, Ed. *High on a Hill: A Book of Chinese Riddles.* New York: Philomel, 1980. illus. by author. unp. $8.95. Gr. 1–5.

A beautifully produced collection of traditional riddles heard by the editor-illustrator during his childhood in China. The riddles are printed in English verse and Chinese characters and the answers appear as each page is turned.

94. Young, Ed, and Beckett, Hilary. *The Rooster's Horns: A Chinese Puppet Play to Make and Perform.* New York: Philomel, 1978. Dist. by U.S. Committee for UNICEF. illus. unp. $5.95. Gr. 1–4.

Outlines for pattern pieces and full directions for making rooster and dragon shadow play figures and for making a "theater" out of two chairs, a sheet and a lamp. Children will need adult help to follow the directions and may first view a shadow play film such as *Chinese Shadow Play* (entry 113) or *The Magic Pear Tree* (entry 127).

95. Young, Ed. *The Terrible Nung Gwama: A Chinese Folktale.* New York: Philomel, 1978. Dist. by U.S. Committee for UNICEF. illus. by author. unp. $5.95. Gr. 1–4.

This story of a monster and a courageous woman is accompanied by delicate illustrations in brown tones accented with pinks.

Audiovisual Resources

An Anthology of Chinese Folk Songs. See entry 230.

97. **Bean Sprouts* (series). 5 ¾" videocassettes, 30 min ea, color,

w/tchr's guides. Loni Ding, 1978–79. Dist. by Great Plains National Instructional Television Library. $55.25 ea. Gr. 2–6.

Produced in cooperation with the Association of Chinese Teachers and Chinese for Affirmative Action, the series features a group of Chinese American children "trying to come to terms with their consciousness of being different." Dramatizations have them exploring their heritage, their neighborhood and city, their interpersonal relations, and their cultural differences and similarities.

98. *Behind the Scenes at the Peking Circus* (How Yukong Moved the Mountains series). 16mm, 16 min, color. Ivens/Loridan, 1976. Dist. by Cinema Perspectives. $275; $50 rental. All ages.

A delightful look, without narration, at the acrobats doing their warmup exercises and practicing high kicks, wire acts, and such unique specialties as balancing a ceramic jar on head or shoulders. A performance in costume concludes the film.

Chairman Mao's 4-Minute Physical Fitness Plan. See entry 231.

99. *China* (World Studies Themes series). broadsheets, 40 transparencies, 1 audiocassette, w/tchr's guide. Heinemann, 1976?. $65; $6.50 ea unit of broadsheets. Gr. 5–8.

Each unit—"Food,""Work,""Family Life,""Village and Town"—presents historical, sociological, and cultural insights, relying heavily on black-and-white illustrations in students' materials and on colorful transparencies. The cassette contains one traditional and one modern story, and some lessons on pronunciation. Important concepts and suggested learning activities using a picture-inquiry method are features of the teacher's guide. The units were prepared by the Inner London Education Authority.

100. *China* (series). 6 filmstrips w/audiocassettes. 62–67 fr ea, 17–21 min ea, color, w/tchr's guide. Activity Records, 1977. Dist. by Educational Activities. $99. Gr. 5–10.

Margaret Rau (see also entries 39, 40, 41, 42, and 43) is the author of this comprehensive set, which is evenly divided between geographical and historical backgrounds, and post-1949 China. "The Land and the People" emphasizes the size of the country and locates its regions, using maps and photography; "Early History" and "Birth of the People's Republic of China" encompass the period from Peking Man to the Boxer Rebellion, and from Sun Yat-sen to 1949, respectively, with the latter strip employing numerous black-and-white archival shots. "Country and City Life" offers vignettes of daily life in the People's Republic. "From the Great Leap Forward to the Cultural Revolution" attempts a portrayal of those two periods of upheaval, while "Facing the Future" touches on the Korean and Vietnam Wars, China's occupation of Tibet, her admission to the United Nations, and the internal political struggle since the death of Mao. The latter two strips introduce material not widely covered elsewhere in this format and for this level. The tone is objective throughout. The teacher's guides—one per strip plus one for the set—print the script and suggest activities. *China—Set 1* (entry 234) and *China—Set 2* (entry 235) cover similar ground in somewhat more advanced fashion.

101. *China. . .A Place of Mystery.* 1 filmstrip w/audiocassette. 65 fr, 15 min, color, w/tchr's guide. Marshfilm, 1972. $24. Gr. 2–5.

The title is unfortunate, but the lively visuals and the female narrator successfully bring home to young children what it is like—or was in 1971 when these pictures were taken—to be a child in China.

102. *China: A Quarter of the World's People* (One World—Many Cultures Series). 80 slides w/1 audiocassette, 15 min, color, w/tchr's guide, student manual, 64-pp. book. Media Tree, 1978. Dist. by Kenneth E. Clouse. $59.95. Gr. 5 up.

The teacher's guide suggests some two dozen topics to be discussed after viewing the set with the accompanying narration, or to be presented as student-produced slide shows using selections from the set and independent research. Students may get pointers on production of such a show from the enclosed manual and data from the enclosed book, *China in Pictures* (entry 34) and those listed in the teacher's guide bibliography. The teacher guide identifies each slide and gives the complete script, which makes reference to the recent drive for economic modernization. The visuals are from farms, schools, stores, and cities, and could be supplemented from slide sets of the National Council for Geographic Education (entries 108, 116, and 136).

103. *China: People, Places and Progress* (Series). 6 filmstrips w/6

audiocassettes. 52–71 fr ea, 9–10 min ea, color, w/tchr's guide. Prentice-Hall Learning Systems, 1974. $105. Gr. 3–5.

The strips "Peking," "Kwangchow," "Shanghai," "Tientsin," and "Dahli Commune" profile boys or girls living in those places, while "Hong Kong" portrays the proprietor of a floating fish store, a refugee from the People's Republic. None of the segments entitled with the name of a city is actually about that city. Rather, it serves as a vehicle for bringing out points about daily life in the People's Republic (pre-1976) that are common to all its cities. "Hong Kong" does, however, clear up the confusion of the same name being applied variously to the colony, one of its islands, and the city located on that island. Life in China is presented as flawless throughout, and there are many oversimplifications—some of them misleading, as when the Little Red Soldiers are likened to Cub Scouts. Lively choral singing by Chinese youngsters introduces each segment. The fifty-five page teacher's guide states learning objectives for each, reprints the entire narration, and supplies evaluation tests and extensive activity suggestions for each unit. The latter are essential for differentiating several of the filmstrips, which are very similar in content.

104. *China: The Land and Its People* (series). 4 filmstrips w/4 audiocassettes. 55–60 fr ea, 12–15 min ea, color, w/tchr's guide. January Productions, 1979. $64 ser.; $16.50 ea. Gr. 5–9.

"How the People Use the Land" compares the geographical setting and climate of China and the United States, then contrasts the ways in which each uses its land. "The Rural Commune" does a good job of explaining the origin of the commune concept in Mao's ideas, the development of communes, the organization into brigades and production teams, the small industrial workshops, and the health and other services provided. "Country Boy, City Girl" profiles two thirteen-year-olds, one living on a commune, the other in an industrial city, and their family and school lives. "A Cultural Heritage" unsuccessfully and jumpily attempts to present the blend of the old and the new that is China. The meager teacher's guides supply script, supplemented with discussion questions and suggested activities, some of which are difficult to carry out.

105. *China Today.* 1 filmstrip w/audiocassette, 52 fr, 17 min, color, w/script. Outdoor Pictures, 1980. $20; $32 slides w/audiocassette. Gr. 4 up.

Don't depend on the dull narration, which is really just a series of captions. Many are excessively simplistic, others betray a narrow viewpoint.

106. *China's People.* 8 photographs, 13" × 18", color, w/tchr's guide. Encyclopedia Britannica, 1978. $19.50. Gr. K–6.

The photographs show people at work in a restaurant, store, and factory, on a wheat farm, and embroidering silk, as well as soldiers, dancers, and children in school. On the back of each there is related information; the teacher's guide lists vocabulary and makes suggestions for classroom uses, related activities, and questions. *Mainland China Today* (entry 128) is probably a better value.

107. *Chinatown* (Five Families Series). 1 filmstrip w/audiocassette or disc. 62 fr, 7 min, color, w/tchr's guide. Scholastic, 1972. $28; $94.50 ser. Gr. K–4.

Portrays the daily activities of a San Francisco Chinatown family.

108. *Chinese Agriculture: A Study of Communes.* 60 slides, color, w/script. National Council for Geographic Education, 1978. Dist. by Great Plains National Instructional Television Library. $43.50. Gr. 5 up.

Without a teacher's guide, this set could most profitably be used as a supplement to others, or for student- or teacher-produced slide presentations. See also entry 102.

109. *Chinese Fairy Tales.* 1 12" LP or audiocassette. Caedmon, 1973. $7.98. Gr. 1–5.

Siobhan McKenna reads seven tales from Isabelle Chang's collection by the same title (entry 62).

Chinese Folk Dances. See entry 240.

110. *Chinese Folktales.* 6 filmstrips w/6 audiocassettes, 46–52 fr ea, 7–9 min ea, color, w/tchr's guide. Coronet, 1973. $115; $25 ea. Gr. 2–5.

Contains "Heavenly Flower Man," "Magic Brocade," "Three Hairs of the Buddha," "A Strange Cave of Gems," "Lo-Sun, the Blind Boy," and "Clever Man and the Landlord." The thrust of the teacher's guide is toward values education and some learning about traditional China. Open-ended questions for discussion follow the synopsis of each story. Each is illustrated in a distinct style; all are read by a male narrator with an accent.

111. *Chinese Folktales, Legends, Proverbs and Rhythms.* 2 12" LPs or audiocassette. CMS Records, 1973. $7.95. Gr. 1–5.

Anne Pellowski, the noted storyteller, tells nursery rhymes, counting rhymes, a legend of the Kitchen God, and other tales. Sources for the selections are given on the jacket.

Chinese Four-Minute Exercises. See entry 242.

112. *The Chinese of Taiwan* (series). 2 filmstrips w/2 audiocassettes. 95–106 fr ea, 10 min ea, color, w/tchr's guide. Mass Communications, 1977. $50; $25 ea. Gr. 5–10.

One of the very few filmic media available on Taiwan, this set adequately depicts the geographic setting, brief history, and present conditions on the island. Taiwan's "successful technological culture," blending Western and traditional Chinese values, comes through. Unfortunately, the meager teacher's guide raises only questions that compare Taiwan with the United States, not the more relevant ones that would compare it with the People's Republic. The guide also provides a synopsis of the narration, and questions involving map study and recall. Confucianism and ancestor worship are dealt with in the first strip, "Origins, Religion and Education," along with Buddhism and Taoism. It also gives glimpses of schools and universities and is narrated alternately by male and female voices. "Agriculture, Industry and Leisure" shows a country less than forty percent agricultural, with modern buildings and TV soap operas.

113. *Chinese Shadow Play.* 16mm, 10min. Wan-go Weng, 1955. Dist. by Pictura. $175; $20 rental. Gr. 2 up.

After watching a performance of the folktale *The White Snake Lady,* viewers are taken backstage to see how shadow puppets made of translucent material are manipulated. This truly affective film makes one want to know more about Chinese puppetry. That can be done by following the instructions in Young's *The Rooster's Horns* (entry 94). *The Magic Pear Tree* (entry 127) is another film of a folktale shadow play.

114. *Chinese Tales* (series). 4 filmstrips w/4 audiocassettes. 65–81 fr ea, 15–18 min ea, color, w/tchr's guide. Schloat, 1973. Dist. by Clearvue. $60; $17 ea. Gr. 3–8.

These adaptations of traditional Chinese folktales offer a unique feature: a "postscript" on the theme of each fable. The one following "Kan-han and the Evil Dragon" explores Chinese dragons as symbols, with eighteen frames and narration. In "The Magic Brush of Po Ling" (see also entry 82), there is an interview with an artist on traditional brush strokes and painting. In "Clever Girl and the Marvelous Jacket" traditional and contemporary Chinese dress styles are considered; and "The Great Quest of Yenkang" treats Chinese cooking, with its genius for making the most of whatever is available.

The filmstrips are based on a Foreign Languages Press publication and reflect the art style of the original. The superb seventy-one-page illustrated teacher's guide states student learning objectives, relates the stories to actual events, explains Chinese symbolism, prints the script and an additional article by the artist interviewed, and in its final section supplies a complete sourcebook for extended follow-up activities.

Courts, Tombs, and Dragons. See entry 243.

115. *The Dragon Wore Tennis Shoes.* 16mm, 9 min. Diane Li, 1976. Dist. by Cambridge Documentary Films. $140. Gr. 3 up.

As we view colorful scenes from the Chinese New Year's parade in San Francisco and watch the frantic preparations for the event, we share in the joy and excitement. One of the boys chosen to carry the dragon narrates, explaining the dragon's construction and telling the legends that relate to it. If you can't get to the parade, watch this charming film.

116. *Education in the People's Republic of China.* 40 slides, color, w/script. National Council for Geographic Education. n.d. Dist. by Great Plains National Instructional Television Library. $31. Gr. 5 up.

Without a teacher's guide this set could most profitably be used as a supplement to others, or for student- or teacher-produced slide presentations. See also entries 125, 135, 483, and 491.

117. *The Families of Hong Kong* (Families of Asia series). 1 filmstrip w/audiocassette, 75 fr, 9 min, color, w/tchr's guide. Encyclopedia Britannica, 1975. $19.50; $99.50 ser. Gr. 4 up.

Children's activities in families of different social status are emphasized.

118. *Family in China* (Families Around the World series). 1 filmstrip w/audiocassette, color, w/tchr's guide. Science Research Associates, 1977. $21.10; $165 ser. Gr. 4 up.

Daily activities are profiled in this program from a series of eight.

119. *Folktale Classics from Other Lands* (series). 4 filmstrips w/audiocassettes, 64–79 fr, 9 min ea. color, w/tchr's guide. BFA, 1976. $70. Gr. 2–5.

Includes "The Seven Brothers" (78 fr).

120. *Folktales of China* (series). 6 filmstrips w/audiocassettes. 44–68 fr ea, 8–15 min ea, color, w/tchr's guide. Q-Ed Productions, 1977. $109; $3 tchr's guide if purch. sep. Gr. K–5.

A superb thirty-page teacher's manual directs attention to folktales from other cultures with themes parallel to those in this collection, and provides teacher background, scripts, a synopsis of each tale, learning objectives, vocabulary, and suggested activities. The series contains these stories: "The Story of Shih-Chieh," "The Bank of the Celestial Stream," "The Great Flood," "The Gossiping Animals," "The Wishing Stone," and "A Jar Full of Ants." The art work is unexceptionable. For a book with a similar thrust, see Shah's *World Tales* (entry 85) and *Rabbit in the Moon* (entry 561).

121. *Himalayan Adventure.* 80 slides w/audiocassette & carousel, color. Crystal Productions, 1976. $75. Gr. 5 up.

122. *Hong Kong.* 1 filmstrip W/audiocassette, 51 fr, 14 min, color. Outdoor Pictures, 1980. $20; $32 slides w/cassette. Gr. 4 up.

Entry 105 is from the same producer.

Hong Kong: A Family Portrait. See entry 248.

123. *Hong Kong* (One World—Many Cultures series). 80 slides w/audiocassette, 15 min, color, w/tchr's guide, student manual, transparency master, 64-pp. book. Media Tree, 1979. $59.95. Gr. 5 up.

See *China: A Quarter of the World's People* (entry 102) in the same series for general format.

Hong Kong Today. See entry 249.

House of Sixty Fathers. See entry 223.

124. *Industrial China.* 16mm, 13 min, color. Jens Bjerre, 1974. Dist. by Pictura. $200; $25 rental. Gr. 5 up.

One of the few, if not the only, treatment of this subject in a visual format for a younger age group, this didactic film takes a fairly close look at factory organization, and participatory management in large plants and also at smaller industry connected with agricultural communes. Students are shown performing daily work assignments, as was required during and after the Cultural Revolution.

It's Always So in the World. See entry 252.

125. *Keep Fit, Study Well, Work Hard.* 16mm, 12 min, color. Cary Lu, 1973. Dist. by Churchill. $180. Gr. 4 up.

Performances of dance and music and a foot race are the few instances of individual or small group activities seen in this profile of a Chinese school. The greater portion of the footage shows schoolyard calisthenics and marching, unison chanting and singing in classrooms with fixed seats, and assembly line work by students. Paint flaking off walls, and blackboards are also unfamiliar features for most North American viewers.

126. *Life in a Chinese Commune.* 16mm, 13 min, color. Jens Bjerre, 1974. Dist. by Pictura. $200; $25 rental. Gr. 4 up.

The commune pictured here engages in large-scale horse and stock breeding, providing scenes that are a change from the rice and wheat farming more commonly seen. Commune organization is clearly explained in the lecture-type narration, which also stresses the free medical care, the care for old people, and the absence of hunger. The conclusion that a commune is "just like any community anywhere where people work and live together" may be questioned. See also "The Rural Commune" in the filmstrip set *China: The Land and Its People* (entry 104) and *Something for Everyone* (entry 260).

127. *The Magic Pear Tree.* 16mm, 5 min, color. Wan-go Weng, 1970. Dist. by Pictura. $125; $15 rental. Gr. K–4.

This satisfying folk tale of kindness and generosity rewarded is done in shadow puppet animation. See also *Chinese Shadow Play* (entry 113).

128. *Mainland China Today.* 16 photographs, 12½" × 17", color, w/chart & tchr's guide. David C. Cook, 1973. $7.75. Gr. K–6.

Pictured scenes of the Great Wall, pedicarts, buses, a harvest, homes, family meals, children and parents at school, industry, painting, musical instruments, and others are suitable for wall display. The chart outlines Chinese history to 1949. The superb 39-page teacher's guide is a sourcebook of data supporting each unit, including related folktales and poems, and has suggestions for activities for both K–2 and 3–8. While the section on "Leaders" and the listings of resource materials are dated, the rest of this set could make a good starting point for a unit on China.

129. *Marco Polo (Age of Exploration and Discovery* set). 1 filmstrip w/audiocassette, 51 fr, 13 min, color, w/tchr's guide. Coronet, 1975. $25; $115 set. Gr. 5 up.

A clear and straightforward account of trade between Asia and Europe in the thirteenth century, the Kublai Khan empire (Yuan dynasty) and the Polos' position there, and Marco Polo's overland return trip to Venice. The teacher's guide summarizes the program's content, sets out student objectives, and suggests topics for further study. Some stereotyping of facial features appears in the visuals.

130. *Marn-ling and the Chinese Musical Instruments.* 1 12" LP. Dist. by Children's Book and Music Center. $6.98. Gr. 1–5.

Demonstrations of Chinese flute, harp, violin, banjo, zither, lute, and mouth organ are woven into a slight story framework. Photos of the instruments are included. See also *The Magic of Chinese Music* (entry 568).

131. Marn-Ling Sees the Chinese Lion Dance. 1 12" LP w/poster. Dist. by Children's Book and Music Center. $6.98. Gr. 1–5.

Cantonese and Mandarin songs with dance instructions and words in transliterated Chinese and English, and sounds of a Chinese New Year's parade in Hawaii.

Mind, Body, and Spirit. See entry 256.

132. **My Family Business.* 16mm, 12 min. Films, Inc., 1979. $210; $25 rental; $160 videocassette. Gr. 3–5.

This segment from the *Zoom* television series, originally filmed in 1975, includes a five-minute section, "Chinese Restaurant," that profiles a young Chinese immigrant working in her family's business.

133. *My Name Is Susan Yee.* 16mm, 12 min, color, w/tchr's guide. National Film Board of Canada, 1977. Dist. by Media Guild. $195; $18 rental. Gr. 3–6.

This refreshing film, narrated by Susan, shows her doing things all children do—going to school, shopping with her mother, sleigh riding—but she also helps her family make jewelry boxes on a piecework basis. She attends a multiracial classroom in an urban renewal area of Montreal, and she comments on the changes in her slowly disappearing neighborhood. A one-page teacher's guide provides a synopsis, viewing suggestions, and comprehension and discussion questions.

Myths of China. See entry 257.

134. *A Night at the Peking Opera.* 16mm, 20 min, color. Film Images, 1959. $325; $30 rental. Gr. 4 up.

Explaining that Chinese audiences need no program notes because the characters in traditional Chinese opera are "as familiar as Donald Duck," the narrator refers to its long history and outlines the conventions of make-up and costume. We then view acrobatic dances and mime sequences from three traditional operas. Though the film is thoroughly enjoyable on its own, viewing would be enhanced by collateral reading of the monkey legends as told in *Havoc in Heaven* (entry 71) and other books (entries 81 and 89). See also *In Rehearsal at the Peking Opera* (entry 494).

One Hundred Entertainments. See entry 258.

135. *People's Republic of China* (series). 5 filmstrips w/5 audiocassettes, 47–53 fr ea, 9–13 min ea, color, w/tchr's guide. Centron, 1978. $97.50. Gr. 5–10.

This set, apparently completed before post-Mao changes became known, presents a positive view of the accomplishments of the People's Republic, set against the country's history. But it also issues warnings against assuming that all of China is like the model sites shown to foreign visitors. "The Middle Kingdom and Modern China, Parts I and II" present a survey of Chinese history to the establishment of the People's Republic. Unfortunately, the brief reading from Marco Polo's writings that starts it off is done in a fake Italian accent that is unnecessary and offensive. The remaining three strips deal with contemporary China: "Education: China's Hope" examines elementary and secondary schools, and the role of ideology and of work experience; "The Millions in the Cities" notes Shanghai's industrial role and Beijing's (Peking) as the seat of government, and details living conditions; "The Millions on the Farms" discusses agricultural techniques and processing as well as living conditions. The twenty-four-page teacher's guide states objectives for each portion, clearly outlines content, and suggests discussion questions and activities. *China—Set 1* (entry 234) and *China—Set 2* (entry 235) are comparable units.

136. *The People's Republic of China: Aspects of Life and Society in the New China.* 60 slides, color, w/script. National Council for Geographic Education. n.d. Dist. by Great Plains National Instructional Television Library. $43.50. Gr. 5 up.

Without a teacher's guide, this set's most profitable use may be as a supplement to others, or for student- or teacher-produced slide presentations.

Silkmaking in China. See entry 259.

Son of the Ocean. See entry 261.

137. *Strangers in a Strange Land* (Heritage Stories set). 1 filmstrip w/audiocassette, 56 fr, 12 min, color, w/tchr's guide. United Learning, 1975. $22; $95 set. Gr. 4 up.

The soundtrack is the female narrator's moving testimonial to her grandfather who came to "The Golden Mountain" only to endure the hardships of railroad construction and discriminatory treatment. She also touches on her own growing up in Chinatown, conveying a strong sense of family. The cartoon visuals, unfortunately, don't do justice to the narration, and historical photographs assembled in several books (e.g., entry 336) would make a better supplement. The teacher's guide states student objectives and stresses comprehension and extending activities.

138. *Tales of China and Tibet. 1 12" LP or audiocassette. Caedmon, 1972. $7.98. Gr. 1–5.

Siobhan McKenna reads seven tales from a collection by Isabelle Chang. (See also entry 62.)

139. *Tangram. 16mm, 3 min, color, w/book. Pyramid, 1975. $100; $175 video; $25 rental. Gr. 3 up.

Animation introduces the endless possibilities presented by tangram puzzles. Viewing may be followed up by actual puzzle construction, following suggestions in the 126-page book *Tangramath* supplied with the film, and others (e.g., entries 26, 54).

140. *Tea Clipper Race* (game). York, England: Longmans, 1973. 12pp. w/tchr's guide. Gr. 5–9.

This board game is designed to teach world geography, ocean currents, ports, wind systems, and the situation in the 1860s when the last of the clipper ships raced to bring each year's first crop of tea from China to England. No mention is made of the product—opium—that was traded for the tea.

Traditional Handicrafts. See entry 263.

141. *Treasury of Chinese Folk Tales* (series). 4 filmstrips w/4 audiocassettes. 35–72 fr ea, 8–14 min ea, color, w/tchr's guide. Spoken Arts, 1976. $89.95; $28.95 ea. Gr. K–4.

Only one of the stories is a traditional one, *Monkey Subdues the White-Bone Demon* (for the book see entry 81). The others extol child heroes and heroines of contemporary China and its various regions: *The Little Sisters of the Grasslands* (for the book see entry 79), *The Battle with the Giant Sturgeon,* and *The Great Hunt.* The illustrations are cartoon-style. The full text of narrations is given in the teacher's guide, which also has vocabulary and pronunciation, motivation suggestions, comprehension questions, and follow-up activities, some of them quite impractical.

142. *The Wangs* (American Families series). 1 filmstrip w/audiocassette. 46 fr, 7 min, color, w/tchr's guide. Coronet, 1972. $25; $115 set. Gr. 4–6.

The strip follows an ordinary family to religious observances in a Buddhist temple, shopping in Chinatown, a (multiracial) tenants' meeting, and a session of teaching brush stroke technique to their children.

143. *With a Town Family in Taiwan* (Living in Asia Today set). 1 filmstrip w/audiocassette, 51 fr, 11 min, color, w/tchr's guide. Coronet, 1972. $25; $145 set. Gr. 4–6.

This strip shows daily activities and gives data on geography and culture.

144. *A World Nearby: Hong Kong* (series). Cross-Cultural Studies. 3 filmstrips w/2 audiocassettes, 58–88 fr, 14–16 min, color, w/tchr's guide. Guidance Associates, 1976. $89.50. Gr. 4–7.

Focusing throughout on children, the two sound filmstrips in this set portray Hong Kong's busy streets and harbor, its housing developments, fishing and farming, and school and family life. Part III consists of frames showing similar scenes, each with one or more printed questions. The questions aid and test students' comprehension of the two earlier strips. Additional questions and activities related to each frame are found in the eighty-nine-page teacher's guide, which also gives the text of the Part I and II narrations. Comparisons are made with experiences familiar to North American children, rather than with life in the People's Republic.

Part 2
Materials for the Middle
School–Junior High

Books

Nonfiction

Titles in this section are either specifically published for this age group or are adult books deemed suitable because of the subject matter or its presentation. Books annotated in Part 1, Materials for Primary–Elementary Grades, that are also appropriate for this level are cross-referenced. Additional titles listed in Part 3, Materials for Senior High–Adults, may also be considered appropriate, but they are not specifically indicated here.

Besides books, including several textbooks, this section annotates periodicals and print materials such as "Jackdaw" and similar kits, and sets of dittomasters.

145. Appel, Benjamin. *Why the Chinese Are the Way They Are.* Boston: Little, 1973. illus. maps. 182pp. o.p. Gr. 7–12.

The author may not explain "why the Chinese are the way they are," but he presents an understandable if cursory overview of Chinese history, helped by many maps, that is friendly to the People's Republic. There is a good chapter on the Long March.

146. Archer, Jules. *China in the Twentieth Century.* New York: Macmillan, 1974. illus. 230pp. $7.95. Gr. 7–12.

This political history of China from the Boxer Rebellion through the fall of Lin Biao (Lin Piao) in 1973 is evenly presented in easily understood language by a journalist who is the author of several other books on Chinese and other Asian subjects. The content is about equally divided between the pre- and post-1949 periods, and is served by a fine index.

147. Archer, Jules. *The Chinese and the Americans.* New York: Hawthorn, 1976. 227pp. o.p. Gr. 8–12.

While the emphasis is on Sino-American foreign relations, the journalist-author focuses also on the opium trade, missionaries, Chinese immigrants in the United States, the Boxer Rebellion, the Korean and Cold Wars, the Vietnam years, détente, and on United States relations with Taiwan (from 1854 on). There is considerable information about Americans who disagreed with the official pro-Chiang policy of the war years, and who went to Yenan to interview Mao in his hideaway. A four-page chronological table of U.S.–Chinese interactions between 1784 and 1975, and a good index are included.

148. *Asia 1981 Yearbook.* Hong Kong: Far Eastern Economic Review, 1981. Dist. by China Books & Periodicals. illus. 320pp. $10.95. Gr. 7 up.

China, Hong Kong, and Taiwan are covered in separate sections in this annual, which is chock-full of data on the economy, politics, construction projects, and prominent personalities. The two-column format is on newsprint, and there is advertising.

149. *Axelbank, Albert. *The China Challenge.* New York: Watts, 1978. 85pp. $5.90. Gr. 7–12.

This book presents a visit to the People's Republic, with interviews and an overview of its accomplishments.

Barker. *The Glorious Age of Exploration.* See entry 2.

150. Batterberry, Michael. *Chinese and Oriental Art.* New York: McGraw-Hill, 1968. illus. 192pp. $9.95. Gr. 7 up.

About eighty pages are devoted to China and contain 179 illustrations of painting, sculpture, architecture, ceramics, and other art objects up to the end of the eighteenth century. The accompanying text, in good-sized print, explains the significance of the objects in lay terms. See also Moore's *The Eastern Gate* (entry 192).

151. Beers, Burton F., ed. *Chiliying: Life in a Rural Commune in China.* People of Asia Series. Raleigh, N.C.: North Carolina State University, 1979. illus. 69pp. $3 pap.; $.50 tchr's guide. Gr. 6–8.

Developed by North Carolina teachers in 1976, this three- to four-week unit reprints Chinese children's stories, songs, cartoons, and selections from Foreign Languages Press publications to bring home the values and ways of life on a commune in Central China. The geographic setting, crops, schools, barefoot doctors, women's roles, and family life are among the topics of the fourteen chapters, most of which end with suggestions for reinforcement activities or discussion questions.

152. Beers, Burton F. *China in Old Photographs, 1860–1910.* New York: Scribner, 1978. illus. 160pp. $17.50. Gr. 7 up.

Authentic photographs from the collections of the Museum of the American China Trade (entry 574). A similar title is Capa's *Behind the Great Wall of China* (entry 161).

153. *Boardman, Fon W. *Tyrants and Conquerors*. New York: Walck, 1977. illus. maps. 183pp. $8.95. Gr. 7–12.

Biographies of the third century b.c. Qin Shih Huang Di (Ch'in Shih Huang Ti) and of the thirteenth-century Genghis Khan are among the ten profiles here that address the question whether power and ruthlessness inevitably go together. Emperor Shih unified a group of warring states and created the imperial system that continued for over two thousand years.

154. Bonavia, David. *Peking*. New York: Time-Life Books, 1978. illus. 200pp. $10.95. Gr. 5 up.

Striking color photos from a quarter-page to a double-page spread in size, plus archival black-and-whites from the pre-1911 period, depict just about every aspect of life in China's capital, from early morning Tai Ji Quan (T'ai Chi Ch'uan) to evening at the Opera. Several winter scenes are reminders that Beijing is on the same latitude as Philadelphia. There are "picture essay" sections of each chapter on "shopping in a planned economy," "citizens in training" (schools), the Imperial Palace, and other topics. A similar title is MacFarquhar's *The Forbidden City* (entry 186).

155. Borgese, Elisabeth Mann. *Seafarm: The Story of Aquaculture*. New York: Abrams, 1980. illus. 236pp. $35. Gr. 7 up.

China has practiced fish farming for two thousand years and today produces one-half of the world's farmed fish, we learn in the brief chapter that deals with China. The index turns up additional references to seaweed farming, the export of Chinese aquaculture technology to Mexico, and related topics. This is a subject of unique significance, not widely covered in the popular literature.

156. *Bown, Colin. *The People's Republic of China* (kit). 26 broadsheets. 80pp. total. Exeter, N.H.: Heinemann Educational Books, 1975. $6.95. Gr. 7 up.

Documentary and photographic archive materials illustrate the course of events from 1950 to the mid-1970s, with special attention to China's relations with other countries. Suggested questions make this a useful supplement to books with more depth. It is a good tool for classroom discussion of such topics as the Great Leap Forward, Tibet, China's India War, the war in Indochina, the Cultural Revolution, education, women's roles, nuclear capability, relations with the U.S. and U.S.S.R., admission to the United Nations, Hong Kong, and the economy.

157. *Bown, Colin, and Edwards, Tony. *Revolution in China, 1911–1949: History Broadsheets* (kit). 21 broadsheets, 2–4pp. ea. Exeter, N.H.: Heinemann Educational Books, 1974. Dist. by Social Studies School Service. $6.95. Gr. 7–12.

Excerpts from primary and secondary sources, as well as maps and charts, illustrate the rise of nationalism, the founding of the Communist Party, the Long March, U.S. involvement in China's Civil War, the victory of the Communists, and other topics. Suggested discussion questions keyed to the reading and a summary sheet are included.

Boyd. *Rulers in Petticoats.* See entry 5.

Buell. *The World of Red China.* See entry 7.

158. Burati, Robert, and Pettelkay, Harald. *Hong Kong.* This Beautiful World. New York: Kodansha, 1971. illus. maps. 138pp. $4.95 pap. Gr. 7 up.

Eighty-eight colorful photographs portray not only the city but also the outlying islands, the traditional ways of the people engaged in farming and fishing, the cottage industries, and life on sampans. There is a separate section on Macao. The text is easy to read, but without an index or a detailed table of contents, it is difficult of access.

159. Butts, Miriam, and Heard, Patricia. *The American China Trade: "Foreign Devils to Canton," 1783–1843* (kit). 12 exhibits, 6 broadsheets, contents brochure. Jackdaw. New York: Viking, 1974. $5.95. Gr. 7–12.

This kit consists of facsimile reproductions of ships' journals, a carpenter's certificate, and other documents, maps, and portraits, plus printed materials supplying data on the China trade, with suggested questions. It supplements Tamarin's *Voyaging to Cathay* (entry 213) and Carpenter's *The Old China Trade* (entry 162) with primary sources.

160. Cameron, Nigel. *China Today.* New York: Watts, 1974. illus. 128pp. $6.90. Gr. 7–12.

The liberally illustrated and very pro-People's Republic text in three-column format covers such aspects of Maoist China as its agriculture, industry, science, medicine, governmental structure, performing arts, minorities, and foreign relations. Political indoctrination and the Cultural Revolution receive some attention, and there are sections on Beijing and Shanghai, and a brief historical sketch, accompanied by art reproductions. The description of archaeological finds since the 1950s is of interest.

161. Capa, Cornell, ed. *Behind the Great Wall of China: Photographs from 1870 to the Present.* New York: Graphic Society, 1972. illus. unp. $12.50. Gr. 7 up.

The catalog of an exhibit at the Metropolitan Museum of Art of work by noted photographers, and by Edgar Snow (entries 398, 399), the most recent dated 1964. See also Beers's *China in Old Photographs* (entry 152).

162. Carpenter, Francis R. *The Old China Trade: Americans in Canton, 1784–1843.* illus. by Demi Hitz. New York: Coward-McCann, 1976. 152pp. o.p. Gr. 6–10.

The author's association with the Museum of the American China Trade (entry 574) lends authority to this full and detailed history. Observations on the effect of the China trade on industry in the United States and on the development of the West are noteworthy, as are the detailed stylized line drawings. See also Tamarin's *Voyaging to Cathay* (entry 213).

163. Carter, Michael. *Crafts of China.* New York: Doubleday, 1972. illus. 144pp. $9.95. Gr. 7 up.

A profusely illustrated, exhaustive sourcebook for puppetry, embroidery, enameling, lacquer work, basketry, kites, papercutting, jade carving, weaving, pottery, etc. Instructions are provided in some chapters. See also Stalberg's *Chinas's Crafts* (entry 212).

164. *The Cave Home of Peking Man.* Beijing: Foreign Languages Press, 1975. Dist. by China Books & Periodicals. illus. maps. 52pp. $1.95 pap. Gr. 7 up.

The discovery of a cave with remains in the 1920s and further excavations in the 1950s are recounted, followed by descriptions of stone and bone implements, and Peking Man's use of fire and his hunting and gathering culture. There is also a summary of other sites and findings explored between 1957 and 1972. The book is printed on better quality paper and with better color and black-and-white illustrations than most from this publisher.

165. *China.* 9 ditto masters. n.d. Dist. by Social Studies School Service. $6. Gr. 7–12.

The contents touch on geography, Imperial China, relations with the West prior to 1912, Republican China, culture and society, economy, government, and foreign relations, and includes a political map. Use with care, as portions may contain obsolete data.

166. *China: All Provinces and Autonomous Regions.* Zheng Shifeng, and others. New York: McGraw-Hill, 1980. illus. maps. 285pp. $60. Gr. 5 up.

Since the only other extensive source of visuals on the diversity of China's regions is an even more expensive film (entry 232), this coffee-table book is included despite its steep price, and in expectation of its being available at more reasonable cost from remainder dealers in the future. Disregard the text, but use the over two-hundred exquisite color photographs to illustrate other books on China's geography (see entries 172, 291, 292) or on China in general.

167. *China Pictorial.* Dist. by China Books and Periodicals. illus. 12/yr. $10; $38 airmail. Gr. 4 up.

This excellent source for pictures of people, places, natural features, and the arts contains brief articles. This and the following two titles are official organs of the People's Republic.

168. *China Reconstructs.* Dist. by China Books & Periodicals. illus. 12/yr. $8; $16.20 airmail. Gr. 7 up.

Articles on politics, culture, the arts, medicine, industry, and nationalities, are illustrated with color photographs. Collections of articles are published from time to time (see entries 289, 315, 363). There are editions of this official publication in other European languages and in Arabic.

169. *China Sports.* Dist. by China Books & Periodicals. illus. 6/yr. $8; $29 airmail. Gr. 7 up.

Of particular interest to fanciers of table tennis and of Chinese exercises and martial arts, this official magazine carries news and features about all sports practiced in China, profiles of athletes, and articles about technique.

170. *The Chinese War Machine: A Technical Analysis of the Strategy and Weapons of the People's Republic of China.* New York: Crescent Books, 1979. Dist. by China Books & Periodicals. illus. maps. tables. 184pp. $14.95. Gr. 7 up.

Over two hundred photographs and sketches of planes, naval vessels, soldiers, combat training, etc., and three-column text provide exhaustive detail on the history of the Chinese armed forces, ground forces, navy, air force, weapons, and defense and foreign policies.

171. Chu, Daniel. *China.* World Cultures. rev. ed. New York: Scholastic, 1980. illus. maps. tables. 240pp. $3.95 pap. *Teaching guide, $4 pap.; *Spirit masters, $11.95. Gr. 7–12.

This text, updated as of mid-1979, surveys China's geography, history, religion, arts, culture, and traditions. It includes several pages on overseas Chinese in Southeast Asia, a topic not often touched on in material for this age level, and separate chapters on Sun, Chiang, and Mao, as well as a chapter on Taiwan. There are clear maps, statistical tables, and over one hundred black-and-white photographs from European and United States sources. A spelling and pronunciation guide helps with both Pinyin and Wade-Giles transliteration; the latter is employed in the text.

172. Chung, Chih. *An Outline of Chinese Geography.* Beijing: Foreign Languages Press, 1978. Dist. by China Books & Periodicals. illus. maps. 186pp. $3.95. Gr. 7 up.

Straightforward text, with only minor ideological overtones, treats China's administrative divisions, nationalities, landforms, rivers and lakes, climate, soils, deserts, vegetation, mammals and birds, agriculture, industry, and communications and transport. Foldout physical and political maps and a separate section of black-and-white photographs are included. There is no index. This title replaces *China—A Geographical Sketch* (1974).

Cooke. *Taiwan, Island China.* See entry 9.

173. Crook, Welton J. *Abacus Arithmetic: How to Perform Some Calculations on the Chinese Abacus.* Palo Alto, Calif.: Pacific Books, 1958. Dist. by China Books & Periodicals. illus. 69pp. $2.95 pap. Gr. 5 up.

Clear illustrations and directions for performing the four arithmetic operations and calculating square and cube roots are provided. There is no index.

174. deKeijzer, Arne J., and Kaplan, Frederic M. *The China Guidebook; a Traveler's Guide to the People's Republic of China.* 1979–80 ed. New York: Lippincott, 1979. illus. maps. tables. 304pp. $12.95; $8.95 pap. *1980 ed., $14.95; $10.95 pap. Gr. 7 up.

Three parts deal with traveling to China, traveling in China, and cities and sites included in general tours. The first part provides just about all the advice a potential traveler from the United States or other Western countries would want, from names and addresses of organizations sponsoring tours, visa procedures, and what to wear, to a transliteration glossary of place names, Pinyin pronunciation guide, and helpful phrases. Part II consists of brief essays of what to expect on typical group visits to schools, health care facilities, art and archaeological sites, and the Canton Trade Fair. Sightseeing information for thirty-four cities and other sites in Part III includes some street maps. Black-and-white photographs, a foldout map, and selective reading lists appropriate for the nonspecialist are included. For other guidebooks see entries 181 and 188.

Dietz. *Folksongs of China, Japan and Korea.* See entry 10.

175. Doeringer, Franklin (and others). *The People of East Asia.* New York: Sadlier, 1973. illus. maps. 116pp. $4.44 pap. Gr. 5–10.

A colorful, attractive presentation with excellent maps and informative photographs. Comprehension and discussion questions are part of the caption of each illustration, and accompany the text in the margin. End-of-chapter reviews extend the questioning, while the end-of-the-book review is intended to test students' understanding of leading concepts in anthropology, sociology, history, geography, economics and political science. While the focus is on all of East Asia, the material on China and Taiwan is easily located. Update this title with more recent sources.

176. *Dupuy, Trevor N. *Military History of the Chinese Civil War*. New York: Watts, 1969. illus. 110 pp. $4.90. Gr. 6 up.

One of a series of military histories by the author.

177. *Edmonds, I.G. *Mao's Long March: An Epic of Human Courage*. New York; Macrae, 1973. 152pp. $6.50. Gr. 7 up.

A sympathetic account by an author experienced in writing for this age group.

178. Edmonds, I.G. *Taiwan—The Other China*. Indianapolis, Ind.: Bobbs-Merrill, 1971. illus. map. 160pp. o.p. Gr. 7 up.

This straightforward historical account from the sixteenth century discovery by the Portuguese on unfortunately does not include a chronological table. Reference is made to Chinese legends of the island's origins. The illustrations are black-and-white photos.

179. *Eunson, Ruby. *The Soong Sisters*. New York: Watts, 1975. 136pp. $5.90. Gr. 7 up.

The three American-educated daughters of an American-educated Chinese Methodist businessman married, respectively, Sun Yat-Sen, Chiang Kai-Shek, and H.H. Kung, a member of the Nationalist government under Chiang. Mme. Chiang became particularly well-known in the West. Mme. Sun had considerable influence in the People's Republic, where she died in 1981.

180. Fitch, Florence Mary. *Their Search for God: Ways of Worship in the Orient*. New York: Lothrop, 1947. illus. 160pp. $7.92. Gr. 6 up.

The book jacket makes this appear to be directed at a younger audience than it actually is. Text and 155 black-and-white photographs describe Chinese social and religious customs and observances such as respect for parents and for learning, holidays, marriage customs, the Kitchen God, and Buddhist shrines and monastic life. Emphasis is on the teachings, not the lives, of Confucius, Lao-Tzu, and Buddha, and on Confucianism as a force in Chinese culture.

181. *Fodor's People's Republic of China*. 1981 ed. New York: McKay, 1981. illus. maps. tables. 514 pp. $15.95; $11.95 pap. Gr. 7 up.

Travel tips and background information are given on history, the arts, food, crime and security, the media, ethnic-groups, and other topics. Charts illustrating China's political system, including its army and the Communist Party, and a table of common signs and their meaning are handy features. Sightseeing notes on major cities, and a thirty-six-page chapter on business and trade with China are included.

Glubok. *The Art of China.* See entry 13.

Goldston. *The Long March.* See entry 14.

Hammond. *China: The Land and Its People.* See entry 18.

182. Hantula, James Neil. *China.* Global Insights: People and Cultures Series. Columbus, Ohio: Merrill, 1980. illus. maps. 136pp. $4.20 pap. Gr. 7–12. R.L. 8.

This text seeks to present Chinese culture and history from Chinese points of view. It features colorful illustrations, excerpts from many primary sources (both Western and Chinese), and questions to encourage inquiry and aid comprehension and review. Chapter headings include "'We' and 'They'," "The Arts, " "Agriculture," "The Peasant," "The Upper Class," "The Confucian Heritage," and "China after Mao." "The Chinese Revolution" takes but little note of nineteenth-century Western imperialism, however. "The Other China" elicits student comparisons of the People's Republic and Taiwan. China's ethnic diversity receives no mention. See also *Where Is the Flowery Kingdom?* (entry 586) by the same author.

Hawley. *Chinese Folk Designs.* See entry 19.

183. *Hoobler, Dorothy and Thomas. *U.S.-China Relations Since World War II.* New York: Watts, 1981. 104pp. $7.45. Gr. 6–10.

An impartial account, and the only one for this age level, of the United States's fluctuating relations with the People's Republic and the Republic of China.

Hughes-Stanton. *See Inside an Ancient Chinese Town.* See entry 23.

Jennings. *China.* See entry 25.

Johnston. *The Fun with Tangrams Kit.* See entry 26.

Knox. *Ancient China.* See entry 29.

Lamb. *Genghis Kahn and the Mongol Horde.* See entry 30.

Leckie. *The War in Korea.* See entry 31.

184. Liston, Robert. *Women Who Ruled: Cleopatra to Elizabeth II.* New York: Messner, 1978. 192pp. $7.79. Gr. 7–12.

The Dowager Empress Ci Xi (Tzu Hsi, 1834–1908) is one of fourteen women rulers past and present who are profiled here (pp. 134–143).

185. Long, Jean. *How to Paint the Chinese Way.* New York: Sterling, 1979. illus. 127pp. $13.95. Gr. 7 up.

The principles of flower and landscape painting were formulated fifteen hundred years ago and are clearly explained here in text and graphic illustrations. The book covers equipment, the technique of brush strokes, the use of various intensities and shades of black as well as of color, the artist's seal (chop), and mounting. It complements Wong's *Oriental Watercolor Techniques* (entry 447).

186. MacFarquhar, Roderick. *The Forbidden City.* Wonders of Man. New York: Newsweek, 1972. illus. 172pp. $14.95. Gr. 6 up.

Profuse color and black-and-white illustrations and a two-column open format invite browsing in this story of Beijing's palaces through the ages of Chinese history. Extracts from what foreign visitors, past and present, have had to say about the Forbidden City are assembled in a separate section. Bonavia's *Peking* (entry 154) is a comparable title.

187. McKown, Robin. *The Opium War in China, 1840–1842: The British Resort to War in Order to Maintain Their Opium Trade.* World Focus Book. New York: Watts, 1974. illus. maps. 66pp. $4.47. Gr. 7 up.

The events are presented as "a painful and shameful example of Western imperialism." Noteworthy features include a list of participants on the page preceding the title page. The illustrations are in black-and-white.

188. Malloy, Ruth Tor. *Travel Guide to the People's Republic of China.* rev. ed. New York: Morrow, 1980. illus. maps. bibl. 366pp. $17.50; $12.95 pap. Gr. 7 up.

What distinguishes this from other guidebooks are the author's family ties to China. It moreover offers superior reference features in a detailed table of contents (five pages), coverage of over ninety tourist destinations in encyclopedic style, forty-five pages of phrases with more content than some separately published books, fifteen pages on Chinese designs, and a thirteen-page summary of Chinese history. Note also the separate chapter addressed to overseas Chinese, and the advice in "Learn about your own country" (good for any traveler to any foreign country). Addresses, the usual tips for travelers, and good bibliographies are included in this revision, which contains almost double the number of pages of the 1975 edition.

189. Marshall, S.L.A. *Military History of the Korean War.* New York: Watts, 1963, illus. 90pp. $4.90. Gr. 7 up.

China's historic relation to Korea and the advance of Chinese troops across the border in 1950 are briefly reported. The author, a military historian, omits the political causes of General MacArthur's dismissal, and his intention to invade China. The book is primarily for military strategy buffs who are willing to work through the difficult text. Leckie's *The War in Korea, 1950–1953* (entry 31) covers the China aspect more fully.

190. Martin, Christopher. *The Boxer Rebellion.* New York: Abelard, 1968. illus. maps. 175pp. $6.95. Gr. 7–12.

This book was written during the period of the Cultural Revolution, which the author ascribes to the same "anti-foreignism" that started the Boxer uprising. Duiker's *Cultures in Collision* (entry 306) is a more authoritative account.

191. Meltzer, Milton. *The Chinese Americans.* New York: Crowell, 1980. illus. map. 181pp. $8.95. Gr. 5–10.

Rarely has the story of the overwork, underpay, and near-peonage conditions of the Chinese railroad workers been told so dramatically. Employers of the Chinese in the goldmines, on California farms and on the railroad exploited their skills and technical knowledge, returning only contempt. The Chinese fought back on occasion and gained some important legal victories, but the achievement of a fair degree of equal rights came only in the 1960s. Even so, sweatshops are still a fact of life in Chinatowns.

The author has written other books on civil rights and racial injustice, and has done his homework. The lively and fast-paced text includes an excellent and well-illustrated discussion of factors that can lead to stereotyping, and is supplemented by instructive black-and-white photographs. Relevant legal documents are found in Tung's *Chinese in America* (entry 413).

192. Moore, Janet G. *The Eastern Gate: An Invitation to the Arts of China and Japan.* New York: Philomel, 1979. illus. 296pp. $24.95. Gr. 7 up.

Approximately ninety pages on the arts of China and twenty on Chinese literature provide a thematic introduction and "an invitation to enter the gate" for those outside the Eastern cultural realm. Profuse illustrations help the reader explore nature and the arts, landscape painting, the ceramic tradition, and the relation of art to Chinese philosophy, writing, and poetry. Considerable coverage of recent archaeological discoveries is provided.

Moore. *China in Pictures.* See entry 34.

193. Moskin, Marietta. *In Search of God: The Story of Religion.* New York: Atheneum, 1979. illus. 142pp. $10.95. Gr. 6 up.

A thematic examination of major religions and how each deals with death, good and evil, sin, the origin of the earth and of life, and similar universals, this unique volume can serve to promote pluralist attitudes toward religion.

Nach. *Hong Kong in Pictures.* See entry 35.

Nancarrow. *Early China and the Wall.* See entry 36.

Newton. *The First Books of Kings.* See entry 37.

194. *Norman, Marjorie, and Evans, Peter. *China: A Cultural Heritage* (kit). 9 exhibits, 4 broadsheets, w/tchr's guide. Jackdaw. New York: Viking, 1974. Dist. by Center for Teaching About China. $5.95. Gr. 7 up.

Good photos and prints of Chinese art illustrate the rich Chinese cultural heritage, from Confucius to the Cultural Revolution.

195. *Perrin, Linda. *Coming to America: Immigrants from the Far East.* New York: Delacorte, 1980. illus. 160pp. $9.95. Gr. 7–12.

From the Gold Rush to the present is covered. A history of immigration laws appears in the Appendix.

196. Petersen, Gwenn B. *Across the Bridge to China.* New York: Elsevier-Nelson, 1979. illus. 243pp. $8.95. Gr. 8 up.

The narrative by a fictional character who appears to be a composite of Chinese Americans expresses reactions to the New China by young persons with family ties there. It presents unique points of view on education, life in Canton, life in a commune, etc., and is at times critical, at other times admiring. Black-and-white photographs were taken by the author on a 1978 trip.

197. *Poole, Peter A. *China Enters the United Nations: A New Era for the World Organization.* World Focus Book. New York: Watts, 1974. illus. 77pp. $4.90. Gr. 7 up.

Chinese and Western perspectives are represented. See also the documentary United Nations film *China's Chair* (entry 487).

198. Printz, Peggy, and Steinle, Paul. *Commune: Life in Rural China.* New York: Dodd, 1977. illus. maps. 192pp. $6.95. Gr. 7 up.

The authors visited a commune in South China to make a television documentary, *China Commune* (16mm, 35 min, color, 1973; available from film rental libraries). Their report in book form is equally as telling and factual, and is replete with on-the-spot interviews, data, and black-and-white photographs showing young and old going about their daily activities. It provides insight into the organization and administration of the commune, its products, rural education, medical care, and the lifestyles of its people, including relations between the sexes. It provides good follow-up to such visuals illustrating communes as *Chinese Agriculture: A Study of Communes* (entry 108), *China—Set 1* (entry 234), *China: The Land and Its People* (entry 104), *Something for Everyone* (entry 260).

199. Purcell, Hugh. *Mao Tse-Tung.* New York: St. Martin's, 1977. illus. 96pp. $6.95. Gr. 7 up.

This British import objectively sets Mao's life and accomplishments in the contexts of Chinese history and Marxist ideology, in a manner and format suitable to a wide age range. Mao's typical behavior of setting himself apart from others is pointed out. Mao quotes are sprinkled in the margins where appropriate, and there are brief identifications of Jiang Qing (Chiang Ching), Zhou, Lin Biao, Sun and others. The approximately fifty full-page and smaller black-and-white photos are of China's last boy emperor, Pu Yi, the Long March, Mao's Yangtze swim, street scenes from the nineteenth and early twentieth centuries, of children building their own school, and much else.

Rau. *Our World: The People's Republic of China.* See entry 40.

200. RIUS. *Mao for Beginners.* Del Rio, Eduardo, ed. Trans. from Spanish. New York: Pantheon, 1980. illus. 171pp. $8.95; $2.95 pap. Gr. 9 up.

A sympathetic and humorous primer on Mao and Maoism in comic-book style.

201. *Roberson, John R. *China from Manchu to Mao.* New York: Atheneum, 1980. illus. 191pp. $10.95. Gr. 6–12.

Photographs illustrate this overview, which emphasizes the twentieth century, to 1976.

202. Romualdez, Daniel. *China: A Personal Encounter with the People's Republic.* Englewood Cliffs, N.J.: Prentice-Hall, 1977. illus. 164pp. $25. Gr. 6 up.

Amateur photos and very readable text are by the teenage son of the Philippine ambassador to the People's Republic, who visited cities and farms in 1975 and 1976.

203. Rugoff, Milton. *Marco Polo's Adventures in China.* Horizon Caravell Book. New York: American Heritage, 1964. illus. 152pp. o.p. Gr. 6 up.

The superb and varied illustrations will be of interest to younger students, though the text will not be accessible to most of them.

204. Schafer, Edward H. *Ancient China*. Morristown, N.J.: Silver-Burdett, 1967. illus. maps. tables. 191pp. $10.95. Gr. 6 up.

The history of the period from 1500 B.C. to A.D. 907 is lavishly illustrated with art reproductions. Several pages on the art of printing and "picture essays" on the Bronze Age, Buddhism in sculpture, women's roles, and painting punctuate the various chapters.

205. Schell, Orville, and Escherick, Joseph. *Modern China: The Story of a Revolution*. New York: Knopf, 1972. illus. 147pp. $5.99; $1.95 pap. Gr. 5–10.

Quotes from Chinese and Western sources are skillfully blended into the clear and straightforward text, which traces the origin of the 1949 Revolution to the inequalities of traditional Chinese society and to Western colonialism. The authors are well-disposed toward the PRC and quite uncritical of Mao and of the Cultural Revolution. The book includes black-and-white photographs. Schell is the author and editor of a number of adult books on China (see entries 286, 389, 390).

206. Seeger, Elizabeth. *Eastern Religions*. New York: Crowell, 1973. illus. 213pp. $10. Gr. 6 up.

The chapter entitled "The religions of China" (pp. 103–156) outlines the concepts of Yin and Yang, the teachings of Confucius and Lao Tzu, ceremonies, popular beliefs, the relationship between Confucianism and Buddhism, and the impact of Western influences. A separate chapter treats Buddhism. Black-and-white photographs show shrines, ceremonies, etc.

207. Sidel, Ruth. *Revolutionary China: People, Politics, and Ping-Pong*. New York: Delacorte, 1974. illus. map. 178pp. $6.95. Gr. 6 up.

The author and her husband traveled in China in 1971 and 1972 and became converts. This is a report of what she saw and learned; it stresses the contrast between the past and the present—in health, opium addiction, schooling, work, nutrition, politics and foreign relations. There is a chapter on Norman Bethune, the Canadian doctor who served with the Communist armies in 1938–39. Black-and-white photos and papercut illustrations are included.

208. Spencer, Cornelia. *Chiang Kai-shek: Generalissimo of Nationalist China*. New York: Day, 1968. illus. 253pp. o.p. Gr. 7–12.

This is a fictionalized, pro-Nationalist portrait, but the facts are there. It includes black-and-white photographs. The author, the sister of Pearl Buck (see entries 6, 454) was born in China.

209. Spencer, Cornelia. *China's Leaders in Ideas and Action.* Philadelphia, Pa.: Macrae Smith, 1966. map. 190pp. o.p. Gr. 7–12.

Profiles of a dozen outstanding Chinese range in time from Confucius to Zhou Enlai and include, in addition, the leader of the Taiping Rebellion; an eleventh-century administrator, Empress Ci Xi (Tzu Hsi); three Emperors, Sun, Chiang, Mao; and the language reformer James Yen.

210. Spencer, Cornelia. *The Land and People of China.* New York: Lippincott, 1972. illus. 159pp. $8.95. Gr. 7–12.

This chronological account of Chinese history offers about the right amount of detail for secondary school use. It ends with the China visit of the U.S. ping-pong team in 1971, and uses now passé terms such as "Mainland China" and "Nationalist China."

211. Spencer, Cornelia. *Sun Yat-Sen; Founder of the Chinese Republic.* New York: Day, 1967. illus. 191pp. o.p. Gr. 7–12.

The text notes the social standing of Sun's family, early influences on him, and his idealism and disappointments, and includes some fictional dialogue. Black-and-white illustrations and a four-page chronology are additional features.

212. Stalberg, Roberta Helmer, and Nesi, Ruth. *China's Crafts: The Story of How They're Made and What They Mean.* New York: Eurasia Press, 1980. Dist. by China Books & Periodicals. illus. map. 200pp. $9.95 pap. Gr. 7 up.

Collectors and shoppers may be the intended audience, but this is a value-packed reference volume for students and teachers as well. The chapter on symbols has extensive woodcut and papercut illustrations, and other chapters deal with pottery, jade, silk weaving and embroidery, lacquerware, cloisonné, metalwork, glass, and folk and regional arts. It contains color and black-and-white plates.

Sung. *An Album of Chinese Americans.* See entry 50.

Sung. *The Chinese in America.* See entry 51.

213. Tamarin, Alfred, and Glubok, Shirley. *Voyaging to Cathay: Americans in the China Trade.* New York: Viking, 1976. illus. 202pp. $10. Gr. 6–10.

This text on the China trade by a husband-and-wife team is first choice both for its superior selection of art works and for its vivid writing style. Glubok is the author of many successful art history books for beginners, including *The Art of China* (entry 13). About 185 black-and-white reproductions of contemporary illustrations include prints and engravings of ships, ports in China and the United States, homes of mandarins and ship captains, portraits, Chinese prints demonstrating pottery and silk manufacture, and even photographs of Northwest Coast Indians with Chinese coins (sea otters were trapped there for sale to China). The coverage is through the clipper ship era. See also Carpenter's *The Old China Trade* (entry 162).

214. Topping, Audrey. *The Splendors of Tibet.* New York: Sino Publishing Co., 1980. Dist. by China Books & Periodicals. illus. 185pp. $25. Gr. 7 up.

History, religion, economy, and government are covered in the text but the mainstay is the color photographs of cities, communes, people, palaces and temples. The slant is pro-People's Republic. For photographs of an older Tibet, see Tung's *A Portrait of Lost Tibet* (entry 215).

215. Tung, Rosemary Jones. *A Portrait of Lost Tibet.* New York: Holt, 1980. illus. 224pp. $19.95. Gr. 7 up.

The mainstay of the book is black-and-white photographs of people, places and practices, taken by a World War II secret mission to Tibet. The fairly brief text starts off heavy with Tolstoyan mystique (a grandson of Tolstoy was a member of the mission) but does give good accounts of the way of life, the religion, and the festivals of traditional Tibet. There is no index.

Van Note. *Tangrams, Picture-making Puzzle Game.* See entry 54.

216. Vlahos, Olivia. *Far Eastern Beginnings.* New York: Viking, 1976. illus. 292pp. $10.95. Gr. 7–12.

Since material on Tibet is not easy to come by, the chapter on that region is of value. Two others deal with Chinese culture and history ("Great

China") and village life ("Village China"). The book is engagingly written, with a continental view.

217. Werstein, Irving. *The Boxer Rebellion: Anti-Foreign Terror Seizes China, 1900.* World Focus Book. New York: Watts, 1971. illus. maps. 65pp. $4.90. Gr. 7–12.

The author, an experienced writer of nonfiction books for the general public and for young people, deftly summarizes the background of China's long self-sufficiency, the missionary overtures, and the trade relations that led to the Opium Wars. After a brief account of the Taiping Revolt of the 1850s, the bulk of the volume objectively and clearly reports on the sequence of events starting with the Sino-Japanese War and ending with the defeat of the Boxers. The illustrations are in black-and-white.

Wolff. *Chinese Writing.* See entry 58.

218. Wong, Jade Snow. *Fifth Chinese Daughter.* New York: Harper, 1950. illus. 246pp. $9.87. Gr. 5 up.

The classic autobiography of a San Francisco girl growing up in two cultures. Her portrayal has been criticized by activists as overly nostalgic. For a film verison see *Jade Snow* (entry 253). *No Chinese Stranger* (entry 219) is the sequel.

The World's Great Religions. See entry 59.

219. Wong, Jade Snow. *No Chinese Stranger.* New York: Harper, 1975. 366pp. $10.95. Gr. 7 up.

This sequel to *Fifth Chinese Daughter* (entry 218) reports on Wong's adult life and a trip to China.

220. Zetterholm, Tore. *China: Dream of Many.* New York: Sterling, 1978. illus. 240pp. o.p. Gr. 6 up.

Hundreds of color photos show art works, theater, daily life, street scenes, landscapes, homes, families, and games. The sparing text gives some historic hackground but emphasizes the present. It is more journalistic than Morath and Miller's *Chinese Encounters* (entry 368).

Fiction, Folklore, Poetry

221. Carlson, Dale. *The Beggar King of China.* New York: Atheneum, 1971. 185pp. o.p. Gr. 6 up.

A story set in fourteenth-century China.

222. Cordell, Alexander. *The Traitor Within.* New York: Nelson, 1973. illus. 126pp. o.p. Gr. 5–9.

The "traitor within" is the fear experienced by the fourteen-year-old hero as Taiwanese spies threaten to infiltrate his commune. He overcomes it and proves his loyalty and courage. The story is told in the first person and is based on actual incidents.

223. DeJong, Meindert. *House of Sixty Fathers.* New York: Harper, 1956. illus. 189pp. $8.79. Gr. 5–8.

A Chinese boy, separated from his family during the Japanese occupation, is reunited with them with the help of an Allied unit. A dramatized recording is available (entry 250).

224. Huggins, Alice M. *The Red Chair Waits.* Philadelphia, Penn.: Westminster, 1948. illus. 256 pp. o.p. Gr. 5 up.

The heroine is a teacher in a missionary school and must deal with the problem of having to marry a man chosen for her by her parents when she was a child.

Lao Tzu. *Tao Te Ching.* See entry 461.

Lewis. *Moment of Wonder.* See entry 77.

Liu. *Sunflower Splendor.* See entry 462.

225. Monjo, F.N. *The Porcelain Pagoda.* New York: Viking, 1976. 243pp. $10. Gr. 7 up.

The fictional journal of a girl accompanying her ship captain father to Canton in the 1820s, this historical novel is solidly based on research of the China trade and skillfully recreates its environment.

Roberts. *Chinese Fairy Tales and Fantasies.* See entry 469.

Shah. *World Tales.* See entry 85.

Tung. *One Small Dog.* See entry 87.

226. Yep, Laurence. *Child of the Owl.* New York: Harper, 1977. 217pp. $7.95: Dell, $1.50 pap. Gr. 7–12.

227. ———. *Dragonwings.* New York: Harper, 1975. 248pp. $8.95; $2.95 pap. Gr. 7–12.

228. ———.*Sea Glass.* New York: Harper, 1979. 208pp. $8.95. Gr. 6–8.

A Chinese immigrant kite-maker is the hero of *Dragonwings,* narrated by his son, and set in the San Francisco of the early 1900s. It illuminates the then prevailing white prejudice as well as Chinese family life and customs. How present-day Chinese-American teenagers come to terms with ethnic identity is the theme of the other two stories.

229. *Young, Alida. *Land of the Iron Dragon.* New York: Doubleday, 1978. 213pp. $7.95. Gr. 7 up.

The indignities suffered by Chinese railroad workers are dramatized in this story.

Audiovisual Resources

Acupuncture: An Exploration. See entry 472.

230. *An Anthology of Chinese Folk Songs.* 1 12" LP. Folkways. 1963. $8.98.

Performed by Ellie Mao.

Barefoot Doctors of Rural China. See entry 477.

Behind the Scenes at the Peking Circus. See entry 98.

231. *Chairman Mao's 4-Minute Physical Fitness Plan.* Millbrae, Calif.: Celestial Arts, 1973. illus. 64pp. 7" LP disc. Dist. by China Books & Periodicals. $3.95 pap. Gr. 4 up.

The exercises are pictured and described; the record has counting and music. This title is comparable to *Chinese Four-Minute Exercises* (entry 242).

China. See entry 100.

232. *China: A Portrait of the Land.* 16mm, 18 min, color, w/tchr's guide. Magnum, 1967. Dist. by Encyclopedia Britannica. $285. Gr. 7-12.

Exquisite work by the Swiss filmmaker René Burri and pleasing narration introduce the regions of China, their resources, and their unique characteristics. Scenes of logging may startle viewers who think of China in terms of rice paddies. A teacher's guide lists the film's sequences, with a synopsis for each, suggests discussion topics, and notes new vocabulary.

China: A Quarter of the World's People. See entry 102.

233. *China: Education for a New Society.* 16mm, 15 min, color, w/tchr's guide. Jens Bjerre, 1976. Dist. by Encyclopedia Britannica. $230. Gr. 7-12.

Footage of China's young people in schools, on farms, at sports centers, and at "Children's Palaces" demonstrates the persistent indoctrination of the Mao years. Some sports and farm scenes appeared in an earlier film by the same filmmaker. A teacher's guide provides a content summary and suggests pre- and post-viewing activities.

234. *China—Set 1: A Cultural Approach* (series). 5 filmstrips w/5 audiocassettes. 52-63 fr ea, 7-8 min ea, color, w/tchr's guide, 27 ditto masters. United Learning, 1980. $98. Gr. 6-12.

This set and its companion *An Historical Approach* (entry 235) are self-contained packages. The thirty-three-page teacher's guide states objectives for the unit and for each lesson within it, suggests comprehension and discussion questions (with expected answers), and prints the script. Accompanying ditto masters provide for follow-up activities and pre- and post tests and quizzes for each lesson (answer keys are in the teacher's guide). Additional projects are suggested, few involving reading or research. Component portions are "The Land," pointing to China's geography as her destiny; "A Sea of People," showing the "teeming millions" at work, at play and in school; "Daily Life," pointing out that living and housing conditions that seem shabby by our standards are vastly better than what most Chinese knew until the recent past; "Communes," again contrasting old and new; "Philosophy, Education, and Government," contrasting Mao Zedong's life and teachings with Confucianism. The occasional terminology "Mainland China" and the concluding statement "they see the complete victory of Communism, both at home and abroad, as their life's work" lend a slightly jarring note. See *China* by Margaret Rau (entry 100) for a comparable unit.

235. *China—Set 2: An Historical Approach* (series). 5 filmstrips w/5 audiocassettes. 50–72 fr ea, 9–15 min ea, color, w/tchr's guide, ditto masters. United Learning, 1980. $98. Gr. 6–12.

This set and its companion *A Cultural Approach* (entry 234) are self-contained packages. The forty-five-page teacher's guide states unit and lesson objectives; suggests comprehension and recall questions, discussion topics (with expected outcomes), and research projects; and prints the script. Accompanying ditto masters provide related activities, timelines, lesson quizzes, and a unit test (answer keys are in the teacher's guide). The visuals are from many sources, professional and amateur. Component portions are "China: Times of Elegance and Decay," surveying China's history from approximately 1500 B.C. to the late nineteenth century; "Crisis and Calamity: From Revolution to Liberation," continuing from the late nineteenth century to 1949; "Reshaping a Nation," dealing with the policies of Mao and his successors; "Art: A Barometer of Culture," a history of Chinese art from prehistoric pottery through Communist poster art; "China as a World Power," exploring China's relations with the Soviet Union, the United States (including references to Korea), African countries, Japan, and other Western nations, and China's wars with India and Vietnam. This strip and *Reshaping a Nation* present material not widely covered for this age group in a visual format. *China* by Margaret Rau (entry 100) and *The People's Republic of China* (entry 135) also offer historical approaches.

China: The Land and Its People. See entry 104.

236. *China: The One-Billion Society.* 1 filmstrip w/audiocassette, color, w/tchr's guide. 74 fr, 18 min, Current Affairs, 1979. $29.50. Gr. 7–12.

This brief overview begins by picturing examples of the flowering of

Chinese civilization, science, and technology of the past, then turns to the country's continuing labor-intensive agriculture and recent drives toward industrialization and modernization. Trade-offs of physical well-being and health versus regimentation and lack of freedom are addressed, and there is speculation about the coming Westernization. The teacher's guide contains the script (read by a female narrator), introduction and background, suggested questions, activities, and topics for papers, and a quiz.

Chinese Agriculture: A Study of Communes. See entry 108.

237. *Chinese Americans: Realities and Myths.* 4 filmstrips w/4 audiocassettes, color, w/tchr's guide, student book. Association of Chinese Teachers, 1977. Dist. by Social Studies School Service. $52. Gr. 7 up.

The history of Chinese Americans, current conditions, and stereotyping and prejudice in the past and present are treated here. The cassettes are in Cantonese and English. The book contains related source materials.

238. *Chinese Classic Instrumental Music.* 1 10" LP. Folkways, 1950. $7.98.

239. *Chinese Cooking: Pepper Steak, Rice, Cucumber Salad.* 1 filmstrip w/audiocassette. 97 fr, 23 min, color, w/tchr's guide. Encore, 1977. $25. Gr. 7–12.

Cutting, slicing, and cooking in a wok are clearly shown in close-ups and explained in the narration by a (female) instructor in Chinese cooking. The guide states objectives, gives a synopsis of the narration, and provides recipes and cooking directions.

240. *Chinese Folk Dances.* 16mm, 10 min, color. Wan-go Weng, 1955. Dist. by Pictura. $175; $20 rental. Gr. 4 up.

Two dances, performed by a professional dancer.

241. *The Chinese 49ers.* 1 filmstrip w/audiocassette. 50 fr, 10 min, color and b&w, w/tchr's guide. Multi-Media Productions, 1973. $25. Gr. 7 up.

How the Chinese came to California and how they were treated—with friendliness when their labor was needed, with hostility when they were seen as a threat—is told with sympathy by a female narrator and illustrated with stills from contemporary anti-Chinese pamphlets. The teacher's guide outlines the program, states its themes and student objectives, and suggests discussion questions and activities. This is a revision of the same producer's 1972 release *The Other 49ers*.

242. *Chinese Four-Minute Exercises.* 1 audiocassette, 2 posters, 23 × 35 in. ea, w/tchr's guide. Activity Records, 1977. Dist. by Educational Activities. $9.95. Gr. 4 up.

Recorded music and (female) voice directions are given for a series of eight exercises that involve each part of the body, and that are a part of the physical fitness program of the People's Republic. The two posters suitable for wall display show a leotard-clad young girl in each of the positions—a somewhat inauthentic note, since the exercises can be, and in China are, done in street clothes, and since Chinese clothing generally is quite figure-concealing. See also *Chairman Mao's 4-Minute Physical Fitness Plan* (entry 231) and *Friendship First, Competition Second* (entry 568).

The Chinese of Taiwan. See entry 112.

Chinese Shadow Play. See entry 113.

Chinese Tales. See entry 114.

243. *Courts, Tombs and Dragons.* 1 filmstrip w/audiocassette. 58 fr, color, w/tchr's guide. Bear Films, 1968. Dist. by Educational Activities. $19. Gr. 5–12.

China's history to 1644 is presented through its art, pictured on captioned frames. The accompanying narration offers considerable detail, and is reprinted in full in the teacher's guide, which also shows black-and-white prints of each frame. References to the present and some of the teaching suggestions are dated. Use as a complement to Glubok's *The Art of China* (entry 13) and to materials dealing with Chinese history.

244. *Crisis in Asia.* (World History from 1917 to Present (series). 16mm, 20 min, b&w. British Broadcasting Corporation, 1970. Dist. by Time-Life. $160; $70 video; $25 rental. Spanish soundtrack available. Gr. 7 up.

Made at a time when the People's Republic was regarded as the archenemy and reflecting that view, this focuses on U.S. efforts to "contain" Asian communism, the Korean war, and Chinese intervention in it.

Education in the People's Republic of China. See entry 561.

245. *The Football Incident* (How Yukong Moved the Mountains series). 16mm, 21 min, color. Joris Ivens, 1976. Dist. by Cinema Perspectives. $350; $50 rental. Gr. 7 up.

Unlike most films with footage of Chinese schools, this one features teenagers, and could be an excellent vehicle for North American high school students' gaining insight into the lives of their Chinese contemporaries. The slight plot revolves around a playground teacher–student dispute, and its settlement by extensive classroom discussion. The discussion ends with a public apology by the accused student to the teacher. Students may notice everyone wearing loose pants and shirts, the boys in crewcuts, the girls in pigtails and without make-up or jewelry. The question may be raised as to what extent more recent Western influences in China, as reported in Orville Schell's book (entry 390), have affected dress styles. The film was produced in France and French lines occasionally and disturbingly intrude on the soundtrack.

246. *From War to Revolution* (World History from 1917 to Present series). 16mm, 20 min, b&w. British Broadcasting Corporation, 1970. Dist. by Time-Life. $125; $12 rental. Spanish soundtrack available. Gr. 7 up.

China's political history from the early 1900s to 1949 is traced in this film, which includes footage of the Long March and the 1930s peasant mobilization campaigns.

The Good Earth: Farming Sequence. See entry 492.

The Good Earth: Woman Sequence. See entry 493.

247. *The Great Bronze Age of China: An Exhibition from the People's Republic of China.* 40 slides w/audiocassette. 30 min, color. Metropolitan Museum of Art, 1980. $19.95. Gr. 7 up.

Includes slides of recently excavated life-size terra cotta figures from the tomb of the first Emperor of Qin, and bronzes from earlier periods.

248. *Hong Kong: A Family Portrait.* 16mm, 59 min, color. National Geographic, 1979. $495; $395 (video). Gr. 5 up.

The film captures Hong Kong's transformation, since the 1950s, into a manufacturing center, partly as a consequence of the influx of millions of refugees from the People's Republic, and the perseverance of tradition alongside pervasive Westernization.

249. *Hong Kong Today.* 16mm, 16 min, color, w/tchr's guide. World Vision Educational Resources, 1980. Dist. by International Film Bureau. $295; $22.50 rental; $210 videocassette. Gr. 5 up.

The viewpoint and the male narrator's accent are British, and the general thrust is toward the tourist. Yet this film does in a short span of time hit the main aspects of the housing, population, religious practices, economy and agriculture, and life in Hong Kong today.

250. *House of Sixty Fathers.* 1 12" LP, 44 min. Newberry Award Records, 1973. $7.95. Gr. 5–8.

Dramatization of the book by DeJong (entry 223).

251. *How We Got Here: The Chinese.* ¾" videocassette, 29 min, color. Doni Ling, 1976. Dist. by PBS Video. $175; $55 rental. Gr. 7 up.

Interviews, dramatizations, period photographs, and music create a portrait of Chinatown residents in major United States cities.

Inside the New China. See entry 495.

252. *It's Always So In the World* (The Human Face of China series). 16mm, 28 min, color, w/tchr's guide. Film Australia, 1979. dist. by Learning Corporation of America. $450; $40 rental. Available on videocassette. Gr. 5 up.

This human interest profile of a three-generation family living in one of the new settlements on the outskirts of Shanghai includes a family picnic and school scenes from a special boarding school for promising athletes. There is repeated emphasis on the theme that China is coming out of its earlier austerity, that there is now consumer demand for cameras and television, not just for bicycles, and a concern for personal appearance. A two-page teacher's guide supplies a summary, before-viewing activities, and after-viewing discussion questions focusing on comparisons with the United States.

253. *Jade Snow. 16mm, 27 min, color. Films, Inc., 1976. $400; $35 rental; $300 videocassette. Gr. 5 up.

A film version of Fifth Chinese Daughter (entry 218), a favorite Chinese-American autobiography.

254. Jung Sai: Chinese American (Storm of Strangers series). 16mm, 29 min, color, w/tchr's guide. Macmillan, 1977. $385; $35 rental. Gr. 7 up.

A young Chinese American sets out to discover her heritage by interviewing older immigrants and finds that Chinese American immigrants came to the United States for much the same reasons as did those from Europe. The teacher's guide provides background information and a synopsis of the contents, and suggests discussion and comprehension questions.

255. The Mao Legacy: China at the Crossroads. 1 filmstrip w/audiocassette. 65 fr, 20 min, color, w/tchr's guide. Current Affairs, 1980. $29.50. Gr. 7 up.

This illustrated lecture examines China's geopolitical situation vis-a-vis other Asian countries (including the Soviet Union) and speculates on whether it or Japan will emerge as a superpower. The teacher's guide contains some background information, but no script or clearly defined objectives.

Marco Polo. See entry 129.

256. Mind, Body and Spirit (The Human Face of China series). 16mm, 28 min, color, w/tchr's guide. Film Australia, 1979. Dist. by Learning Corporation of America. $450; $40 rental. Available on videocassette. Gr. 5 up.

The film views China's three-pronged approach to health care: programs for universal physical fitness, public sanitation, and the availability of inexpensive medical care. It notes that the traditional health exercises, once reserved for the upper classes, are now performed by everyone, and that diseases of deprivation such as schistosomiasis have been wiped out. Barefoot doctors are shown at work in the field and in clinics. A two-page teacher's guide provides a summary, previewing activities, and post-viewing discussion questions focusing on comparisons with the United States.

Misunderstanding China. See entry 501.

257. **Myths of China* (World Mythology series). 1 filmstrip. 44 fr. Merit Audio Visual, 1980. $9. Gr. 6–8.

The captions tell traditional legends and stories while the visuals show art works representing mythical beings and other characters in the stories.

A Night at the Peking Opera. See entry 134.

258. *One Hundred Entertainments* (The Human Face of China series). 16mm, 28 min, color, w/tchr's guide. Film Australia, 1979. Dist. by Learning Corporation of America. $450; $40 rental. Available on videocassette. Gr. 5 up.

This documentary of an acrobatic troupe in Xian (Sian), capital of Shanxi province, shows members in practice, in performance, on tour to a rural commune, and at home. They explain that acrobats were popular street performers in the old China who only gained respectability under communism. Though theirs is said to be an art form free of politics, one notes the artists helping out the farmers on their visit to the commune. There is also some background on the history and the sights of Xian. The viewer keeps wishing for more shots of the performers and less talk. A two-page teacher's guide provides a summary and before- and after-viewing discussion questions.

People's Republic of China. See entry 135.

The People's Republic of China: Aspects of Life and Society in the New China. See entry 136.

259. *Silkmaking in China.* 16mm, 13 min, color. Atlantis Productions. n.d. $175. Gr. 5 up.

Silk production in a commune setting is shown, from the breeding of the worms, through processing, spinning, weaving, and embroidery. Art works interspersed with the photography clearly indicate that much of the process is unchanged over the centuries. Though the soundtrack is in spots poorly coordinated with the visuals, this is an instructive film. The Chinese genius for letting nothing go to waste shows up again: the dead silk worms find a final use as fish food on the commune's fish farm.

260. *Something for Everyone* (The Human Face of China series). 16mm, 28 min, color, w/tchr's guide. Film Australia, 1979. Dist. by Learning Corporation of America. $450; $40 rental. Available on videocassette. Gr. 5 up.

A profile of a rural commune in southern China, this film offers little new to add to earlier films about communes or filmstrips such as "The Rural Commune" (entry 104).

261. *Son of the Ocean* (The Human Face of China series). 16mm, 28 min, color, w/tchr's guide. Film Australia, 1979. Dist. by Learning Corporation of America. $450; $40 rental. Available on videocassette. Gr. 5 up.

A trip by boat down the Yangzi (Yangtze) River provides a travelogue of scenery and life along the river and insight into the lives of the passengers and crew, and the river's role in Chinese history. The two-page teacher's guide has a format similar to others in this series (see entries 252, 256, 258).

Tangram. See entry 139.

262. *A Town by the Yangtze.* 16mm, 10 min, color. Wan-go Weng, 1955. Dist. by Pictura Films. $175; $20 rental. Gr. 7 up.

The nostalgic portrait of the producer's hometown sees nothing but positive values in the traditional China where "the present is past and the past is present" and life never changes. It provides some balance to the more common totally negative view of the past.

263. *Traditional Handicrafts* (How Yukong Moved the Mountains series). Joris Ivens, 1976, released 1980. Dist. by Cinema Perspectives. $275; $40 rental. Gr. 4 up.

In traditional China ancient handicraft skills were passed on from father to son; today they are taught to young workers in collective workshops. Old legends and myths still provide the subjects, however. This appealing film permits an over-the-shoulder look at ivory sculpture, painting inside a bottle, and the manufacture both of curios for export and of studio quality art. The craftsman's use of his hand as palette as he fashions a delicate clay figurine will intrigue quite young viewers.

Part 3
Materials for
Senior High–Adults

Books

Nonfiction

Most of the books noted in this section are trade books for the general reader. Others are college texts and books by scholars that are suited for reference use by high school students or that serve to round out subject coverage. Pamphlets from both private organizations and government agencies, including Congressional committees, offer good value. Many of the books listed in Part 2, Materials for Middle School–Junior High Grades, will be of interest to this age group also, and that section should be referred to. In it will be found textbooks for this level (entries 171, 175, 182), in addition to the ones listed below (entries 293, 314, 324, and 325), as well as kits and similar sets for classroom use.

264. *Alexander, Garth. The Invisible China: The Overseas Chinese and the Politics of Southeast Asia.* New York: Macmillan, 1974. 272pp. $7.95. Gr. 11 up.

A journalistic account.

265. Allen, Steve. *"Explaining China."* New York: Crown, 1980. illus. 339pp. $14.95. Gr. 9 up.

Allen's introduction and concluding "Thoughts on China and America" make this a travelogue to be noticed. They represent an intelligent generalist's appraisal of what is good and what is bad about Communist China, achieving a reasoned understanding. Since the author comes from the world of the mass media rather than that of scholarship, his language is easy to follow. The bulk of the book tells the impressions gained on his 1975 trips with his China-born wife, and with his son, and is accompanied by black-and-white photographs. A detailed table of contents and a careful index complete the book.

266. *Ancient and Medieval Science.* (History of Science series). ed. by René Taton. New York: Basic, 1963. illus. tables. 551pp. o.p. Gr. 11 up.

"Ancient Chinese Science," by A. Haudricort and J. Needham, recounts Chinese accomplishments in astronomy, biology, mathematics, and physics prior to 300 A.D. and relates them to Confucian and Taoist teachings. Hoyt (entry 340) and Mason (entry 362) are other works on the history of science that take notice of Chinese accomplishments.

267. Arnold, Eve. *In China.* New York: Knopf, 1980. illus. 201pp. $30. Gr. 9 up.

An album of studio quality photographs of Chinese landscapes, people, life and work, from a 1979 trip. The text is not up to the quality of the pictures. Compare Morath and Miller's *Chinese Encounters* (entry 368) and Zetterholm's *China: Dream of Many?* (entry 220).

268. *A Barefoot Doctor's Manual: A Guide to Traditional Chinese and Modern Medicine.* Seattle, Wash.: Cloudburst, 1977. Dist. by China Books & Periodicals. illus. 372pp. $8.95 pap. Gr. 12 up.

A translation of an official 1970 Chinese manual, this title details the human body and its systems; discusses principles of personal and public hygiene, diagnostic and therapeutic techniques, birth control, and medicinal plants; and surveys the diagnoses and treatment of common diseases, infections, parasitic diseases, gynecologic and pediatric conditions, and much else. It includes line drawings of anatomical structures, an appendix on Chinese herbal medicines and patent medicines, and a glossary. It is more readable than the 1974 translation of the same manual by the National Institutes of Health (entry 437).

269. Barnett, A. Doak. *China and the World Food System.* Washington, D.C.: Overseas Development Council, 1979. tables. 115pp. $5 pap. Gr. 11 up.

Noting that China's food production increases have lagged behind the average for Asia, the author, a leading China scholar, sees a pressing need for China's full participation in the solution of worldwide food problems. No index is provided. See also *The Role of Science and Technology in China's Population/Food Balance* (entry 422).

270. Belden, Jack. *China Shakes the World.* New York: Monthly Review Press, 1970. Dist. by China Books & Periodicals. 524 pp. $6.95 pap. Gr. 11 up.

Belden came to China in 1933 as a sailor and remained, working with General Stilwell during the early part of World War II. This is his eyewitness account, first published in 1949, of what he saw of the Civil

War between Communists and Nationalists upon his return in 1946. The introduction is by Owen Lattimore.

271. Bloodworth, Dennis. *The Chinese Looking Glass.* rev. ed. New York: Farrar, 1980. 448pp. $8.95 pap. Gr. 11 up.

The purpose of the author, a journalist in the Far East whose wife is Chinese, is "to try to explain what makes the Chinese tick . . ." This collection of thirty-six essays blends personal experiences, anecdotes, and the writings of others into a potpourri of Chinese life and customs, history and politics, science and superstition. A chronological table and a thoughtful bibliography complement it, and an index helps to pinpoint specific topics, including the effects of Mao's death. A selective reading could be rewarding.

272. Bonavia, David. *The Chinese.* New York: Lippincott & Crowell, 1980. illus. 290pp. $12.95. Gr. 9 up.

The chief of the London Times Beijing bureau, and a former correspondent in the Soviet Union, here summarizes his insights into contemporary China. His topics include agriculture, cities and countryside, marriage and family, medicine, "the new consumerism," population policy, government, law, education, overseas Chinese, mass media, Chinese communism, and foreign policy, and are made accessible by a good index. There is an insert of black-and-white photos.

273. Bouc, Alain. *Mao Tse-tung: A Guide to His Thought.* Trans. by Paul Auster and Lydia Davis. New York: St. Martin's, 1977. 232pp. $10. Gr. 10 up.

A biographical account serves to introduce an analysis of Mao's interpretation of the dictatorship of the proletariat, the class struggle, and his ideas concerning leadership, economics, foreign policy and imperialism, women, and the Soviet Union. Thirty pages of excerpts follow. Terrill's *Mao* (entry 408) is a more recent biography.

274. Cameron, Nigel. *Barbarians and Mandarins: Thirteen Centuries of Western Travelers in China.* Chicago, Ill.: University of Chicago Press, 1976. illus. 443pp. $7.95 pap. Gr. 11 up.

Quotes from travelers' writings and period illustrations enhance this well-documented story that asks "who are the barbarians?" Its scope extends from a seventeenth-century Syrian through the 1930s.

275. Capon, Edmund. *Art and Archaeology in China.* Dist. by Cambridge, Mass.: The MIT Press, 1977. illus. maps. tables. 180pp. $25; $9.95 pap. Gr. 11 up.

Originally published in Australia to accompany the official Chinese Archaeological Exhibition and "to introduce some of the recent finds which have so dramatically brought ancient China to life," the handsomely produced and formated volume traces China's art from paleolithic times to 1368 A.D. with 118 color plates arranged in chronological chapters, each introduced by several pages of close print. Introductory chapters treat relations between China and the West, and archaeology in China, noting the Communist regime's extensive support of excavations. *New Archaeological Finds in China* (entries 373, 374) is a more modest account of recent excavations. See also the film *Old Treasures from New China* (entry 503) about the same exhibition, and the slide set *The Great Bronze Age of China* (entry 247) about a later one.

276. Chai, Chu & Winberg. *The Changing Society of China.* New York: New American Library, 1969. 278pp. $1.95 pap. Gr. 9 up.

This comprehensive survey for the general reader is organized to make it readily accessible for reference use. It addresses geographic background, the historical experience, ethnic origins and racial amalgamation, fundamental concepts, government in Imperial, Nationalist and Communist China, social structure, family (including ancestor worship), communes, law, philosophy, religion, literature, language, and art. Finally, there is a survey of change and revolution since the mid-1800s, with concluding observations on change and continuity in Chinese society.

277. Chai, Winberg. *The Search for a New China: A Capsule History, Ideology, Leadership of the Chinese Communist Party, 1921–1974.* New York: Putnam, 1975. maps. tables. 316pp. o.p. Gr. 11 up.

After an introduction tracing the Party's origins to the Opium Wars, Boxer Rebellion, Sun Yat-sen, warlord politics, and Japanese aggression, separate chapters trace the Party's birth, the collaboration with the Nationalists, the Long March, the peculiarly Chinese brand of Communism, the Cultural Revolution, and the period immediately after it. Approximately half the book is taken up with documents (the 1969 Constitution of the Party, reports by Lin Biao and Zhou Enlai, and others), and there is a chronology of the events of the Cultural Revolution.

278. Chang, Raymond. *Speaking of Chinese.* New York: Norton, 1978. illus. 197pp. $10.95. Gr. 9 up.

The logic and construction of Chinese language and writing are explained in relaxed and easily understood style and illustrated by facsimile pages from Chinese books and ideographs in the margins. Proverbs in Chinese and English illustrate sentence construction. The chapter on calligraphy provides insight into writing as an art form. Historical tables and tables of common elements (radicals) are included.

279. *Chen, Jack. *The Chinese of America: From the Beginnings to the Present.* New York: Harper, 1980. 274pp. $15.95.

Chinese immigrants not only built railroads; they also worked in gold mines, wineries, fisheries, on farms and in cities. The familiar story of their deprivation of both legal rights and human dignity is retold up through the present, with new insights into Chinese-American institutions.

280. Chen, Jack. *The Sinkiang Story.* New York: Macmillan, 1977. illus. maps. 386pp. $17.95. Gr. 10 up.

The story of China's westernmost province and the locus of the ancient Silk Road is told from an official People's Republic perspective. The author sees it as "the melting pot of history" from A.D. 220 to 1850, after having been mentioned as early as 500 B.C. in a Greek manuscript. He includes a glossary, a gazetteer, and a superior chronological table of Chinese history.

281. Chen, Jack. *A Year in Upper Felicity: Life in a Chinese Village during the Cultural Revolution.* New York: Macmillan, 1973. illus. 383pp. $8.95. Gr. 9 up.

The author was born in China and returned there after being reared in the West Indies. Here he tells of the farm activities for each season of the year (1969–70) he spent on a commune.

282. Chesneaux, Jean. *China from the Opium Wars to the 1911 Revolution.* New York: Pantheon, 1976. 412pp. $17.95; $6.95 pap. Gr. 11 up.

283. _____. *China from the 1911 Revolution to Liberation.* New York: Pantheon, 1977. 372pp. $17.95; $6.95 pap.

284. _____. *China: The People's Republic, 1949–1976.* New York:. Pantheon, 1979. maps. 255pp. $15; $4.95 pap.

These massive volumes by a professor at the Sorbonne are suitable for reference use and contain original source materials. Of interest are the chapters "China in 1840," "China in 1885," and "China in 1949." The last volume clearly notes the various stages in the history of the People's Republic to 1976 and its changing policies.

285. "China: Education and Society," *Theory Into Practice.* Vol. 27, no. 5 (December 1978). $2.50 pap. Gr. 12 up.

An entire issue devoted to China's education.

286. *The China Reader.* New York: Random. 4 vols. Gr. 11 up. vols. 1, 2, 3: Schurmann, Franz, and Schell, Orville, ed. vol. 1: *Imperial China* (1967, 287pp., $3.95 pap.); vol. 2: *Republican China* (1967, 369pp., $3.95 pap.); vol. 3: *Communist China* (1967, 667pp., $4.95 pap.). vol. 4: Milton, David and Nancy, ed. *People's China.* (1974, 659pp., $4.95 pap.).

The editors compiled the first three volumes "to further our rational understanding of China"—a brave undertaking in 1967. Indispensable sourcebooks, they bring together primary and secondary sources, Chinese and Western, representing many points of view. Volume 1 covers the eighteenth and nineteenth centuries; volume 2, 1901–1949, with selections by Sun Yat-sen, Chiang Kai-shek, Lu Hsun, Mao Zedong, Edgar Snow, General Joseph Stillwell, Theodore White, General Albert Wedemeyer, William Bullitt, and Dean Acheson, for example. Volume 3 has Edgar Snow's 1965 interview with Mao, among many other excerpts dealing with Communist China's foreign and domestic policies, ideology, daily life, economy and trade, science and technology, minorities and borders. Volume 4's focus is on the 1966–1972 period, specifically communes, administration, economy, education, health, the Cultural Revolution, ideology, foreign policy, and "views of China" from France, Africa, and the USSR. The majority of sources are People's Republic spokesmen or friendly observers. James Reston's (*The New York Times*) interview with Zhou Enlai is notable.

287. *China Traveler's Phrasebook.* Eurasia Press, 1980. Dist. by China

Books & Periodicals. illus. 192pp. $5.95; $11.95 including audiocassette. Gr. 9 up.

Two thousand words and phrases are shown in English, in simplified Chinese characters, in Pinyin romanization, and in phonetic transcription. Background is given on the history and characteristics of the Chinese language.

288. *China: U.S. Policy Since 1945*. Washington, D.C.: Congressional Quarterly, 1980. maps. tables. 387pp. $10.95 pap. Gr. 9 up.

An invaluable sourcebook not only for U.S.-China relations but for internal developments in China as well. One half the pages are taken up with a chronology of the People's Republic and the Republic of China from a "Before 1945" summary to January 1980, and are preceded by a parallel chart of Chinese and world history. The biography section carries one- to two-page articles on major figures (Communist and Nationalist), and briefer ones on U.S. policy makers, Nationalist leaders, and Communist leaders that were relatively obscure at the time of writing, including Zhao Ziyang. Finally there are reprinted here relevant documents, speeches, and other statements—the Constitution of the People's Republic, the "Four Modernizations" announcement, the China Aid Act of 1948, Taiwan–U.S. treaties, the Tonkin Gulf Resolution, and many others. Summaries and tables on a variety of subjects from acupuncture to pandas to Vietnam are placed throughout the two-column text.

289. *China's Minority Nationalities: Selected Articles from Chinese Sources*. Modern China series No. 3. Red Sun, 1977. Dist. by China Books & Periodicals. illus. maps. 256pp. $3.95 pap. Gr. 11 up.

Reprints of articles, with black-and-white photos, from *China Reconstructs* (entry 168) and Foreign Languages Press publications, and of speeches by Chinese officials. No index.

290. *The Chinese Revolution—The Early Stages*. Beijing: Foreign Languages Press, 1976. Dist. by China Books & Periodicals. 5 vols., $7.95 pap.; $1.95 ea. Gr. 11 up.

The set contains *The Opium War* (131pp.), *The Taiping Revolution* (188pp.), *The Reform Movement of 1898* (136pp.), *The Yi Ho Tuan Movement of 1900* (133pp.), and *The Revolution of 1911* (174pp.). They represent the official Maoist interpretation of the overthrow of the Man-

chu dynasty and earlier revolutionary attempts of the Chinese people,
See also Tung's *An Outline History of China* (entry 412).

291. Chu, Yu-kuang. *A Demographic and Economic Geography of China.* Saratoga Springs, N.Y.: Empire State College, 1974. 62pp. $1.75 pap. Gr. 11 up.

This sequel to *A Physical and Political Geography of China* (entry 292) deals with population trends, and agricultural and industrial development.

292. Chu, Yu-kuang. *A Physical and Political Geography of China.* Saratoga Springs, N.Y.: Empire State College, 1974. maps. 97pp. $1.75 pap. Gr. 11 up.

This programmed text designed for individual study encompasses geopolitics, topography, climate, ethnology, and political factors, and takes up in detail each region of China, including Taiwan, and Tibet and other autonomous regions. It is a companion volume to *A Demographic and Economic Geography* (entry 291).

293. Clark, James I. *China.* Peoples and Cultures series. Evanston, Ill.: McDougal, Littell. 1976. illus. map. 162pp. $5.80 pap.; $1.50 tchr's guide. Gr. 9–12.

The three portions of this attractive text describe "An ancient civilization," "China in the hands of foreigners," and "A new society." Numerous black-and-white photos, a two-column format, a free-flowing narrative including excerpts from Chinese literature and Western writings, and a full index are plus features. The eighteen-page student's guide (by James M. Edwards) identifies the major concepts of each chapter, suggests study questions, and lists important names and terms.

294. Clubb, Oliver Ed. *Twentieth Century China.* 3rd ed. New York: Columbia, 1978. bibl. 554pp. $22.50; $9 pap. Gr. 12 up.

A thorough, scholarly work by the last U.S. Consul General in Beijing after the Communist takeover, it is accessible for reference use by the general reader, and contains helpful bibliographic notes. The final chapter is entitled "China after Mao."

295. Cohen, Joan L., and Cohen, Jerome A. *China Today and Her An-*

cient Treasures. 2nd ed. New York: Abrams, 1980. illus. maps. 416pp. $35. Gr. 9 up.

Addressed chiefly to prospective visitors, the book seeks to present China's "artistic heritage . . . in the context . . . of today." Several hundred color photographs of palaces, monuments, art works, homes in cities and towns, communes, and day nurseries accompany the text, which gives a chronological account of Chinese history. Events since the mid-1970s, when the first edition appeared, are assessed in the introduction, which calls for a "more sober" view. The final chapter deals with "The Arts in People's China." Compare *Horizon Book of the Arts of China* (entry 338).

296. *Constitution of the People's Republic of China.* Beijing: Foreign Languages Press, 1978. Dist. by China Books & Periodicals. 41pp. $2.95; $1.50 pap. Gr. 9 up.

Adopted in 1978, and about the same length as the U.S. Constitution, its four chapters outline General Principles, Structure of the State (national and local government), Rights and Duties of Citizens, and National Flag, National Emblem and the Capital. Citizens' duties include "support(ing) the leadership of the Communist Party. . . ."

297. Costello, Mary. "China's Opening Door." *Editorial Research Reports,* September 8, 1978.

Costello's summary is an assessment of the policies of Hua Gofeng (Hua Kuo-feng) and Deng Xiaoping (Teng Hsiao-ping), with a look back at criticism of Mao during the Great Leap Forward and the Cultural Revolution. This was written just before President Carter's announcement of the normalization of diplomatic relations between the People's Republic and the United States.

298. Costello, Mary. "Sino-Soviet Relations." *Editorial Research Reports,* February 4, 1977.

Costello provides an even summary of the two countries' competition for world influence and the genesis of the present relationship in Mao's early grievances against the Soviet Union, and the role of the United States. The article ends with various commentators speculating on "American policy in a Tripolar world."

299. Coye, Molly Joel, and Livingston, Jon, ed. *China: Yesterday and*

Today. The George School Readings on Developing Lands. 2nd ed. New York: Bantam, 1979. maps. 576pp. $2.95 pap. Gr. 9–Adult.

An anthology of over 100 selections by Chinese and foreign writers on Chinese culture (including fables and poetry), history, and politics. Writings by Chiang Kai-shek, Mao, and Confucius are represented.

300. *Creating a New Chinese Medicine and Pharmacology.* Beijing: Foreign Languages Press, 1977. Dist. by China Books & Periodicals. illus. 82pp. $1 pap. Gr. 11 up.

Black-and-white photos and text describe treatments combining traditional Chinese with Western techniques for the relief of fractures, intestinal obstructions, appendicitis, ulcers, gall bladder diseases, and cataracts. *Scaling the Peaks in Medical Science* from the same sources (1972, illus., 69pp. $.75) contains reports on Mao-inspired alleged cures for deafness, poliomyelitis, and burns, on acupuncture anaesthesia, rejoining of severed limbs, pharmacology, and other topics.

301. Curtin, Kate. *Women in China.* New York: Pathfinder Press, 1975. illus. 95pp. $8; $2.45 pap. Gr. 11 up.

The author writes from a feminist and socialist point of view, and sees sexual inequality and double standards continuing in the People's Republic. After examining women's place in the old society, the volume traces changes and adjustments in recent policy relating to women, population, birth control, abortion, education of women, their place in the labor force and in politics. No index.

302. *Ding, Shu De. *The Chinese Book of Table Tennis.* New York: Atheneum, 1981. illus. 192pp. $9.95. Gr. 9 up.

Ping pong is a national sport in China. This work lets us in on the history of the sport in China, strategies of play, and Chinese training techniques.

303. *Doncaster, Islay. *Traditional China.* St. Paul, Minn.: Greenhaven, 1980. illus. 32pp. $6.60; $2.60 pap. Gr. 10 up.

Photos and excerpts from original documents.

304. Draper, Thomas, ed. *Emerging China.* Reference Shelf, vol. 52, no. 1. New York: Wilson, 1980. 240pp. $5.75. Gr. 9 up.

Twenty-seven excerpts from books, pamphlets and periodical articles on the subjects of U.S.-China relations and Chinese foreign trade, history, Overseas Chinese in Southeast Asia, and life inside the People's Republic of China, including the legal system, cultural life and performing arts, population policy, and the status of women and of older people. There is no index. One or two of the selections are reprinted from the earlier volume in the same series, Isenberg's *China: New Force in World Affairs* (entry 343).

305. Dreyer, June T. "Ethnic Relations in China." *Annals of the American Academy of Political and Social Science*, vol. 433, pp. 100–111. September 1977. Gr. 10 up.

A one-half page abstract precedes the article, which summarizes the history of the Han Chinese gaining of dominance, the policies of the Chinese Communist Party, the effects of the Great Leap Forward and the Cultural Revolution, and the outlook for the future. Dreyer is the author of the standard scholarly work *China's Forty Millions: Minority Nationalities and National Integration in the People's Republic of China* (Cambridge, Mass.: Harvard, 1977. 333pp. $14). See the map *Peoples of China* (entry 537) for pictorial representations.

306. Duiker, William J. *Cultures in Collision: The Boxer Rebellion.* San Rafael, Calif.: Presidio Press, 1978. illus. maps. 226pp. $12.95. Gr. 10 up.

This political and military history traces the revolt's origins in imperialist practices and its legacy, and is enhanced by sketch maps, reproductions of contemporary prints, pleasing typography, and bibliographies.

307. Durdin, Tillman, ed. *New York Times Report from Red China.* New York: Quadrangle, 1971. 367pp. o.p. Gr. 9 up.

Dispatches sent by *The New York Times* correspondents James Reston and Seymour Topping in 1970 convey American attitudes toward the China of that period.

308. Eberhard, Wolfram. *A History of China.* 4th ed. Berkeley, Calif.: California, 1977. illus. maps. 388pp. $5.95 pap. Gr. 10 up.

The latest edition of this standard work incorporates new knowledge gained as a result of recent archaeological excavations. It "attempts to pay more attention to social and cultural developments than to purely political history; to try to find out how the 'common man' lived and not only how the leaders lived." One chapter each is devoted to the Republic (1912-1948) and to present-day China, the latter written before Mao's death. Clear subdivisions of each chapter make this closely printed volume suitable for reference, and a full index enables the tracing of topics such as agriculture, education, and administration through the various periods of Chinese history.

309. *Ebrey, Patricia Buckley, ed. *Chinese Civilization and Society: A Sourcebook.* Glencoe, Ill.: Free Press, 1981. 575pp. $19.95; $10 pap. Gr. 10 up.

Letters, diaries, newspaper articles, folktales, stories, excerpts from books, and other primary sources in translation are arranged chronologically, from 1766 B.C. to 1979. Gittings's *A Chinese View of China* (entry 322) serves a similar purpose with smaller scope.

310. Eckstein, Alexander. *China's Economic Revolution.* New York: Cambridge University Press, 1977. tables. 340pp. $19.95; $9.95 pap. Gr. 11 up.

A quite academic work, treating China's economic heritage, policies, organization, foreign trade, resource allocation, and related topics. The final chapter, "The Chinese Development Model," offers a summary and critical appraisal. It is reprinted in the government publication *The Chinese Economy Post-Mao* (entry 426).

311. "Education in China." *Journal of General Education.* vol. 26, XXVI, no. 3 (Fall 1974). Pennsylvania State University Press, 1974. $2 pap. Gr. 12 up.

This issue consists of accounts of visits by members of a delegation from the university. See also Parker's *What Can We Learn From the Schools of China* (entry 382). Educational policies have changed in the years since this was published.

312. *Encyclopedia of China Today.* ed. by Frederic M. Kaplan and others. rev. ed. New York: Harper, 1980. illus. maps. tables. 336pp. $37.50. Gr. 11–Adult.

This oversized, comprehensive reference emphasizes politics and economics, while also including sections on geography, population and culture. Some fifty concise biographies of postwar leaders, analysis of the governmental structure, texts of the 1978 State Constitution and the 1977 Communist Party Constitution, and chronologies for 1970–78 are among the notable features. The introduction is by John S. Service, the former U.S. diplomat who was in disgrace during the McCarthy period.

313. Fairbank, John K. *The United States and China.* 4th ed. Cambridge, Mass.: Harvard, 1979, illus. maps. tables. bibl. 606pp. $18.50; $6.95 pap. Gr. 12 up.

No one engaged in the serious study of China can do without this standard work by one of the foremost authorities in the United States, first published in 1948 "to explain China to Americans." Its scope extends from prehistory to the present, but the emphasis is on the long revolutionary process that changed the old Confucian order under the impact of Western intrusions and led to the rise of the Communist party. Relations between the United States and the People's Republic are traced through the shifts in policies of each country, and through the Korean and Vietnam wars. Of particular note is the ninety-page definitive bibliographic essay, with a separate table of contents and an author index, which assays mostly academic books dealing with every aspect of traditional and modern Chinese life and Chinese–American relations.

314. Fairbank, John K.; Reischauer, Edwin; and Craig, Albert M. *East Asia: Tradition and Transformation.* Boston: Houghton; 1978. illus. maps. tables. 982pp. $18.95. Gr. 11 up.

A college text that makes an excellent reference on China, Hong Kong, and Taiwan, it traces the spread of Chinese civilization to Vietnam and Korea and states that the four East Asian nations (the fourth is Japan) are more unlike each other than the various national subunits in the West.

315. Fan, K.H. & K.T. *From the Other Side of the River: A Self-Portrait of China Today.* Garden City, N.Y.: Doubleday, 1975. 429pp. o.p. Gr. 9 up.

Reprints from *Peking Review, China Reconstructs* (entry 168) and other People's Republic publications are arranged in topical sections, each briefly introduced, on family and marriage (including excerpts from the Marriage Law), women, children and youth, schools, communes, cities, minority nationalities, economic principles, agriculture, industry, commerce and finance, environmental protection, higher education, and political ideology. It is an excellent sourcebook for leaning Chinese views firsthand. There is no index. The periodicals from which the selections are taken are available for subscription through China Books & Periodicals (entry 562).

316. Fitzgerald, Charles P. *The Chinese View of Their Place in the World*. New York: Oxford, 1966. 80pp. o.p. Gr. 11 up.

Essays on ancient and modern Chinese history are written from a Chinese point of view. See Gittings's *A Chinese View of China* (entry 322) for the writings of Chinese authors. There is no index.

317. Frolic, B. Michael. *Mao's People: Sixteen Portraits of Life in Revolutionary China*. Cambridge, Mass.: Harvard University Press, 1980. map. 278pp. $15. Gr. 11 up.

The author, a student of the Soviet Union who also served in the Canadian embassy in Beijing in 1974–75, interviewed more than two hundred refugees and travelers from the People's Republic to Hong Kong. The incidents selected from those interviews are told here in the narrators' own words, and each is introduced with a brief background sketch. Though the author started with considerable skepticism about the People's Republic, these stories are not rabidly anti, but they do expose cracks in the facade. No index is provided.

318. Fryer, Jonathan. *The Great Wall of China*. New York: Barnes, 1977. illus. maps. 207pp. $12. Gr. 9 up.

Readable text, line maps, art reproductions, and black-and-white photographs briefly survey archaeology in China, trace the course of Chinese history, and chronicle the building and maintenance of the Wall for almost two thousand years, from the third century B.C. to the 1600s. The book also covers the construction of the Great Canal, and devotes twenty pages to Westerners' impressions of the Great Wall.

319. Garside, Roger. *Coming Alive: China After Mao*. New York: McGraw-Hill, 1981. illus. 458pp. $12.95. Gr. 11 up.

Writings from the "Democracy Wall" that went up in Beijing in early 1976 are quoted in this sympathetic and optimistic account of the liberalization China experienced after the deaths of Zhou Enlai and Mao Zedong. The author is a British diplomat who was stationed in Beijing from 1976 to 1979. There is an interesting chapter, "But what is socialism?," on China's economy.

320. Gentzler, J. Mason. *A Syllabus of Chinese Civilization.* 2nd ed. New York: Columbia University Press, 1972. maps. 107pp. $5 pap. Gr. 9 up.

Chinese history is given in outline form, with extensive detail. Outline maps show the extent of agricultural areas and territory ruled by various dynasties, also the provinces now in existence.

321. *Ginneken, Jaap van. *The Rise and Fall of Lin Piao.* New York: Avon, 1977. 348pp. $2.50 pap.

Lin Biao (Lin Piao) a defense minister of the People's Republic in the 1950s, was one of Mao's most loyal aides until their falling-out in 1971. He died shortly thereafter in a mysterious plane crash.

322. Gittings, John. *A Chinese View of China.* New York: Pantheon, 1973. illus. 216pp. $6.95; $2.95 pap. Gr. 11 up.

Thirty-four excerpts from contemporaneous Chinese sources, extending from 800 B.C. through the Cultural Revolution and including poetry and prose, are illustrated with black-and-white photographs of portraits, posters, and other graphics. The first eight selections are from the period prior to the Opium Wars; the rest deal with nineteenth-century trade and other interaction with the West, the Boxer Rebellion, Sun Yat-sen, the Republican period, Mao, and the People's Republic. There is no index. The book supplements Fan's *From the Other Side of the River* (entry 315). Ebrey's *Chinese Civilization and Society: A Sourcebook* (entry 309) is a more recent and more ambitious anthology.

323. Gittings, John. *The World and China, 1922–1972.* New York: Harper, 1974. 303pp. o.p. Gr. 9 up.

A sympathetic British correspondent, Gittings gives an explanation of the foreign policies of the People's Republic as rooted in China's victimization by imperialist powers. The prologue, which recounts the introduction of cigarette smoking and tobacco growing in China by British and American interests, serves as a case study in point. Of special interest are the chapter on the Korean War, giving the Chinese side in that conflict, and the one on "Mao and the Soviet Union," providing the ideological background for the current enmity between the two countries.

324. Gross, Susan Hill, and Bingham, Marjorie Wall. *Women in Traditional China: Ancient Times to Modern Reform.* Hudson, Wisc.: Gary E. McCuen Publications, 1980. illus. 120pp. $7.95; $3.95 pap; $.95 tchr's guide. Gr. 9–12.

325. ———. *Women in Modern China: Transition, Revolution and Contemporary Times.* Hudson, Wisc.: Gary E. McCuen Publications, 1980. illus. 106pp. $7.95; $3.95 pap; $.95 tchr's guide. Gr. 9–12.

The first volume speculates on a possible prehistoric Chinese matriarchy, and notes women as warriors, rulers, at court, and the role of educated women, before describing in detail the lives of most women in traditional China. The second volume traces reform movements from 1700 on, including the influence of Christian missionaries, and takes note of special conditions in Tibet and under the Manchu, finally focusing on women in the People's Republic. Plentiful black-and-white photographs, charts, summaries, review questions, glossaries, and full bibliographies are features of these volumes in the series *Women in World Area Studies.* An accompanying sound filmstrip *Women in China* (117 fr, 19 min, $24.95) brings together archival and contemporary visuals.

326. Hammond, Ed. *Coming of Grace: An Illustrated Biography of Zhou Enlai.* Berkeley, Calif.: Lancaster-Miller, 1980. illus. map. 177pp. $14.95; $8.95 pap. Gr. 9 up.

This admiring, at times flowery, biography shows Zhou frequently in the role of peacemaker, adjusting conflicts within the Chinese Communist Party, and as statesman. It relies heavily on black-and-white newsphotos, which are most welcome since many are unique and not readily found elsewhere.

327. Hammond, Ed. *To Embrace the Moon: An Illustrated Biography of Mao Zedong.* Berkeley, Calif.: Lancaster-Miller, 1980. illus. map. 175pp. $14.95; $8.95 pap. Gr. 9 up.

Mao's unique gift for leadership comes through clearly in this account, which also raises many questions about his policies and intention. Over one hundred black-and-white newsphotos from Chinese and other sources are included.

328. Han, Suyin. *The Crippled Tree.* New York: Bantam, 1972. map. 502pp. o.p. Gr. 9 up.

Dr. Han, part Chinese and part Belgian, practices medicine in Singapore. Her writings blend China's twentieth-century history with her own autobiography and generally reflect the thinking of the currently leading faction within the People's Republic. This particular volume focuses on the period from 1885 to 1913. It has several sequels.

329. Han, Suyin. *Lhasa, The Open City.* New York: Putnam, 1977. illus. map. 180pp. o.p. Gr. 9 up.

This travelogue, with black-and-white photos by the author, of her visit in 1975, delves into the history of Tibet, its occupation by China and subsequent flight of the Dalai Lama, and the improvements in living conditions since 1951. The viewpoint is totally uncritical, and laudatory of the People's Republic.

330. Harding, Harry, Jr. *China and the U.S.: Normalization and Beyond.* New York: Foreign Policy Association, 1979. illus. maps, tables. 32pp. $1.50 pap. Gr. 10 up.

Noting that normalization of relations with China has not ended the debate over U.S. policy toward that country, the author examines the issues involved in implementing the present policy, as it relates to trade, scientific and educational exchanges, and military and strategic considerations. Possible future courses for Taiwan are also explored. Joint statements and statements by each country, including Taiwan, are reprinted. The tone is even, the style readable, the theme to "avoid unrealistic or sentimental expectations." Black-and-white photographs, cartoons, and graphic illustrations of economic and military data lend interest. There is no index. It is jointly published with The Asia Society (entry 579). See also *China and America: Past and Future* (entry 377).

331. Hatano, Sumi. *Cooking from Mainland China: 158 Authentic Recipes from the People's Republic of China.* New York: Barron's, 1979. illus. 133pp. $9.95. Gr. 9 up.

There are less expensive Chinese cookbooks on the market, but the luscious full-color illustrations of finished dishes and the black-and-white photos depicting technique give this one unique instructional value. Its visuals are superior to those of any film or filmstrip seen and include pictures of Chinese ingredients. There is a good section on how to prepare ingredients. Included are recipes for meats, vegetables, egg and chicken, fish and shellfish, and rolls and buns.

332. Hellerman, Leon, and Stein, Alan L., eds. *China: Readings on the Middle Kingdom.* New York: Washington Square Press, 1971. 332pp. $1.25 pap. Gr. 10 up.

Extracts from Chinese and Western sources, including treaties and other documents, prose and poetry, range over all of Chinese history and culture. One or more selections are included on language, geography, oracle bones, traditional agriculture, land distribution, civil service examinations, Western observers, and much else. One-third of the pages pertain to contemporary China.

333. Hinton, Harold C. *The Far East and Southwest Pacific.* 1978 ed. Washington, D.C.: Stryker-Post, 1978. illus. maps. tables. 99pp. Dist. by Social Studies School Service. Annual. $2.95. Gr. 9 up.

This annually revised overview includes chapters on China (including Taiwan) and Hong Kong, each full of current data on area, population, economy, and politics, as well as geographical and historical summaries.

334. *Hinton, Harold C. *An Introduction to Chinese Politics.* 2nd ed. Huntington: Krieger, 1978. 336pp. $13. Gr. 11 up.

This is the definitive text, with revisions for the post-Mao period. The first edition (1973) contained sections dealing with the traditional Chinese political system, the rise of the Communist Party, factionalism within the Party, the Cultural Revolution, the armed forces, foreign policy, and the question of Taiwan. Intended for the college level, the book is useable by high school students for reports on specific topics.

335. Hinton, William. *Fanshen: A Documentary of Revolution in a Chinese Village.* New York: Monthly Review Press, 1966. 637pp. Random, $5.95 pap. Gr. 11 up.

Hinton went to China as a United Nations Relief and Rehabilitation Administration worker and remained to teach English at a university. When land reform was instituted in Communist-held territory, he went to observe and take notes. His notes were confiscated when he came to the United States in the 1950s and returned to him only after lengthy legal maneuvers. This close study remains a classic description of land reform in one North China village. See *The Dragon's Village* (entry 456) for an autobiographical novel dealing with the same period.

336. Hoexter, Corinne K. *From Canton to California: The Epic of Chinese Immigration.* Englewood Cliffs, N.J.: Four Winds, 1976. illus. 304pp. $9.95. Gr. 9 up.

The first half of this volume, which is really two books in one, tells the story of the Chinese immigrant railroad workers and miners, excellently illustrated with contemporary prints and photographs from collections of historical societies. The second half is a biography of a Chinese–American newspaper editor and community leader.

337. Hookham, Hilda. *A Short History of China.* New York: New American Library, 1972. illus. maps. 381pp. $2.25 pap. Gr. 9 up.

This readable chronological account of events from prehistoric times on, with attention to traditional social structures, beliefs, the examination system, agriculture, and other aspects of Chinese life, is illustrated with black-and-white portraits and photographs. Regrettably, neither the incomplete index nor the table of contents provide needed access. See also Eberhard's *A History of China* (entry 308) and Hucker's *China to 1850* (entry 341).

338. *Horizon Book of the Arts of China.* Froncek, Thomas, ed. New York: American Heritage, 1969. illus. maps. tables. 380pp. $20. Gr. 9 up.

A visual feast of Chinese architecture, bronze, calligraphy, ceramics, cloisonné, crafts, furniture, gold and silver, jade, lacquer, painting, printing, rubbings, sculpture, silk, tapestry, textiles, woodcuts—every form of arts and crafts. The presentation is topical, and supplemented by a chronological table. The text consists of brief chapter introductions, general introductory essays, informative captions for each of hundreds of illustrations, and excerpts from classic Chinese writings on painting as an expression of harmony with nature.

339. Howe, Christopher. *China's Economy: A Basic Guide.* New York: Basic Books, 1978. maps. tables. 248pp. $16; $4.95 pap. Gr. 11 up.

An authoritative overview for the nonspecialist of population and human resources, organization and planning in industry and in communes, agriculture, industry, transportation, foreign trade, incomes, prices, and the standard of living. Clear organization and close indexing make this a suitable reference source to supplement publications of the Congressional Joint Economic Committee (entries 424, 425, 426, and 427.)

340. Hoyt, Edwin P. *A Short History of Science.* New York: Day, 1965. illus. 256pp. o.p. Gr. 9 up.

"Science in the Far East" is covered on pages 35–61. Other general works on the history of science that recognize Chinese science are Mason's *A History of the Sciences* (entry 362), and *Ancient and Medieval Science* (entry 266).

341. *Hucker, Charles O. *China to 1850: A Short History.* Stanford, Calif.: Stanford University Press, 1978. 162pp. $2.95 pap. Gr. 9 up.

A chronological introduction to traditional China and Chinese civilization.

342. Hucker, Charles O. *Some Approaches to China's Past.* Washington, D.C.: American Historical Association, 1973. 71pp. $2. Gr. 12 up.

A chronological overview of China's history and a discussion of the country's growth into a bureaucratic autocracy.

343. Isenberg, Irwin, ed. *China: New Force in World Affairs.* Reference Shelf, vol. 44, no. 5. New York: Wilson, 1972. 219pp. $5.75. Gr. 9 up.

This book contains selections from the flurry of articles and pamphlets that resulted from the 1972 Nixon China visit, reprints of the 1966 Chinese Communist Party statement on the Cultural Revolution, and summaries of the Cultural Revolution by the Foreign Policy Association and the League of Women Voters. There is no index. For a later issue of the same series see *Emerging China* (entry 304).

344. Jia, Lanpo. *Early Man in China.* Beijing: Foreign Languages Press, 1980. Dist. by China Books & Periodicals. illus. 60pp. $6.95 pap. Gr. 11 up.

Fairly specialized descriptions of major fossil discoveries and archaeological sites in China occasion speculation about possible links with contemporaneous Mediterranean and other cultures. There is no index. Many color and black-and-white photographs are included.

345. Kahn, Ely Jacques. *The China Hands: American Foreign Service Officers and What Befell Them.* New York: Viking, 1975. 315pp. o.p. Gr. 11 up.

Kahn's book is a readable group profile of the State Department career men who in the 1940s advised the Department of the Chinese Communists' strength and counseled against dealing exclusively with the Chiang Kai-shek regime. Their careers were effectively ended, but the expertise of at least some of them is again appreciated as the result of the more recent détente with the People's Republic. Among them are authors represented in this guide, such as John Service (entry 312) and Oliver Clubb (entry 294).

346. *Kallgren, Joyce, ed. *The People's Republic of China after Thirty Years: An Overview.* Berkeley, Calif.: University of California Press, 1979. 122pp. $5 pap. Gr. 11 up.

A collection of five essays about China's political institutions, economy, and foreign and public policy.

347. Kessen, William, ed. *Childhood in China.* New Haven, Conn.: Yale, 1974. illus. 236pp. $15; $4.95 pap. Gr. 12 up.

A group of U.S. child-study experts visited China in 1973 and here report on the contrasts with American conditions: the stability of children's lives; their evident skills at a young age in complex dance routines, painting and sculpture; the orderliness of classrooms and cleanliness of streets. Chapters on the Chinese family, nurseries, kindergartens, primary and middle schools, language development, and health and nutrition are illustrated with black-and-white photographs.

348. Lattimore, Owen and Eleanor. *Silks, Spices, and Empire: Asia Seen through the Eyes of Its Discoverers.* New York: Delacorte, 1968. 340pp. o.p. Gr. 9 up.

In line with the Lattimores' nonchauvinist outlook, their readable anthology comprises the writings of Asian and European travellers, the earliest being a Chinese from the second century B.C. The earliest European writer is Pliny. Significantly, the final section, covering 1815–1914, is entitled "When the white man was a burden." The title is helpful for learning to see Asia from an Asian perspective, as is Mirsky's *The Great Chinese Travelers* (entry 367) and Cameron's *Barbarians and Mandarins* (entry 274).

349. Lautz, Terry E., ed. *Asia: Half the Human Race—A Viewer's Guide.* New York: Asia Society, 1979. Dist. by Social Studies School Service. illus. maps. 105pp. $3.50 pap. Gr. 11 up.

Published to accompany a thirty-program series broadcast in 1979 on CBS's Summer Semester, part one of this booklet provides a brief synopsis of each lecture, followed by questions and reading suggestions. Six of the lectures dealt with China and Taiwan, exploring legacies of Imperial China, Mao's China, the future, and relations with the United States. Part two consists of summaries of the history and present conditions of each country, including eight pages on China and two on Taiwan.

350. Lee, Sherman. *A History of Far Eastern Art.* rev. ed. New York, Abrams, 1973. illus. 532pp. $20.95. Gr. 11 up.

Chapters on Chinese art from Neolithic times through the Sung Dynasty are included in this book, which is illustrated with black-and-white photographs and color plates.

351. Leys, Simon. *Chinese Shadows.* New York: Viking, 1977. 220pp. $10. Baltimore, Md.: Penguin, $2.50 pap. Gr. 10 up.

The author, a Belgian China-scholar, didn't find much to his liking when he visited the People's Republic shortly after the Cultural Revolution. Since the index carries no entries for "agriculture," "health," "exercise," "nutrition," and other areas of publicized accomplishments of the Mao period, it is difficult to contrast and compare his statements with those of commentators of a more friendly disposition, but they do provide a counterweight.

352. Li, Dun J. *The Ageless Chinese: A History.* 3rd ed. New York: Scribner, 1978. illus. maps. 629pp. $17.50; $10.95 pap. Gr. 12 up.

The introduction places China in its geographical setting, and there are also chapters on philosophers and on traditional (i.e., early nineteenth-century) society in addition to straightforward political and social history. Approximately one quarter of the total is devoted to the period from 1911 on. See also Eberhard's *A History of China* (entry 308).

353. Li, Veronica Huang. "Trade with China." *Editorial Research Reports*, December 5, 1980.

Reviews historical background, Chinese policies since Mao's death, and prospects under the Reagan presidency.

354. Li, Victor H. *Law without Lawyers: A Comparative View of Law in the United States and China.* Boulder, Colo.: Westview, 1978. illus. 102pp. $16.50; $7.50 pap. Gr. 11 up.

China's ways of dealing with criminal offenses and settling civil disputes are described in language accessible to nonlawyers. The author, who is a leading authority, makes some observations about the shortcomings of the U.S. legal system, and in the final chapter summarizes the differences—and similarities—between the two. There have been changes in legal practice in the People's Republic since this was written, and updating is required. No index is provided.

355. *Living in China.* San Francisco: China Books & Periodicals, 1979. 341pp. $5.95 pap. Gr. 11 up.

A collection of nineteen articles by visitors to the People's Republic from Canada, the United States, France, New Zealand, and other countries, and by a returned Chinese student. It includes a contribution by Felix Greene, who produced one of the first documentaries to present the People's Republic favorably—*One Man's China* (1972, available from rental libraries). There is no index.

356. Lo, Ruth Earnshaw, and Kinderman, Katharine S. *In the Eye of the Typhoon.* New York: Harcourt, Brace, 1980. illus. 288pp. $12.95. Gr. 11 up.

This account of one academic family's hardships during the Cultural Revolution contains excessive personal detail, but it does give insight into the anti-intellectualism and repression of that period. There is no table of contents or index.

357. *Loescher, Gil and Ann D. *China: Pushing Toward the Year 2000.* New York: Harcourt, 1981. illus. 160pp. $10.95.

By the authors of *The Chinese Way* (entry 358).

358. Loescher, Gil and Ann D. *The Chinese Way: Life in the People's Republic of China*. New York: Harcourt, 1974. illus. 206pp. $7.95. Gr. 9 up.

The authors are an academic with credentials in Chinese area studies and his wife, a teacher. Their friendly, but even, text, plus their own black-and-white photographs, recount their stay in the People's Republic. There are chapters on life in the countryside, life in the city, women and the family, health and medicine, recreation and sports, economic development, communications, the Army, language, and education. See also Watson's *Living in China* (entry 442).

359. Manaka, Yoshio, and Urquhart, Ian A. *The Layman's Guide to Acupuncture*. New York: Weatherhill, 1972. Dist. by China Books & Periodicals. illus. tables. $3.95 pap. Gr. 11 up.

The authors are a Japanese medical doctor and a Scottish-born lay practitioner of acupuncture. On the premise that "it is not necessary to believe the ancient Chinese philosophy underlying acupuncture to practice it successfully but only to accept it as a working hypothesis," they state the illnesses for which the three-thousand-year-old Chinese medical technique is indicated, and the biorhythms known to its practitioners. Clear text and detailed body charts make this an understandable exposition of acupuncture's principles and diagnostic and treatment procedures, and of moxibustion and massage. Black-and-white plates illustrate techniques, including the use of acupuncture points for self-defense. There is no index.

360. Mao Zedong. *Quotations from Chairman Mao Tsetung*. Beijing: Foreign Languages Press, 1972. Dist. by China Books & Periodicals. 312pp. $1. Gr. 9 up.

This is the "Little Red Book" that inspired both the accomplishments and the excesses of Maoist China.

361. *The Marriage Law of the People's Republic of China*. 3rd ed. Beijing; Foreign Languages Press, 1973. Dist. by China Books & Periodicals. 10pp. $.50. Gr. 7 up.

The text of the law adopted in 1950 that states the rights and duties of husband and wife, and of parents and children; the conditions for obtaining a divorce; and has a chapter devoted to the maintenance and education of children after divorce. Contrast the rights granted women by this law with their oppressed status in China's traditional society, demonstrated, for example, in *The Dragon's Village* (entry 456).

362. Mason, Stephen F. *A History of the Sciences.* New rev. ed. New York: Collier, 1962. 638pp. $5.95 pap. Gr. 11 up.

One of the few general histories of science that takes cognizance of the science and technology of the Chinese, in a fifteen-page chapter. Others include Hoyt's *A Short History of Science* (entry 340) and *Ancient and Medieval Science* (entry 266).

363. *Medicine in China.* Beijing: China Reconstructs, 1979. Dist. by China Books & Periodicals. illus. 68pp. $.95. Gr. 9 up.

Fourteen articles that appeared in *China Reconstructs* (entry 168) between 1975 and 1979 describe surgery, microsurgery, cancer research and treatment, malaria treatment, health care for women and children, and the work of medical teams in Tibet. A similar work from the same source is *Cooperative Medical Service Is Fine* (1977, 76pp., $1.25 pap.), a description of the collective rural health care system.

364. Middleton, Drew. *The Duel of the Giants: China and Russia in Asia.* New York, Scribner, 1978. 241pp. $10.95. Gr. 11 up.

The military correspondent of *The New York Times* examines the strategies of the two superpowers on the Asian continent, who have a background of "four centuries of rivalry." The author terms China the "unarmed giant" and finds its strategic thinking unduly influenced by the glorification of the infantry and memories of the Long March.

Milton. *People's China.* See entry 286.

365. Milton, David and Nancy Dall. *The Wind Will Not Subside: Years in Revolutionary China, 1964–1969.* New York, Pantheon, 1976. illus. 397pp. $4.95 pap. Gr. 9 up.

The Miltons taught English at the Foreign Language Institute in Beijing during those years and here share what they observed of the Cultural Revolution. Their black-and-white photos accompany this sympathetic, yet questioning, story, full of personal detail. It is a standard, perhaps classic, account of the period.

366. Milton, Joyce. *A Friend of China: Portrait of a Journalist.* New York: Hastings House, 1980. illus. maps. 126pp. $8.95. Gr. 9 up.

This sympathetic biography of Agnes Smedley (see entry 396) traces her growing up in a Colorado mining town, her unsuccessful marriages, and her finally "finding herself" as a correspondent in China for a German newspaper in the 1920s. Both her early life and her later accomplishments are viewed from a '70s feminist viewpoint. With sufficient background material lightly introduced, maps, and many contemporary black-and-white photographs, this is an attractive introduction to the rise of Mao and the Chinese Communists during the Long March and Civil War periods.

367. Mirsky, Jeannette, ed. *The Great Chinese Travelers.* Chicago, Ill.: University of Chicago Pr., 1964. 309pp. $4.50 pap. Gr. 9 up.

To prove that the "Age of Discovery" did not begin with Columbus, the editor has here collected reports by Chinese explorers beginning in A.D. 1000. They travelled overland to Central Asia and the Near East and to India, and by sea to the Indian Ocean and Africa. The final chapter excerpts what Chinese scholars wrote about the West after those countries moved in to occupy much of China in the nineteenth century. Unfortunately, there is no index. The Lattimores' *Silks, Spices and Empire* (entry 348) is a similar anthology. See also Steiner's *Fusang* (entry 402).

368. Morath, Inge, and Miller, Arthur. *Chinese Encounters.* New York, Farrar, 1979. illus. 255pp. $25. Gr. 9 up.

These pages are about equally divided between text and a sensitive photographic journal of the husband-and-wife team's trip in 1978. There are pictures of school, street, and factory scenes, the palace in Beijing, the ubiquitous bicycles, stores, farms, narrow streets, Sun Yat-sen's home, fishing boats, and harvesting. Zetterholm's *China: Dream of Many* (entry 220) is similar, though more journalistic. Arnold's *In China* (entry 267) is the most artistic.

369. *Morton, W. Scott. *China: Its History and Culture.* New York: Lippincott & Crowell, 1980. illus. 304pp. $12.95. Gr. 9 up.

An introduction for the general reader.

370. Munro, Eleanor. *Through the Vermillion Gates: A Journey into China's Past.* New York, Pantheon, 1971. illus. 139pp. o.p. Gr. 9 up.

Munro describes discoveries of seventh- to ninth-century Chinese artifacts and sites by early-twentieth-century explorers and archaeologists.

371. Myrdal, Jan. *The Silk Road: A Journey from the High Pamirs and Ili through Sinkiang and Kansu.* New York: Pantheon, 1980. illus. maps. 292pp. $15. Gr. 9 up.

Myrdal's boyhood dreams came true when he followed the Silk Road starting from coastal China all the way to Kansu province in the Northwest. His wife, Gun Kessle, took the black-and-white photographs. Their earlier books had proved them to be friends of the People's Republic.

372. Needham, Joseph. *Shorter Science and Civilization in China.* Abridged by Colin A. Ronan. Vol. 1. New York: Cambridge, 1978. tables. 325pp. $24.95; $12.95 pap. Gr. 12 up.

The abridgement of Needham's monumental work is itself encyclopedic. The chapter on "The travelling of science between China and Europe" is of unique interest, however, stating that "there is no doubt that China was in the circuit" for the general diffusion of knowledge as early as the time of Aristotle. The routes for interchanges of scientific information from about 1000 B.C. on are described. Two tables display the transmission of inventions from China to the West, and of many fewer from the West to China, noting time lags of from one to eighteen centuries.

373. *New Archaeological Finds in China: Discoveries during the Cultural Revolution.* Beijing: Foreign Languages Press, 1974. Dist. by China Books & Periodicals. illus. 72pp. $2.95 pap. Gr. 11 up.

374. *New Archaeological Finds in China (II): More Discoveries during the Cultural Revolution.* Beijing: Foreign Languages Press, 1978. Dist. by China Books & Periodicals. illus. 127pp. $2.95 pap. Gr. 11 up.

Each book contains from ten to sixteen articles reporting on various digs through the mid-1970s, and many color and black-and-white illustrations of better quality than is usual for books from this publisher. It is a relatively inexpensive way of looking at objects that have been seen in Western countries as part of a traveling exhibit, and of learning of their significance in Chinese history. See also Capon's *Art and Archaeology in China* (entry 275) and the filmstrip set *China: Inside the People's*

Republic of China (entry 484). *The Great Bronze Age of China* (entry 247) and *Old Treasures from New China* (entry 503) are additional relevant titles.

375. *New China's First Quarter-Century.* Beijing: Foreign Languages Press, 1975. illus. 209pp. Dist. by China Books & Periodicals. $2.95 pap. Gr. 9 up.

These twenty-three articles from Chinese newspapers are predictably laudatory of China's economy, lack of inflation, mining and industry, education, medical services, railroad building, flood control, women's status, and science and technology.

376. Newnham, Richard. *About Chinese.* Baltimore, Md.: Penguin, 1973. 188pp. $2.95 pap. Gr. 11 up.

The unique features and history of spoken and written Chinese and how they affect Chinese thought, and language reform are explained in this introduction for the nonspecialist.

377. Oksenberg, Michel, and Oxnam, Robert B. *China and America: Past and Future.* New York: Foreign Policy Association, 1977. Headline Series no. 235. illus. 80pp. $2 pap. Gr. 9 up.

The complex web of facts and fancy that has historically underlain United States–China relations is competently summarized for the nonspecialist. The booklet was written before normalization. Discussion questions are suggested. There have been several earlier titles about China in the same series. See also Harding's *China and the U.S.: Normalization and Beyond* (entry 330).

378. Oksenberg, Michel; Oxnam, Robert, eds. *Dragon and Eagle: United States–China Relations, Past and Future.* New York: Basic, 1978. maps. 384pp. $15. Gr. 11 up.

A companion volume to Terrill's *The China Difference* (entry 407), this collection of fourteen essays by the editors and other experts examines American perceptions of China, and Chinese perceptions of America preparatory to extensive analyses of Sino-American relations, with reference to culture, science and technology; foreign trade; and Japan, the Soviet Union, Taiwan, and South and Southeast Asia.

379. *Orleans, Leo A., and Davidson, Caroline, eds. *Science in Contemporary China.* Stanford, Calif.: Stanford University Press, 1980. 640pp. $35. Gr. 11 up.

An authoritative anthology of twenty-eight essays on the role of science and the state of the art of various disciplines.

380. Oxnam, Robert B., and Bush, Richard C., ed. *China Briefing, 1980.* Boulder, Col.: Westview Press, 1980. illus. map. tables. 126pp. $14.50; $6.50 pap. Gr. 11 up.

Published in cooperation with the China Council of The Asia Society (entry 566), this collection consists of eight essays by scholars written for and distributed to U.S. journalists assigned to China. They chart politics, economics, art, literature, and foreign policy since 1978, and profile Deng Xiaoping and politics in Taiwan. An appendix supplies biographical sketches of Chinese Communist leaders. It is typewriter-composed.

381. *Painter, Desmond. *Mao Tse-Tung.* St. Paul, Minn.: Greenhaven, 1980 (1977). 32pp. $6.60; $2.60 pap. Gr. 10 up.

Painter supplies excerpts from original documents stating Mao's policies.

382. Parker, Franklin. *What Can We Learn from the Schools of China.* Fastback no. 89. Bloomington, Ind.: Phi Delta Kappa Educational Foundation, 1977. illus. 50pp. $.75 pap. ED 138 534. Gr. 12 up.

The author admires the PRC's success at educating the disadvantaged, instilling altruistic "serve the people" attitudes in its young, and having young people participate in work efforts, and its "can do" approach, while also pointing out deficiencies in higher education and the suppression of dissent. An appendix supplies brief facts, a school summary, and extracts from Mao's observations about education.

383. "The People's Republic of China, 1979." *Current History,* vol. 77, no. 449 (September 1979). map. 96pp. $2. Gr. 11 up.

This issue contains articles by scholars on the economy, the Four Modernizations, the China–Vietnam War, water resources, the future of Taiwan, liberalization, and modernization in industry and agriculture, plus the text of the 1978 Joint Communique establishing diplomatic relations with the United States.

384. *Petrov, Victor P. *China: Emerging World Powers.* 2nd ed. New York; Van Nostrand, 1976. 167pp. $3.95 pap. Gr. 11 up.

The earlier edition (1967) explored China's industrial potential in a college textbook manner.

385. Pye, Lucien W. "China: Ethnic Minorities and National Security." In Glazer, Nathan, ed., *Ethnicity, Theory and Experience.* (Cambridge, Mass.: Harvard University Press, 1975. 531pp. $20; $7.95 pap.) pp. 489–512. Gr. 11 up.

This selection notes that the Han Chinese are not as homogeneous as is commonly believed, and describes the ethnic divisions within that group, as well as discussing the People's Republic's minority policies as a function of national security considerations.

386. Qi, Wen. *China: A General Survey.* Beijing: Foreign Languages Press, 1979. illus. maps. tables. 252pp. Dist. by China Books & Periodicals. $4.95 pap. Gr. 11 up.

This survey provides an introduction, free of ideology, to geography (including population and nationalities), history to 1949, politics, economy, and culture. The chapter on politics summarizes the Constitution of the People's Republic and explains its government and party structure. "Economy" deals with agriculture, industry, communications and transportation, money, banking and public finance, and foreign trade. Education, science and technology, medicine, sports, literature, art and publications are topics in the chapter on culture. Color and black-and-white photos are included. There is no index.

387. Rice, Edward. *Eastern Definitions.* New York: Anchor, 1978. illus. 433pp. $6.95 pap. Gr. 9 up.

This encyclopedic dictionary has entries from one paragraph to several pages in length on persons and concepts relating to Eastern religions, including those of China.

388. Roots, John McCook. *Chou: An Informal Biography of China's Legendary Chou En-Lai.* New York: Doubleday, 1978. 220pp. $8.95. Gr. 11 up.

The author, a China-born *New York Times* correspondent, considers Zhou one of the most accomplished statesmen of our time and has written an admiring and readable biography. See also Hammond's *Coming of Grace* (entry 326).

389. Schell, Orville. *In the People's Republic: An American's First-hand View of Living and Working in China.* New York: Random, 1977. illus. 269pp. $8.95; $3.95 pap. Gr. 10 up.

The author spent two months in 1976 on a commune and in a factory and here tells, in text and black-and-white photographs, his impressions and experiences. Subheads break up the narrative and set off conversations dealing with such human interest topics as dental hygiene, physical appearance, train travel, old age, a barbershop, collective toilet training in a children's nursery, and many others. No index is provided.

390. *Schell, Orville. *Watch Out For Foreign Guests: China Encounters the West.* New York: Pantheon, 1980. 178 pp. $8.95. Gr. 11 up.

A long-time observer of the People's Republic reports on Westernization and other changes observed on a 1978 trip. No index is given.

391. *Schiffrin, Harold Z. *Sun Yat-sen: Reluctant Revolutionary.* Boston: Little, 1980. 280pp. $10.95. Gr. 11 up.

An authoritative biography of the father of China's 1911 revolution.

392. Schram, Stuart, ed. *Chairman Mao Talks to the People: Talks and Letters, 1956–1971.* New York: Pantheon, 1974. 352pp. $4.95 pap. Gr. 9 up.

Mao's simplicity and eloquence come through in these two dozen very readable selections, several of which give insight into what led him to initiate the Cultural Revolution. The editor's introduction and notes accompanying each excerpt will be necessary for students' understanding. No index is provided. See also *Quotations from Chairman Mao* (entry 360) and Bouc's *Mao Tse-Tung: A Guide to His Thought* (entry 273).

Schurmann & Schell. *The China Reader.* See entry 286.

393. Sidel, Ruth. *Families of Fengsheng.* Baltimore, Md.: Penguin, 1974. illus. 163pp. $2.50 pap. Gr. 9 up.

Briskly sketched profiles of families and individuals enliven this admiring report on life, work, schooling, health care, and neighborhood organization in a city. Though based on a 1972 trip, the last chapter raises points that remain pertinent. The intimacy of the Chinese communal lifestyle and resultant control are contrasted with the privacy and alienation in our society. Deprofessionalization is also noted. Black-and-white photos are by Victor Sidel. There is no index.

394. Sidel, Ruth. *Women and Child Care in China: A Firsthand Report.* New York: Hill and Wang, 1972. illus. 207pp. $7.95. Baltimore, Md.: Penguin, $2.95 pap. Gr. 9 up.

This title contrasts the "bitter past" of footbinding, arranged marriages, etc., with women's status now, evidenced by many photographs (black-and-white) of smiling professionals, laborers, and committee members. Observations on marriage, medical care in pregnancy and childbirth, childcare centers, and socialization in nurseries and kindergartens stem from the author's trips in 1971 and 1972, and are quite lacking in skepticism. A chapter comparing collective childrearing practices on an Israeli kibbutz, in the Soviet Union, and in China is also of interest.

395. Smart, Ninian. *The Long Search.* Boston: Little, 1977. 315pp. $17.50. Gr. 11 up.

The chapter on China not only treats traditional religion but also analyzes Maoism as a fourth religion, after tracing the influence of Confucian teachings on Mao. There is no mention of the Communist government's policies toward religious observances. The film series of the same name includes a segment entitled *Taoism: A Question of Balance* (entry 507). The filmstrip series *Asian Man: China* (entry 476) offers a superb treatment of Chinese religion.

396. Smedley, Agnes. *Portraits of Chinese Women in Revolution.* Westbury, N.Y.: Feminist Press, 1976. illus. 203pp. $4.50 pap. Gr. 11 up.

Smedley was an early friend of the Chinese Communist movement, and a war correspondent during World War II. Eighteen selections from her *The Battle Hymn of China* and other writings published during the 1930s and 1940s are collected here, along with photographs taken by her in 1939–40 and published for the first time. A twenty-four-page biographical sketch introduces Smedley. There is no index. For a book-length biography, see *A Friend of China* (entry 366).

397. Snellgrove, David, and Richardson, Hugh. *A Cultural History of Tibet*. Boulder, Colo.: Great Eastern, 1979. illus. 291pp. $11.50 pap. Gr. 11 up.

The theme is that "since 1959 the Chinese rulers have completely destroyed the main springs of Tibetan civilization." For a contrasting point of view, see Han Suyin's *Lhasa, The Open City* (entry 329).

398. Snow, Edgar. *The Long Revolution*. New York: Random, 1971. 269pp. $1.95 pap. Gr. 10 up.

399. ———. *Red Star Over China*. rev. ed. New York: Grove, 1968. illus. 543pp. $10; $4.95 pap. Gr. 10 up.

Snow was a correspondent for the *Saturday Evening Post* when he decided, in 1937, to go and see the "Red bandits" for himself. His was the first account of the Long March to reach the West, and also the first interview with Mao to be published. *Red Star Over China* is an important source document and now a classic; the revised edition includes biographical notes on revolutionary leaders (sixty pages), additional notes, and a twelve-page chronology of 125 years of Chinese revolution. *The Long Revolution* reports later interviews with Mao and Zhou.

400. Solomon, Richard H., and Huey, Talbott. *A Revolution Is Not a Dinner Party*. New York: Anchor, 1975. illus. 199pp. $6.95. Gr. 9 up.

The text and profuse black-and-white illustrations ingeniously explore myths and stereotypes about Chinese food, culture, and ways of life that Americans have entertained since the 1700s, and Europeans since the time of Marco Polo. There are end notes, but no index.

401. Spence, Jonathan. *To Change China: Western Advisers in China, 1620–1960*. Baltimore, Md.: Penguin, 1980. illus. 335pp. $4.95 pap. Gr. 11 up.

The subjects include not only missionaries and teachers, but also Generals Chennault, Stilwell, and Wedemeyer (during World War II), and the Soviet advisers and technicians who served the young People's Republic in the 1950s. It contains black-and-white illustrations, small print.

402. Steiner, Stan. *Fusang: The Chinese Who Built America*. New York: Harper, 1979. 259pp. $17.95; $4.95 pap. Gr. 11 up.

A Chinese may have sailed to the American continent in A.D. 441, and there were ethnic Chinese with Spanish surnames among the Spanish settlers in California. These are among the startling bits of information found in this thought-provoking volume, which regrettably lacks footnotes. The author examines the long history of Chinese trans-Pacific and transcontinental voyages, the China image created by Western travelers and traders, and the experiences of Chinese immigrants who suffered from that image. There is a bibliographic essay on sources.

403. *The Story of Chinese Acupuncture and Moxibustion.* Beijing: Foreign Languages Press, 1975. Dist. by China Books & Periodicals. illus. 40pp. $1.25. Gr. 9 up.

Unlike other books on acupuncture, this one does not deal with technique but explores its history to its origins several centuries B.C. It includes black-and-white illustrations of ancient statues showing acupuncture points, and of treatises describing procedures.

404. *Student's Guide to The Long Search.* Dubuque, Ia.: Kendall–Hunt, 1978. 255pp. $7.95 pap. Gr. 12 up.

This is a text prepared by Miami-Dade (Florida) Community College to accompany the film series *The Long Search* (see entry 507). Chapter Five, "A Question of Balance," outlines major concepts relevant to a study of the religions of China, and provides a capsule summary, followed by questions and suggestions for viewing and reading.

405. Sullivan, Michael. *The Arts of China.* Berkeley, Calif.: California, 1977. illus. 287pp. $9.95. Gr. 11 up.

The standard work, chronologically arranged, on China's cultural history includes revolutionary art. It has pleasing color and black-and-white plates. *Horizon Book of the Arts of China* (entry 338) complements this.

406. Tarling, Nicholas. *Mao and the Transformation of China.* Exeter, N.H.: Heinemann Educational Books, 1977. illus. maps. tables. 45pp. $4.50 pap. Gr. 9–12.

A close study of the evolution of Mao's leadership through the political and factional conflicts of the 1920s to 1940s. Quotes from original sources, with appended discussion questions, are inserted here and there in the text. Many black-and-white photographs and other illustrations, and a readable two- and three-column format make fairly sophisticated subject matter quite accessible. No index is provided.

407. Terrill, Ross, ed. *The China Difference.* New York: Harper, 1979. illus. 335pp. $12.95; $4.95 pap. Gr. 11 up.

Fifteen essays by the United States's foremost China scholars treat the "values, official and unofficial, of the Chinese today" under the headings "The Mind of China," "Tradition and Change," "Daily Life," "The Hand of the State," and "Culture." The contributors shed light on privacy, self-expression, religion, and human rights and due process, as well as art, literature, and theater, urging a flexible and open-minded point of view. The book was commissioned by the Asia Society (see entry 566) along with its companion volume *Dragon and Eagle* (entry 378). The editor is the author of many authoritative books, including *Mao, A Biography* (entry 408).

408. Terrill, Ross. *Mao: A Biography.* New York: Harper, 1980. bibl. 481pp. $17.50. Gr. 9 up.

This lively biography by a most knowledgeable author helps the reader to understand the China in which Mao grew up and the one he created. Ample end notes suggest further reading.

409. *Ting, Wang. *Chairman Hua: The New Leader of the Chinese Communists.* Montreal, Que.: McGill University Press, 1980. 200pp. $19.95; $9.95 pap. Gr. 11 up.

Hua Guofeng (Hua Kuo-feng) served as both Premier of the People's Republic and Chairman of the Communist Party from 1976 to 1980.

410. Townsend, James R., and Bush, Richard C. *The People's Republic of China: A Basic Handbook.* 2nd ed. New York: Council on International and Public Affairs in cooperation with The China Council of the Asia Society, 1981. Dist. by Learning Resources in International Studies. illus. maps. tables. bibl. 112pp. $4.50 pap. Gr. 9 up.

A goldmine of data on the People's Republic. Each chapter—on the land and people, history of the Chinese Revolution, China after Mao, foreign relations and national defense, economic development and foreign trade, material welfare, education and public health, and daily life—begins with a concise introduction and a brief reading list, followed by masses of data in summary form. Charts of the structure of the Chinese Communist Party, and the government, tables illustrating purchasing power, chronologies of the Chinese Communist Movement, of China–U.S. and China–Soviet relations, and biographical sketches are some of the nuggets. An appendix explains the Pinyin Romanization system and gives person and place names in both it and Wade–Giles transliteration. The book is much expanded from the 1979 edition, but it still has no index.

411. Tregear, T.R. *The Chinese: How They Live and Work.* New York: Praeger, 1973. illus. 164pp. o.p. Gr. 9 up.

This clearly written, balanced description compares the present China to that of the past rather than to Western countries. Its coverage ranges from geographical setting, history, population, and language, to agriculture in the diverse regions, fishing, forestry, urban communes, industry, women's roles, education, transportation, amusement, and the arts. One chapter profiles the government and administration, the courts, and the Army. Black-and-white photos are included, and the accessible organization of subject matter is noteworthy.

412. Tung, Chi-ming. *An Outline History of China.* Hong Kong: Jt. Publishing Company, 1979. Dist. by China Books & Periodicals. illus. map. 469pp. $4.95 pap. Gr. 11 up.

Originally published by Foreign Languages Press in 1958, this official version of China's history to 1949 may be compared with accounts by European and American writers. See also *The Chinese Revolution—The Early Stages* (entry 290).

413. Tung, William L. *Chinese in America, 1820–1973; a Chronology and Fact Book.* New York: Oceana, 1974. 150pp. $8.50. Gr. 9 up.

Among the documents reprinted here are the portion of the 1879 California Constitution that stated "No Chinese shall be employed on any state . . .or other public work, except in punishment for crime," earlier California statutes, the Chinese Exclusion Act and its repeal, and California and United States Supreme Court decisions.

414. U.S. Bureau of Mines. *The People's Republic of China, A New Industrial Power with a Strong Mineral Base.* Washington, D.C.: Superintendent of Documents, 1975. illus. maps. 96pp. $3.75. I 28.2.C 44. S/N 024-004-01801-1. Gr. 11 up.

A survey, based on Chinese data, of the country's resources, production, and trade with respect to coal, oil and gas, iron and steel, metals, industrial minerals, and fertilizers and chemicals, with one page each on electric power and "nuclear activities." Three folded maps in a pocket show fuels and power, minerals and metals, and major industrial areas, and there are some forty black-and-white photographs. There is no index, but clear organization and a full table of contents make the information readily accessible. Volume III of the *Minerals Yearbook* issued by the same agency (S/N 024-004-01939-5.I 28.37: 1975) contains additional detailed reports for most countries, including China and Taiwan. More recent data are found in *Oversight of Energy, Science and Technology* (entry 421).

415. U.S. Central Intelligence Agency. *National Basic Intelligence Factbook*. Washington, D.C.: Superintendent of Documents, semi-annual. $8.50 (1980 ed.). PrEx 3.10:N 21/(year). S/N 041-015-00124-8.

Jointly prepared by the CIA, the Defense Intelligence Agency, and the State Department, this is the source for the most current data on population size and characteristics, government, economy, communications, and defense forces for almost two hundred countries. Hong Kong, Taiwan, and the People's Republic of China are each given just over a page. For maps and atlases put out by the CIA see entries 540 and 541; also see *Reference Aids* (entry 435).

416. U.S. Congress. House. Committee on Foreign Affairs. *Sino-American Relations: From the Shanghai Communique to the Present*. Washington, D.C.: Superintendent of Documents, 1980. 12pp. Y4.F76/1: Si 6/3. Gr. 9 up.

Short summaries are given of significant events, statements, and actions on both sides from February 1972 to July 1980.

417. U.S. Congress. House. Committee on International Relations. *China's Birthrate, Deathrate and Population Growth*. Washington, D.C.: Superintendent of Documents, 1977. 31pp. Y4.In 8/16: C 44/3. Gr. 11 up.

This report by Leo Orleans, a long-time student of the population situation in China, notes that traditional values retain some of their force, and assesses their impact on official policies. Arranged marriages, filial piety, and desire for large families and for male offspring have not entirely disappeared from the Chinese scene. The second portion of the booklet reviews progress in public health, especially in rural areas, painting a picture quite at odds with those of films like *Barefoot Doctors of Rural China* (entry 477) and Foreign Languages Press Books.

418. U.S. Congress. House. Committee on International Relations. *A New Realism: Factfinding Mission to the People's Republic of China.* Washington, D.C.: Superintendent of Documents, 1978. 132pp. Y4.In 8/16: C44/5. Gr. 11 up.

Congressmen who visited China in July 1978 report on conversations with Chinese officials about normalization of relations with the United States, and relations with Taiwan, and note a new willingness to get along. There are comments on economic development and modernization, and reprints of assorted documents, but no index.

419. U.S. Congress. House. Committee on International Relations. *Report of a Visit to the People's Republic of China: Report of the Delegation of Congresswomen to the PRC.* Washington, D.C.: Superintendent of Documents, 1976. map. 59pp. Y4.In 8/16: C 44/2. Gr. 11 up.

An account of visits to a commune and to schools, and observations on neighborhood associations, women's organizations, the control of drugs and of prostitution, and the adjudication of disputes. No index.

420. U.S. Congress. House. Committee on Science and Technology. *Manpower for Science and Engineering in China.* Washington, D.C.: Superintendent of Documents, 1980. tables. 36pp. $2.25 pap. Y 4.Sci. 2:96YY. S/N 052-070-05365-8. Gr. 11 up.

A review of China's policies regarding higher education, and their fluctuations since 1949, by Leo Orleans. No index.

421. U.S. Congress. House. Committee on Science and Technology. *Oversight of Energy, Science and Technology in the People's Republic of China.* Washington, D.C.: Superintendent of Documents, 1979. tables. 28pp. $1.75 pap. Y4.Sci 2:96/GG. S/N 052-070-05282-1. Gr. 10 up.

A Congressional delegation touring China in 1979 found its government "clearly disenchanted. . .with. . .'small is beautiful' soft technology" and eager to develop nuclear technology. There follow summaries, derived from secondary sources, of China's resources and technology in coal, oil, electric power generation, nuclear energy, military technology, and—in an appendix—steel, electronics and computers, machine tools, and transportation equipment. Additional appendixes briefly describe current higher education, including training abroad, science and technology cooperation with the United States, foreign trade, and U.S. policy considerations. No index is provided.

422. U.S. Congress. House. Committee on Science and Technology. *The Role of Science and Technology in China's Population/Food Balance.* Washington, D.C.: Superintendent of Documents, 1977. 56pp. $1.70 pap. Y 4 Sci 2:p5H. S/N 052-070-04234-6. Gr. 11 up.

This report by Leo A. Orleans, China Specialist for the Congressional Research Service, finds "China's potential for food production keeping pace with population growth. . .very good," concluding a thorough analysis of methods of population control and of agricultural practices. The applicability of the "China model" to underdeveloped countries is his concern, but on that score he is fairly pessimistic. There is no index. See also Barnett's *China and the World Food System* (entry 269).

423. U.S. Congress. House. Committee on Science and Technology. *Technology Transfer to China.* Washington, D.C.: Superintendent of Documents, 1980. 35pp. $2.25 pap. Y 4. Sci 2:96/TT. S/N 052-070-05344-5. Gr. 11 up.

The Committee's hearings on the problems and possible impacts of technology transfer are summarized and its recommendations to encourage such a process are reprinted. The demands are for equipment and facilities for both light and heavy industry. The booklet also contains background on the PRC's First Five Year Plan, the Great Leap Forward, and the subsequent science policies. No index is provided.

424. U.S. Congress. Joint Economic Committee. *China and the Chinese: A Conpendium of Papers.* Washington, D.C.: Superintendent of Documents, 1976. illus. 139pp. $1.60 pap. Y4.Ec 7:C 44/7. S/N 052-070-03775-0. Gr. 11 up.

Staff reports and reprints of articles by China scholars evaluate the probable impact of Mao's death and discuss China's economic development and Chinese-style socialism. A few black-and-white photos are included. No index.

425. U.S. Congress. Joint Economic Committee. *China: A Reassessment*

of the Economy: A Compendium of Papers. Washington, D.C.:
Superintendent of Documents, 1975. $5.95 pap. Y 4 Ec7:C44/6. S/N
052-070-02995-1. 737pp. Gr. 11 up.

426. ———. *Chinese Economy Post-Mao—Volume 1: Policy and Performance.* 1978. 880pp. $7 pap. Y 4.Ec7:C44/8v.1.S/N 052-070-04726-7.
Gr. 11 up.

427. ———. *People's Republic of China: An Economic Assessment.*
1972. 382pp. $3.95 pap. Y 4.Ec7:C44/4. S/N 052-070-01451-2. Gr. 11
up.

Each volume is a compilation of invited papers, the twenty-seven in the
1978 volume dealing with modernization, Soviet perceptions of Chinese
economic development, specific industries (machine, electric power,
mineral, energy), population growth, science and technology, employ-
ment of women, rural production, agriculture, foreign trade, relations
with Third World countries, and others. It includes "The Chinese
Development Model," a reprint of the summary chapter from a leading
text on the Chinese economy (entry 310). There is no index.

428. U.S. Congress. Senate. Committee on Foreign Relations. *Sino-
American Relations: A New Turn.* Washington, D.C.: Superintendent of
Documents, 1979. tables. 140pp. $2.50 pap. Y4.F76/2:Si 6/2. S/N
052-070-04814-0. Gr. 10 up.

The report by Senator John Glenn on his January 1979 trip with a Congressional team, in part prepared by Committee staff, succinctly surveys
Chinese foreign and defense policy, the economy, and the political scene.
The bulk of the volume is taken up with reprints of the various
statements issued on the occasion of the normalization of relations; of a
Department of Commerce publication, *Doing Business with China;* and
with chronologies of Sino-American relations and events in China.

429. U.S. Department of Agriculture. Economics, Statistics, and
Cooperatives Service. *Agricultural Situation: Review of 1979 and
Outlook for 1980, People's Republic of China.* 1980. 49pp. map. tables.
A 105.10/3-2.6/979-80.

Extensive data on production of grains, cotton, sugar, livestock, fer-
tilizer, and other products indicate gains in 1979 and a projection for
lesser gains in 1980. Mechanization, agricultural policy, and foreign
trade are briefly discussed. Previous reports were published for 1976/77
and 1978/79.

430. U.S. Department of Defense. *Area Handbook for the Republic of China*. Washington, D.C.: Superintendent of Documents, 1972. maps. tables. 729pp. $10. D 101.22:550-60/2. S/N 008-020-00418-9. Gr. 11 up.

The first edition of the *Handbook* was completed in 1967. This 1971 revision produced a work more appropriate to normalization and a Presidential visit, but is now quite dated. Chapters on geography, history, ethnic composition, the traditional social system and family, and science and technology remain of value, and those on the police and the armed forces contain good background information on subjects not frequently covered in depth.

431. U.S. Department of State. *Background Notes*. Washington, D.C.: Superintendent of Documents. illus. maps. tables. $.75 ea.

These frequently updated, concise summaries on 160 countries are issued by the Bureau of Public Affairs, Department of State; they are also available by subscription ($16/year). The series omits Taiwan but includes China and Hong Kong. *China* (1980, 20pp.) is the greatest bargain in data on the country—of course as seen from an official U.S. viewpoint. A natural resources map, statistical tables, a roster of government officials, and an explanation of the Pinyin system of Romanization are features of this overview, which also touches on population, geography, history, the legal system, the economy, education, transportation, and relations with the United States. *Hong Kong* (1978, 4pp.) has coverage similar to the title described above, including land, people, history, government, economy, and foreign relations.

432. U.S. Department of State. *Issues in United States Foreign Policy—People's Republic of China*. Washington, D.C.: Superintendent of Documents, 1972. maps. 44pp. $1.25. S 1.38:206. S/N 044-000-01447-5. Gr. 9 up.

The basic geographical facts given here remain unchanged since the publication date, but the data in the "profile" section need updating from a source such as the *National Basic Intelligence Factbook* (entry 415). A chronology of the Nixon visit in 1972, the text of the Shanghai Communique, a guide to pronunciation, economic and population density maps, and a map showing China's administrative divisions (with an explanation of the meaning of geographical names) are provided in the brief booklet, which replaced the Department's earlier one in the same series, *Communist China* (1969), to reflect the changed U.S.–China relationship.

433. U.S. Department of State. *U.S. Policy Toward China, July 15, 1971 to January 15, 1979.* Publication no. 8967. Washington, D.C.: Superintendent of Documents, 1979. 64pp. $2.20 pap. S 1.38:216. S/N 044-000-01721-1. Gr. 9 up.

The sixty-one documents reprinted in full or in part include statements by U.S. Presidents, Secretaries of State, and other officials at news conferences, in interviews, in speeches, and in toasts, and the China–U.S. Joint Communique of February 1972.

434. U.S. National Defense University. Research Directorate. *A United Front against Hegemonism: Chinese Foreign Policy Into the 1980's,* by William R. Heaton, Jr. National Security Affairs Monograph Series 80-3. Washington, D.C.: Govt. Print. Off., 1980. 55pp. $3 pap. D 5.409:80-3. S/N 008-020-00823-1. Gr. 11 up.

A summary, intended for the U.S. national security community, of determinants of Chinese foreign policy, Chinese foreign policy decisions, and China's relations with the Soviet Union, the United States, and other Asian countries. It includes endnotes.

435. U.S. National Foreign Assessment Center. *Reference Aids.* Individual titles distributed by Photoduplication Service, Library of Congress. Subscription through Documents Expediting Project (DOCEXX), Library of Congress. $225/yr. Pr. Ex 3.10/7:CR. Gr. 9 up.

Among the one hundred or so titles issued each year are *Academies of Sciences and Social Sciences of the People's Republic of China* (79-12497), *Central Government Organizations of the People's Republic of China* (78-13497), *Chinese Communist Party Organizations* (79-14074), *The Chinese Ministry of Foreign Affairs* (79-11830), *The Chinese Ministry of Foreign Trade* (80-10343), *Military Organizations of the People's Republic of China* (80-10320), and *Politburo of the 11th Chinese Communist Party Central Committee* (79-10564). Prepared by the Central Intelligence Agency primarily for the use of other government agencies, these colorful charts display organizational structures and names of incumbents and are frequently reissued with current revisions. They are suitable for wall display.

   Other titles in the series include *China: Agriculture in 1978* (1979), *China: Post-Mao Search for Civilian Industrial Technology* (1979), *China: The Continuing Search for a Modernization Strategy* (80-10248), *Directory of Chinese Scientific and Educational Officials* (1979), *Directory of Chinese Officials: National Level Organizations* (1980), and *Chinese Defense Spending, 1965–79* (1980).

436. U.S. National Institutes of Health. *Acupuncture Anaesthesia in the People's Republic of China, 1973,* by James Y.P. Chen, M.D. DHEW Publication NIH 75-769. Washington, D.C.: Superintendent of Documents, 1975. illus. tables. 105pp. $1.80 pap. HE 20.3702:Ac 912. S/N 017-053-00035-3. Gr. 11 up.

Though written for medical personnel, this report of a 1973 study tour makes profitable reading for lay personnel. It notes that while acupuncture treatment is of ancient origin, its use in anaesthesia dates only to 1958. The use of supplementary drugs, the advantages and disadvantages of acupuncture, and the techniques specific to a wide range of surgical procedures are clearly discussed.

437. U.S. National Institutes of Health. *Barefoot Doctor's Manual.* DHEW Publication NIH 75-695. Washington, D.C.: Superintendent of Documents, 1974. illus. 960pp. $13 pap. HE 20.3708:B23. S/N 017-053-00029-9. Gr. 12 up.

This translation of an official Chinese manual is also available in more readable form from a commercial publisher (entry 268).

438. U.S. National Institutes of Health. *Medicine and Public Health in the People's Republic of China.* Joseph R. Quinn, ed. DHEW Publication NIH 73-67. Washington, D.C.: Superintendent of Documents, 1973. illus. tables. 333pp. HE 20.3702:C44/3. Gr. 11 up.

Contributions by fourteen authors, almost all doctors, describe with clarity traditional Chinese medicine; the role of the family in health care; surgery; acupuncture; pharmacology; public health laws; health care in rural areas; the training of medical personnel; nutrition; disease; cancer research and prevention programs; and population.

439. U.S. Office of Education. *National College Entrance Examination in the People's Republic of China,* by Robert D. Barendsen. OE Publication 79-19138. Washington, D.C.: Superintendent of Documents, 1979. illus. 110pp. $4.25 pap. HE 19.102C:44, S/N 017-080--2-4901. ED 181 776. Gr. 11 up.

The 1978 exam was the first standardized test administered nationwide since 1966, reflecting a shift in educational policy to more competition. Here are translations of the syllabi supplied for each of the subjects included in the test, the tests themselves, and comments comparing the Chinese curricula with corresponding curricula in the United States. High school students may enjoy making their own comparisons. "The

People's Republic of China: What Are Students Studying?" in *Social Education* (vol. 44, no. 3, March 1980, pp.181–197) reprints the review outlines and questions from the Politics and History sections.

440. Vogel, Ezra, and West, Philip. *Social Change: The Case of Rural China.* Episodes in Social Inquiry Series. Boston, Mass.: Allyn and Bacon, 1971. illus. 84pp. Inquire about price. pap. Gr. 11–12.

An introduction explains the concepts of social change and of the transmission of ideas and objects from one culture to another. There follow readings in original sources, mainly translated from the Chinese, arranged to form units on land reform, the family, village health and technology, and the communes, each with an introduction and ending with "questions to explore." One of the few text materials dealing with land reform, this title is of continuing value for in-depth study of agricultural communes. There is no index.

441. Waley, Arthur. *The Opium War through Chinese Eyes.* Stanford, Calif.: Stanford University Press, 1958. 256pp. $7.50. Gr. 9 up.

Refreshingly written, yet thoroughtly researched, this book is an account of the war as seen by the Chinese naval commander charged with suppressing the opium trade, and other contemporary Chinese commentators. The author was a noted scholar and translator of Chinese literature.

442. Watson, Andrew. *Living in China.* Totowa, N.J.: Rowman & Littlefield, 1977. illus. 192pp. $12.50; $2.95 pap. Gr. 9 up.

This handy introduction to the People's Republic and its pre-1976 social institutions is by a former teacher of English there. It is full of solid information on rural and city life, education, culture, medicine, science, industry, and the policy towards both traditional Chinese and Western religions. There are black-and-white photographs included.

443. *Weston, Anthony. *The Chinese Revolution.* St. Paul, Minn.: Greenhaven, 1980 (1977). 32pp. $6.60; $2.60 pap. Gr. 10 up.

Excerpts from original sources document over one hundred years of revolution in China and its background in colonialism, including the Taiping and Boxer Rebellions and civil war between Nationalists and Communists. See also *The Chinese Revolution—The Early Stages* (entry

290) and *An Outline History of China* (entry 412) which are both Foreign Languages Press publications, and the first two volumes of Chesneaux's work (entries 282, 283).

444. White, Theodore, and Jacoby, Annalee. *Thunder Out of China.* New York: DaCapo, 1980 (1946). 331pp. $25; $7.95 pap. Gr. 11 up.

The two *Time* magazine correspondents in China during World War II saw Chiang desperately trying to maintain the old order, while the Communists were responsive to the people and grew in strength. They were sharply critical of United States policy.

445. Witke, Roxanne. *Comrade Chiang Ch'ing.* Boston: Little, 1977. 549pp. $15.

This authorized biography of Mao's widow, Jiang Qing, the chief defendant in the trial of the Gang of Four, is based on personal interviews and thorough research.

446. *Women of China.* Dist. by China Books & Periodicals. illus. 12/yr. $8; $32 airmail. Gr. 9 up.

Feature stories about women's roles and status, and profiles of women achievers, appear in a heavily illustrated format. It is published by the People's Republic.

447. Wong, Frederick. *Oriental Watercolor Techniques.* New York: Watson-Guptill, 1977. illus. 152pp. $18.50. Gr. 9 up.

The Chinese–American artist meticulously covers each stage of painting and all aspects of technique, including brushes, papers, strokes and textures, composition, sketching, special effects, mounting and framing. Calligraphy receives only brief mention and is not illustrated. This and Long's *How to Paint the Chinese Way* (entry 185) complement rather than duplicate each other.

448. Yap, Yong, and Cotterell, Arthur. *The Early Civilization of China.* New York: Putnam, 1975. illus. 256pp. o.p. Gr. 9 up.

449. ———. *Chinese Civilization from the Ming Revival to Chairman Mao.* New York: St. Martin's, 1977. illus. o.p. 256pp. Gr. 9 up.

The pages are closely packed with period illustrations, in color and black-and-white, of art works, buildings, landscape scenes, prints, and others. Somewhat similar to the *American Heritage* format, these are good overviews for the nonspecialist, encompassing from prehistoric times to the Mongol conquest in the first volume, from 1368 to 1976 in the second.

450. Yee, Chiang. *Chinese Calligraphy*. 3rd ed. Cambridge, Mass.: Harvard, 1973. illus. 250pp. $15; $6.95 pap. Gr. 11 up.

A standard text for art students, this covers the origin and construction of Chinese characters, styles, technique, and aesthetics.

451. Yuan, Nathan S.Y. *Crossing the Rubicon: The Story of a Chinese Refugee Family*. Ardmore, Pa.: Dorrance, 1980. 115pp. $5.95. Gr. 9 up.

Yuan had been a government official in Shanghai for over twenty years when the Communists took power in 1949. He fled to Hong Kong and later Taiwan, eventually settling in the United States. A brief return to Shanghai in 1951 confirmed his unreconstructed anticommunism, which permeates this autobiographical document. Previously published in serial form in the Taiwan *Free China Review*, this account provides valuable insight into the state of mind of those who chose life outside the People's Republic. There is no index.

Fiction, Poetry, Fables

". . .*fiction*. . .*deserves fuller recognition and much more constructive utilization.*"—Helen E. Haines, What's in a Novel.
    In this section may be found anthologies of Chinese literature, poetry and drama in translation, and (intentionally) fictional works by non-Chinese.

452. *Asian Pen Anthology*. ed. by F. Sionil Jose. New York: Taplinger, 1966. 358pp. o.p. Gr. 11 up.

Prose and poetry selections from Hong Kong and Taiwan are printed here without commentary.

453. Birch, Cyril, ed. *Anthology of Chinese Literature*. New York: Grove, 1965 and 1972. 2 vols. $3.95 pap. ea. Gr. 10 up.

Poetry, prose and drama selections are included here. About one-sixth of the total number of pages represent the period from 1911 to just after 1949. There is a section on new poets of Taiwan. See also McNaughton's *Chinese Literature* (entry 464).

454. Buck, Pearl S. *The Good Earth.* New York: Crowell, 1931. 323pp. $9.95; $2.50 pap. Gr. 9 up.

The first realistic novel about China and a Pulitzer-prize-winner, it and the feature film based on it shaped the notions of millions in the West. The author had grown up in China, and went on to write many more books on Asian themes for young people as well, for example, see entry 6. For brief excerpts from the movie, see entries 492 and 493.

455. Chen, Jo-hsi. *The Execution of Mayor Yin and Other Stories from the Great Proletarian Cultural Revolution.* Bloomington, Ind.: Indiana University Press, 1978. 220pp. $10.95; $4.95 pap. Gr. 10 up.

The Taiwan-born author chose to live in the People's Republic in 1966 but left, disenchanted, seven years later. The eight stories, some of them personal experiences, are marked by the bitterness of the disillusioned idealist and reveal negative aspects of life in China during the Cultural Revolution. The foreword is by Simon Leys (see entry 351).

456. Chen, Yuan-tsung. *The Dragon's Village: An Autobiographical Novel of Revolutionary China.* New York: Pantheon, 1980. 285pp. $10. Gr. 9 up.

The heroine, who was graduated from a missionary high school, idealistically works to bring land reform to a remote village in northwestern China. She finds living conditions her middle-class up-bringing never prepared her for, and peasants—men and women—distrustful of change. Written in the first person, this is more approachable than *Fanshen* (see entry 335), yet parallels its essential story.

457. *Elegant, Robert S. *Dynasty.* New York: McGraw-Hill, 1977. 625pp. $10.95; Fawcett. $2.95 pap. Gr. 10 up.

The saga of the fortunes of several generations of a Chinese family spans from the early 1900s to the 1960s, and encompasses Communists, Nationalists, Americans, and most major political events. Reviewers found it to be better history than literature.

458. *Elegant, Robert S. *Manchu.* New York: McGraw-Hill, 1980. 592pp. $19.95. Gr. 10 up.

The fortunes of an exiled Englishman at the end of the Ming dynasty are told here.

459. Hsu, Kai-yu, ed. *Literature of the People's Republic of China.* Chinese Literature in Translation. Bloomington, Ind.: Indiana, 1979. 976pp. $37.50. Gr. 10 up.

"The most influential and best examples of new Chinese writing" are selected by the Chinese-born editor, who also wrote the twenty-five-page introduction and commentaries for each selection. They include folksongs, ballads, poetry, and excerpts from novels and operas.

460. Jenner, W.J.F. *Modern Chinese Stories.* New York: Oxford, 1970. 271pp. $4.95 pap. Gr. 10 up.

Twenty stories from twentieth-century China, mainly pre-1949.

461. Lao, Tzu. *Tao Te Ching.* Trans. by Gia-fu Feng and Jane English. New York: Vintage, 1972. illus. unp. $7.95 pap. Gr. 7 up.

A beautiful rendition of eighty-one aphorisms illuminating the way of the Tao. Sensitive black-and-white nature photographs (by English) form a backdrop for the Chinese texts and convey the tranquillity and humility of the sayings.

462. Liu, Wu-chi, and Lo, Irving Yucheng, ed. *Sunflower Splendor: Three Thousand Years of Chinese Poetry.* New York: Anchor, 1975. 630pp. $6.95 pap. Gr. 10 up.

This first-choice anthology spans from 1200 B.c. through Mao Zedong, and has brief biographies, introductory essays, and explanatory notes.

463. Lu Hsun. *Selected Stories.* 3rd ed. Beijing: Foreign Languages Press, 1972. Dist. by China Books and Periodicals. illus. 255pp. $6.95; $4.95 pap. Gr. 10 up.

Lu Xun (Lu Hsun) was trained as a doctor but turned to writing of the life of the ordinary people in the years between the world wars. His sensitive stories have influenced generations of Chinese and help to illuminate the cultural questioning and despair of pre-1949 China. This book is illustrated with black-and-white woodcuts, an art form Lu helped reintroduce to China.

464. McNaughton, William, ed. *Chinese Literature: An Anthology from the Earliest Times to the Present Day*. Rutland, Vt.: Tuttle, 1974. 836pp. $15. Gr. 10 up.

Prose and poetry selections include little from the twentieth century. See also Birch's *Anthology of Chinese Literature* (entry 453).

465. Malraux, André. *Man's Fate*. New York: Random, 1968 (1934). 283pp. $8.95; $2.95 pap. Gr. 11 up.

The classic novel set during the 1927 Communist uprising—and its defeat—in Shanghai.

466. Meserve, Walter J., and Meserve, Ruth I. *Modern Drama from Communist China*. New York: New York University Press, 1970. 368pp. $15; $5.95 pap. Gr. 10 up.

Among the selections are the revolutionary operas *The White-Haired Girl* (published in 1953, set in the 1930s) and *The Red Lantern* (published in 1965, set during war with Japan).

467. Mitchell, John D. *The Red Pear Garden: Three Great Dramas of Revolutionary China*. Boston: Godine, 1973. 285pp. $15; $4.95 pap. Gr. 11–Adult.

Includes a ten-page essay on the staging of Peking opera.

468. Rexroth, Kenneth. *Love and the Turning Year: One Hundred More Poems from the Chinese*. New York: New Directions, 1970. 140pp. o.p. Gr. 10 up.

"I have translated the pieces I enjoyed reading. . .I have avoided poems with references to Chinese historical and literary figures or to Chinese customs and beliefs unknown in the West" (Introduction).

469. Roberts, Moss, ed. and trans. *Chinese Fairy Tales and Fantasies*. New York: Pantheon, 1979. illus. 258pp. $11.95; $4.95 pap. Gr. 7 up.

Selections from traditional folk literature that veil social criticism in sly anecdotes and fables whose butt generally is an official or a greedy rich man. The over one hundred tales here present a view of the Confucian social order from the bottom, and are arranged by general theme: enchantment and magic, folly and greed, animal kingdom, women and wives, ghosts and souls, judges and diplomats. There is a title index.

470. Spence, Jonathan. *The Death of Woman Wang*. New York: Viking 1978. 169pp. $10.95: Baltimore, Md.: Penguin, $2.95 pap. Gr. 11 up.

The events are true and each statement is documented, yet this recreation of poverty, life, and death in seventeenth-century rural China has the power of a well-written and absorbing novel.

471. Van Gulik, Robert. *The Chinese Nail Murders*. Chicago, Ill.: University of Chicago Press, 1977. illus. 209pp. $2.95 pap. Gr. 9 up.

This is one of many Judge Dee mysteries in print. The author was stationed in Tokyo with the Dutch foreign service before World War II. Judge Dee is the exemplar of a Confucian scholar and magistrate, and the stories are in authentic settings in traditional China and quite informative about traditional Chinese law and society.

Audiovisual Resources

472. *Acupuncture: An Exploration*. 16mm, 16 min, color. Filmfair, 1973. $285; $25 rental. Gr. 7 up.

The film covers the philosophical background of acupuncture, its uses in therapy and anaesthesia, and modern experiments and theories that seek to explain why acupuncture works.

Agonies of Nationalism. See entry 480.

473. *The Ancient Chinese*. 16mm, 24 min, color. International Film Foundation, 1974. $420. Gr. 9–Adult.

Still one of the more effective vehicles for giving audiences a feel for China's history, culture, and traditions, this film contains nonnarrated frames of familiar scenes from the People's Republic—red flags, work on the commune, Tai Ji Quan in the streets. They leave the viewer pondering the relation between the old and the new in that country. That relation is emphasized throughout, as centuries-old artistic representations are juxtaposed with photographic footage of continuing practice, be it bowing to one's elders, manufacturing silk, or desert travel by camel. References to simultaneous events in Europe serve to anchor this panoramic view to what is familiar to Western viewers.

474. *An Army Camp.* (How Yukong Moved the Mountains series). 16mm, 57 min, color. Joris Ivens, 1976. Dist. by Cinema Perspectives. $850; $100 rental. Gr. 11 up.

On the outside the barracks in the Chinese army camp near Nanking look like those on any military base, but the ways of this army are different: officers wear no rank insignia (but their jackets have two extra pockets); they are chosen by the soldiers and attend military schools only afterwards; they eat in the same mess hall (at a separate table). Other scenes in this documentary are of sports, weapons practice, housekeeping chores, farming (the Army grows its own food), training in military strategy and revolutionary tactics, and frequent self-criticism meetings. It offers a unique view of an army said to choose only one out of fifteen who apply to enlist.

475. *The Arts of China.* 3 filmstrips, 35 fr ea, color, w/tchr's guide. McIntyre Visual Publications, 1975. $37.50. $12.50 ea. Gr. 11 up.

Photographs of exquisite art works spanning the period from 1000 B.C. to the nineteenth century are assembled here to bring out essential aspects of Chinese art: "The Art of Realism" (chiefly representational paintings of people engaged in various activites); "The Essence of the Brush" (rules and conventions applying to the formation of each stroke are explained; examples are of impressionistic paintings of natural scenes); and "Applied Arts and Sculpture" (examples of work in metal, jade, pottery, lacquer, carvings, and textiles). Identification of each frame and detailed commentary are in the accompanying three booklets, of from twelve to sixteen pages each.

476. *Asian Man: China* (series). 6 filmstrips w/audiocassettes. 82–114 fr ea, 12–18 min ea, color, w/tchr's guide, 10 books, sep. cassette, w/tchr's guide. Encyclopedia Britannica, 1977. $106.95 ser; $175 entire kit. Gr. 9–Adult.

This kit, produced in cooperation with The Asia Society (see entry 566), skillfully and lyrically conveys the essential Chinese themes of harmony and serenity as it surveys history, art, and religion. Background music, calm male and female voices used in the narration, and art works and photographs of the land and people reinforce the theme. "China: The Middle Kingdom" stresses the four-thousand-year continuity and the Chinese sense of history, rather than merely reciting events. The concept of yin and yang is explained. The next three strips, "Confucius and the Peaceful Empire," "Tao: The Harmony of the Universe," and "Buddhism: The Way of Compassion," find the ideas of wisdom, tranquillity and peace common to all three religions and clearly explain sometimes difficult concepts. The development of Chinese science and mathematics is covered in the strip on Tao. "Ch'i: The Arts of China" treats the arts as an expression of culture. The final segment, "Wei Min: For the People," notes the traditional Chinese belief in the people's right to rebel against an emperor not carrying out the "Mandate of Heaven." With many period photographs it traces the application of that principle beginning in the nineteenth century, when the existing dynasty became unable to cope with expanding population, famine, and foreign interference. The final frames look at advances made under the People's Republic. For other visuals on Chinese religion see the film from *The Long Search* series (entry 507), *Chinese Legends: Gods and Prophets* (entry 489), and *Chinese Religion* (entry 490).

Carefully chosen readings in the 159-page student resource book extend and reinforce the teachings of the strips, and the black-and-white illustrations include maps and photographs in addition to art reproductions. The introduction, "Approaching another culture," remarks on Chinese pronunciation, a chronology and bibliography, and materials to accompany the separate audiocassettes *Language and Poetry* and *Introduction to Music* complete the volume. The 131-page teacher's guide outlines a six-week unit, noting the "central topics" for each of the six components, and suggesting related activities, reading, and questions. Approximately half the guide is taken up with small black-and-white reproductions of each frame in the filmstrips, with the text of accompanying narration.

477. *Barefoot Doctors of Rural China*. 16mm, 52 min, color. Diane Li Production, 1975. Dist. by Cambridge Documentary Films. $720; $80 rental. Gr. 7 up.

A stirring documentary of the work of China's paramedics and their training in a combination of Western and traditional Chinese medical techniques. We see a tonsillectomy performed with acupuncture anaesthesia, tooth extraction by acupressure, acupuncture treatment of large animals, and a midwife performing a postpartum checkup on a new mother (with her baby bundled in red). Other barefoot doctors explain birth control methods at a clinic open to married couples only (grandparents' permission is required for abortion in certain cases), while some stationed in a factory keep charts of female employees' menstrual cycles and deliver contraceptive pills accordingly. A pamphlet by Peter Wilenski, *The Delivery of Health Services in the People's Republic of China* (1977) accompanies the film. Compare a more recent and more objective assessment in China's Birthrate, Deathrate and Population Growth (entry 417).

478. *China* (series). Global Cultures and Area Studies. 4 filmstrips w/2 audiocassettes, 81–91 fr ea, 13–19 min ea, color, w/tchr's guide. Educational Design, 1976. $79; $118 if purchased with China After Mao (entry 482). Gr. 9–12.

The separate units are entitled "Introduction and History," "Mao's Vision Implemented," "New Life," and "Education and the Future." After a brief geographical overview, they document the accomplishments of Communist China, contrast the People's Republic with Taiwan and Hong Kong, and make thoughtful comments. Despite the title of the first strip, there is little coverage of China's history. A four-page teacher's guide includes both comprehension and discussion questions and over thirty suggested activities. China After Mao (entry 482) is the sequel, produced by the same team.

479. *China* (World in Focus series). 4 filmstrips w/audiocassettes. 85–95 fr ea, 15 min, color w/tchr's guide. Clearvue, 1981. $60; $17 ea. Gr. 9–12.

More analytical than many filmstrip sets, this one examines post-Mao China critically. "China: A Geographical Survey" deals with agriculture and communes, after briefly establishing the geographical setting. Comparisons with the United States and the Soviet Union are frequent and instructive. "China: Politics and Economy" addresses the "Four Modernizations," and a possible fifth one, democratization. "China: A Day in the Life" follows the life of several individuals, discusses population policies, urbanization, and a new elitism in the cities. All three offer solid information. "China: Culture and Institutions," however, is an unsatisfactory medley of art, religion ("Buddhism" is pronounced as in "bud"), education, and palaces. The teacher's guide lists vocabulary and suggests review and discussion questions and related activities, but unfortunately fails to provide the text of the narration.

480. *China: A Century of Revolution* (series). Includes *Agonies of Nationalism, 1800-1927* (16mm, 23 min, b&w. Metromedia, 1972. Dist. by Films Inc. $275; $35 rental; $210 videocassette. Gr. 9 up); *Enemies Within and Without, 1927-1944* (16mm, 25 min, b&w. Metromedia, 1972. Dist. by Films, Inc. $290; $35 rental; $220 videocassette. Gr. 9 up); and *Communist Triumph and Consolidation, 1945-1971* (16mm, 20 min, b&w. Metromedia, 1972. Dist. by Films, Inc. $250; $30 rental; $190 videocassette. Gr. 9 up).

Theodore White's (see entry 444) documentary, called *China: Roots of Madness* in its first (1967) edition, employs telling newsreel footage to demonstrate how China "moved from the tyranny of Confucius to the tyranny of Mao," and how the United States blundered in its China policy during and after World War II. Scenes of poverty, hunger, death, and destruction follow one another relentlessly in the first two reels, causing the viewer to understand that the citizens of the People's Republic have a good deal to appreciate even in their spartan living conditions. High school students viewing these films will need considerable preparation and direction.

481. **China: A Class by Itself.* 16mm, 52 min, color. NBC, 1979. Dist. by Films, Inc. $600; $50 rental; $420 videocassette. Gr. 9 up.

This film is a documentary of the changes instituted by Deng Xiaoping (Teng Hsiao-ping), especially those in education, with a view to achieving industrialization and modernization.

482. *China After Mao* (series). Global Cultures and Area Studies. 2 filmstrips w/2 audiocassettes. 81 fr ea, color, w/tchr's guide. Educational Design, 1978. $39; $118 if purchased with *China* (entry 478). Gr. 9-12.

"The New Long March" notes the neglect of industrial growth and the pressures for intellectual conformity under Mao, and his successors' plans for modernizing the country by 2000. "Myths, Hopes and Realities" seeks to dispel commonly held misconceptions about today's China. Comprehension and discussion questions are in the teacher's guide. This title is a sequel to *China* (entry 478).

483. *China: Eyewitness Reports from Twelve Western Specialists.* 6 audiocassettes, 15-35 min ea, w/tchr's guide. Visual Education, 1976. $67. Gr. 9-12.

The knowledgeable interviewer, Arlene Posner (see entry 555 and Preface), keeps the conversations flowing smoothly and maintains listener interest. The topics discussed include some on which there is little other material for high school students: "The Legal System," "Thought Reform," "The Role of the Mass Media," as well as "Family Life," "Functions and Nature of Education," "Primary and Secondary Schools," "Medicine and Public Health," "Agriculture," "Daily Life on a Commune," "The Cities," "Child Care," and "Religion." All offer extensive detail but need updating. The teacher's guide summarizes each interview, lists questions for discussion and independent study and suggested reading, and provides a glossary. The set has potential for individual study.

484. *China: Inside the People's Republic* (series). 2 filmstrips w/2 audiocassettes. 82–84 fr, 10 min, color, w/tchr's guide. Mass Communications, 1977. $50; $25 ea. Gr. 9–12.

Taking an approach quite different from other sets with the same or similar titles, this one critically and fairly examines Communist ideology as it pertains to the arts and the interpretation of history. "Ancient Art and History" juxtaposes current and traditional interpretations of Chinese history in the light of recent archaelogical finds, many of which are pictured. The emperors' palaces are now the people's playgrounds. "Art, Politics and Social Revolution Today" critiques Maoist painting and poster art from an artistic standpoint, and illustrates the function of literature and drama, as well as of visual art, in the service of revolutionary change. The teacher's guide has brief synopses and comprehension and discussion questions.

485. *China Talks.* Fairbank, John K. Dist. by Harvard University Press, 1974. 6 audiocassettes w/tchr's guide. $60. Gr. 11 up.

Recorded lectures, including question-and-answer periods, on "The Confucian Social Order," "China and the Barbarians," "Traders, Missionaries, and Diplomats," "The Revolutionary Process," "The People's Republic;" and "A Perspective on Ourselves." Fairbank's vast expertise masterfully relates past and present, as when he notes the Confucian character of present-day practices. His easy delivery places these university lectures at the nonspecialist's comprehension level. The teacher's guide was not seen.

486. *China Transparency–Duplicating Book.* 12 transparencies, 14

ditto masters. Dist. by Social Studies School Service. n.d. $3.95. Gr. 9–12.

Covers geography, Confucianism, the emperors of the Middle Kingdom, the downfall of Imperial China, twentieth-century leaders, and the Communist victory. Use with care as portions may contain obsolete data.

China Traveler's Phrasebook. See entry 287.

487. *China's Chair.* 16mm, 27 min, color & b&w. United Nations, 1971. $330. Gr. 9 up.

This absorbing compilation of important historical footage documents the repeated rejection of the People's Republic from membership in the United Nations, and its eventual admission in November 1971. The Korean conflict is clearly related to the question of which China is to occupy China's chair on the Security Council, and battle scenes punctuate those taking place in the halls of the U.N. China's fears of invasion of its territory are stated as the reason for its troops' strike into Korea.

488. *Chinatown.* ¾" videocassette, 60 min, color. Downtown Community Television Center, 1976. Dist. by WNET/TV. $275. Gr. 9 up.

A well-organized, low-key documentary of New York's Chinatown where cooks, waiters and garment workers earn a hundred dollars for from sixty to seventy hours of work a week. It explores the precarious economics of Chinese laundries and restaurants, the plight of illegal aliens, the Chinese work and savings ethic and drive for academic achievement, as well as the power structure of the community. A growing pride in the accomplishments of Communist China is noted. The program is an excellent corrective to the tourist's vision of Chinatown.

489. *Chinese Legends: Gods and Prophets.* 16mm, 9 min, color. Encyclopedia Britannica, 1973. Dist. by International Film Foundation. $180; $25 rental. Gr. 10 up.

Observances typical of the three major religions in China are pictured and explained.

490. *Chinese Religion.* 180 slides w/text, color. James H. Ware, Jr. Dist. by Visual Education Service, Yale Divinity School. n.d. $60; $15 30-day rental. Gr. 11 up.

Illustrations of religious practices in daily life.

Communist Triumph and Consolidation. See entry 480.

491. *Education in China.* 3 audiocassettes, w/script. Washington, D.C.: National Public Radio, 1979. Dist. by Center for Teaching About China. $15 cassettes; $3 script. Gr. 11 up.

Six programs of discussions with teachers and students relate visits to educational facilities from day care centers through the university level.

Enemies Within and Without. See entry 480.

492. *The Good Earth: Famine Sequence.* 16mm, 13 min, b&w. Teaching Film Custodians, 1943. Rental from Penn State Audiovisual Services. $7.50 rental. Gr. 9 up.

Excerpts from the 1937 feature film based on Pearl Buck's novel (entry 454) depict drought, forced land sales, migration, and starvation. The actors are non-Chinese.

493. *The Good Earth: Woman Sequence.* 16mm, 18 min, b&w. Teaching Film Custodians, 1943. Rental from Penn State Audiovisual Services. $7.50. rental. Gr. 9 up.

Excerpts from the 1937 feature film based on Pearl Buck's novel (entry 454) depict the life of rural women in pre-World-War-II China. The actors are non-Chinese.

494. *In Rehearsal at the Peking Opera.* (How Yukong Moved the Mountains series). 16mm, 32 min. Joris Ivens, 1976. Dist. by Cinema Perspectives. $425; $60 rental. Gr. 9 up.

Nonnarrated acrobatic sequences of a proletarian drama in Chinese opera style are the most interesting portions of this documentary, which unfortunately contains excessive talk.

495. *Inside the New China.* 1 filmstrip w/audiocassette. 109 fr, 19 min, color, 8 transparencies, ditto masters, w/tchr's guide. Educational Audio Visual, 1980. $50. Gr. 7–12.

China since Mao's death and the "Four Modernizations" are examined.

496. *The Korean War: The United Nations in Conflict.* 2 filmstrips w/1 audiocassette, 53 and 59 fr, 9 and 11 min, color & b&w, w/tchr's guide. Multi-Media Productions, 1979. $30. Gr. 9–12.

The story is clearly and objectively told, with considerable detail on the part played by China and the controversy surrounding General MacArthur. Documentary photographs and maps supply the visuals. The script is supplied, and the teacher's manual states student objectives, gives topics for discussion and further study, and lists unfamiliar words, including names of people and places. There is also a blank map and a worksheet.

497. *Looking for America: Chinese Images.* 52 slides w/audiocassette. 16 min, color. China Council of the Asia Society, 1979. $10. Gr. 9 up.

That "the Chinese don't understand us any better than we understand them" is the theme of this searching exploration of Chinese views of Americans from the eighteenth century on. The ways of Americans seemed strange and threatening, yet also friendly and worthy of a degree of imitation. Americans became heroes and deliverers of China in World War II, only to be enemies in the Chinese Revolution of 1949 and the Korean War. "Perceptions and misperceptions can travel both ways across the Pacific," warns this interesting companion program to *Looking for China: American Images* (entry 498). Oksenberg's *Dragon and Eagle* (entry 378) also contains a chapter on Chinese perceptions of the United States.

498. *Looking for China: American Images.* 50 slides w/audiocassette. 18 min, color. China Council of the Asia Society, 1979. $10. Gr. 9 up.

This excellent collection of newspaper cartoons, magazine covers, movie stills, and other visual documents of how Americans have viewed China may be one of the best bargains for stimulating reexamination of stereotypical thinking. The narrator thoughtfully comments on each carefully selected slide, as he traces the mercurial national "journey of the mind" to a China seen as a market (in the eighteenth century), as the Yellow Peril, as the poor and downtrodden, as the Red Peril, and again today as a huge market. Warning that "illusions persist and stereotypes fade slowly," he urges listeners to try to see the Chinese as they see themselves. *Looking for America: Chinese Images* (entry 497) is the companion program. *Misunderstanding China* (entry 501) is a film with a similar theme, and Oksenberg's *Dragon and Eagle* (entry 378) contains a chapter on American perceptions of China.

499. *Mao: Long March to Power* (Leaders of the 20th Century series). 16mm, 24 min, b&w, w/tchr's guide. Learning Corporation of America, 1979. $375; $35 rental. Gr. 9 up.

Mao's rise from self-taught peasant to dictator over a quarter of the human race is interpreted in a telling compilation of newsreel footage and stills, with on-camera comments by *New York Times* correspondent Harrison Salisbury. More than a biography of Mao, this is also a history of his times, and includes absorbing scenes of Yanan (Yenan) and the Long March, of Japanese aggression, of meetings with General Stilwell and other American representatives and with Chiang during and after World War II, and of the Civil War that ended in Communist victory. The two-page teacher's guide carries a synopsis of the film, states instructional objectives, and gives before- and after-viewing questions. *Mao: Organised Chaos* (entry 500) is the sequel.

500. *Mao: Organised Chaos.* (Leaders of the 20th Century series). 16mm, 24 min, b&w, w/tchr's guide. Learning Corporation of America, 1979. $375; $35 rental. Gr. 9 up.

Mao's plans for the role of the Chinese peasant in the Communist revolution were noted in the first of this set of two films (entry 499) and are again emphasized here. This segment searchingly addresses Mao's accomplishment of the seemingly impossible—transformation of a society unchanged for thousands of years. His impact on China is termed the greatest social change ever attempted or effected. Newsreel clips demonstrate Mao's mastery of the uses of power and its symbols. Others explore Mao's ambivalent relations with the Soviet leaders, the takeover of Tibet, his loss of power after the Great Leap Forward, and his recapture of it through the Cultural Revolution and, especially, the Nixon summit. Harrison Salisbury, the commentator, concludes with the observation that "the spirit of Mao will hover over China for years to come" despite the current proceedings against the "Gang of Four." The teacher's guide is similar to that for *Mao: Long March to Power* (entry 499).

501. *Misunderstanding China.* 16mm, 52 min, color. CBS, 1972. $600; $60 rental. Gr. 7 up.

This CBS Special Report, produced by Irv Drasnin and narrated by Charles Kuralt, was produced and shown on the occasion of Richard Nixon's visit to China. It surveys—with clips from Hollywood films, newsreels, cartoons and other illustrations—historic American attitudes toward China, both racist and patronizing, and the merging of the

"Yellow Peril" and "Red Peril" during the Korean War. China's history from 1840 on is also presented. The slide program *Looking for China: American Images* (entry 498) is a similar look at stereotypes. Teaching materials to accompany the film are available from BAYCEP (entry 561).

502. *A Night in the Art Gallery.* 16mm, 18 min, color. Chinafilm. Dist. by Filmakers Library. 1980. $350; $35 rental. Gr. 9 up.

A fetching nonnarrated animation from China apparently intended to be interpreted as an indictment of the anti-intellectualism of the Cultural Revolution. Two bullies destroy and deface the paintings in a museum, but the pictures come to life and the characters help cheerful teams of Red Pioneers and other children restore everything to its previous happy order. A teacher's guide would help.

503. *Old Treasures from New China.* 16mm, 55 min, color. Extension Media Center, University of California, 1977. $650; $50 rental; $575 video. Gr. 11 up.

Art works from the official Chinese Archaeological Exhibition portray China's artistic and technological history from earliest times to 1368. *Art and Archaeology in China* (entry 275) is a book about the same exhibition. *The Great Bronze Age of China* (entry 247) is a museum slide set about a subsequent one.

504. *The Opium Wars: The Trade Wars That Opened China.* 1 filmstrip w/audiocassette, 71 fr, 13 min, color & b&w, w/tchr's guide. Multi-Media Productions, 1979. $25. Gr. 9–12.

The story is told—as the subtitle indicates—from a Western, specifically British, point of view. Visuals are from nineteenth-century British sources, plus some from Chinese ones, and do not always correlate well with the narration. The teacher's manual provides objectives, discussion topics, vocabulary, suggestions for further study, and a test, and relates the topic to present-day drug problems. The program script is also provided. For a book presenting the Chinese position, see Waley's *The Opium War through Chinese Eyes* (entry 441).

505. *Past and Present: China* (series). 7 filmstrips w/audiocassettes, 40 fr ea, 30 min ea, color, w/tchr's guides. McIntyre Visual Publications, 1973–74. $168; $24 ea. Gr. 11 up.

The lecturer brings together a well-chosen assemblage of photographs made on location in China and elsewhere and of artifacts from museums on three continents as he examines Chinese self-sufficiency from 200 B.C. to the present. The perspective is British, the pace demanding, and the narration carries the program. The first four strips, "The Han and T'ang Dynasties," "The Sung and Yuan Dynasties," "The Ming and Early Ch'ing Dynasties," and "The Late Ch'ing and Republican Periods," survey in detail Chinese interaction—political, cultural, scientific, religious—with other countries during those periods. Since internal political events are not the focus, the last strip does not deal at all with the establishment of the Republic, its history, or the establishment of the People's Republic, and it does not mention Sun Yat-sen. China today is the subject of the last three strips. "Town and Country" emphasizes the diversity present in land-forms, climate, language, physical appearance of the population, occupations, resources, and industry. "Politics and Way of Life" notes the pervasiveness of Maoism and includes scenes from the Cultural Revolution. (A two-page insert, dated 1979, traces developments since the deaths of Mao and Zhou Enlai). Several frames of Taiwan and Hong Kong and accompanying commentary sketch their growth since 1950. The final segment, "The Home in Imperial China," illustrates the almost changeless life of the upper classes through the centuries. Separate teacher's guides for each section, plus one covering the series, average twenty-four pages each; they carry background information, and approximate transcripts of the narration for each frame, with footnotes. The series is intended as an introduction to further reading.

506. *The People of "People's China." 16mm, 52 min, color, w/tchr's guide. ABC, 1974. Dist. by Xerox. $620; $415 video. $42 rental from Association Films. Gr. 9 up.

This news documentary contains footage featuring interviews with commune workers, barefoot doctors, soldiers helping with farm work, industrial workers, students and teachers (of the early 1970s). The segment on the People's Liberation Army emphasizes political indoctrination, the relationships between officers and enlisted personnel and between military and civilians, and the Army's role as producer as well as defender, and as servant of the Communist Party. The two-page teacher's guide suggest pre- and post-viewing questions, and related activities.

507. *Taoism: A Question of Balance. (The Long Search series). 16mm,

54 min, color. British Broadcasting Corp. Dist. by Time-Life, 1977. $850; $100 rental; $200 videocassette. Gr. 11 up.

A look at religious observances and rites of passsage, this film was made on Taiwan. *Student's Guide to The Long Search* (entry 404) was prepared to accompany the film series and contains a chapter entitled "A Question of Balance." The filmstrip set *Asian Man: China* (entry 476) offers a superb treatment of Chinese religion. See also *Chinese Legends* (entry 489) and *Chinese Religion* (entry 490).

Women in . . . China. See entries 324 and 325.

508. *Yalu. (board game). Conflict Games, 1977. $11.98. Gr. 9 up.

A military game for two players who represent the United Nations forces and those of the Chinese and North Koreans. The Yalu River forms part of the boundary between Manchuria and (North) Korea. It marked the northernmost penetration of Allied troops after Chinese troops crossed it four months after the beginning of the Korean conflict.

Part 4
Maps and Atlases

Maps and Atlases

Available atlases, wall maps, desk maps, and maps for projection or duplication are listed here with little attempt at selection. The brief descriptions are generally taken from the publishers' catalogs. The maps come from commercial and government sources and are suitable for a range of educational levels.

509. *Asia After World War II.* (World History Maps). map, 50 × 46 in. Rand McNally. $30 folded sheet; $43 w/spring roller.

Shows changes to 1950, the division of Korea, and advances of Communist forces in China.

510. *Asia at the Death of Kublai Khan, 1294.* (World History Maps). map, 50 × 46in. Rand McNally. $30 folded sheet; $43 w/spring roller.

Extent of Mongol Empire, route of Marco Polo, capitals.

511. *Asia 1900* (World History Maps). map, 50 × 46 in. Rand McNally. $30 folded sheet; $43 w/spring roller.

Treaty ports, British and other European control in Asia.

512. *Asian Religions* (Breasted-Huth-Harding series). map, 112 × 81 cm (44 × 32 in). Denoyer-Geppert, 1972. $39 laminated sheet, w/spring roller.

Origin and spread of religions.

513. *Background of World War II.* (World History series). map, 162 × 112 cm (64 × 44 in), w/tchr's guide. Denoyer-Geppert, 1978. $48 laminated paper w/spring roller.

Japanese expansion through 1941. *Includes a timeline and insets of supplemental data.

514. *Barbarian Invasions and World Religions to* A.D. *600.* (World History series) map, 162 × 112 cm (64 × 44 in), w/tchr's guide. Denoyer-Geppert, 1965. $48 laminated paper w/spring roller.

Disturbances on the steppes of Central Asia lead to the invasion of the Roman Empire, China, and India. The map includes a timeline and insets of supplemental data.

515.   Catchpole, Brian. *A Map History of Modern China.* Exeter, N.H.: Heinemann, 1977. Dist. by Center for Teaching About China. illus. maps. tables. 145pp. $5.95 pap.

Approximately half of the over fifty maps and the text and photographs concern the period since 1949. This detailed yet concise history contains a chapter entitled "Overseas Chinese," which treats those populations in Hong Kong, Macao, Taiwan, Malaya, and Indonesia. Other topics include China's relations with the Third World, the Korean conflict, the takeover of Tibet, and disputes with the Soviet Union, and there is a detailed chapter on China in World War II.

516.   *China* (China kit). 2 transparencies w/3 overlays ea, color. Nystrom, 1973. $28 ea.

The slide showing China and North America alongside each other, with overlays illustrating climate and natural resources, makes a unique resource for comparisons. The second one shows China alone, with overlays of population, industrial and agricultural regions.

517.   *China.* map, 40 × 30 in, color, scale: 1:4,500,000. Bartholomew, n.d. Dist. by Hammond. $4.21.

A wall map, sent folded, showing Mongolia, Korea, Taiwan, Northern Laos and Vietnam as well. Political boundaries and physical features are shown.

518.   *China.* activity map, 28 × 41 cm (16 × 11 in). Denoyer-Geppert, n.d. $4 for envelope of 50.

Present boundaries.

519.   *China, Japan.* activity map, 22 × 28 cm (8½ × 11 in). No. 22055. Denoyer-Geppert, n.d. $2.30 for envelope of 50. Also 28 × 41 cm (11 × 16 in), No. 25055, $4.

Present boundaries.

520. *China, Japan. activity map, 28 × 41 cm (11 × 16 in). Denoyer-Geppert, n.d. No. 25955. $4 for envelope of 50.

Pre-World-War-II boundaries.

521. *China: Japanese Domination of the Pacific World, 1905–1945 (Breasted-Huth-Harding series). map, 112 × 81 cm (44 × 32 in). Denoyer-Geppert, 1972. $39 on laminated sheet w/spring roller.

Political and military events.

522. *China, Mongolia. transparency, 1 slide w/4 overlays, color, w/tchr's guide. Hammond, n.d. $5.97.

Correlates with the same publisher's *Intermediate World Atlas. (1976, $3.88)

523. *China (People's Republic of China). map, 163 × 218 cm (64 × 86 in). Denoyer-Geppert, 1975. $165 on paper sheet, cloth-backed, w/ spring roller. No. 15555-14.

A physical–political map showing international and internal boundaries, railroads, canals, and cities graded by population.

524. China Travel Guide. Beijing: Cartographic Publishing House, n.d. illus. maps. unp. Dist. by China Books & Periodicals. $3.95 pap.

A pocket-sized mini-atlas with physical maps of China and separate regions, street maps of cities, and pictures of tourist attractions and other sights, including the Red Flag Canal and the former home of Mao.

525. *Disintegration of Manchu Power, 1865–1905 (Breasted-Huth-Harding series). map, 112 × 81 cm (44 × 32 in). Denoyer-Geppert, 1972. $39 on laminated paper w/spring roller.

Foreign spheres of influence, treaty ports, Sino-Japanese war, Boxer Rebellion.

526. *East and Southeast Asia. map, 72 × 77 in, color, scale: 1:4,000,000. Rand McNally, n.d. $154. cloth backing with spring roller.

A physical map with relief shading and political boundaries shown. It is available in Spanish (also French and German).

527. *East Asia.* map. 163 × 137 cm (64 × 54 in), scale: 1:10,300,000 (1 in = 64 mi). Denoyer-Geppert, 1978. $61 on paper sheet, cloth-backed, w/spring roller;. $74 on laminated paper sheet.

Visual relief in seven colors, showing international boundaries and cities graded by population.

528. *Eastern and Southern Asia about 1775* (World History Maps). 50 × 46 in, Rand McNally. $30 folded sheet; $43 w/spring roller.

China and Chinese Empire during Manchu dynasty; foreign trading ports.

529. *Eastern and Southern Asia about 750* A.D. (World History Maps). 30 × 46 in. Rand McNally. $30 folded sheet; $43 w/spring roller.

530. *Expansion and Decline of Manchu Power, 1644–1864.* (Breasted-Huth-Harding series). map, 112 × 81 cm (44 × 32 in.) Denoyer-Geppert, 1972. $39 on laminated paper sheet, w/spring roller.

Includes military operations of the Opium War and the Taiping Rebellion.

531. Fullard, Harold, ed. *China in Maps.* London: George Philip & Son, 1968. Dist. by Denoyer-Geppert. maps. tables. 25pp. $5.40 pap.

This title is of value for its historical maps, twelve of which trace territorial changes during the dynastic period and three more those from 1912 to the late 1950s. There are also physical (including regional), geologic, soils and climate maps, but those showing economic and population data reflect the 1950s' state of affairs. Use this to supplement Rand McNally's *Illustrated Atlas of China* (entry 532) and other more current maps.

532. *An Illustrated Atlas of China.* New York: Rand McNally, 1972. illus. maps. tables. 80pp. $10.

Double-page maps of the country and each region, including Xinjiang (Sinkiang) and Tibet, are accompanied by a page each of text and black-and-white photos. Additional maps and text define administrative divisions, population, ethnolinguistic groups, transportation and waterways, climate, precipitation, agriculture, metals and minerals, fuels and power, and industry. The geographical meanings of Chinese place names are explained. Based entirely on the CIA's *People's Republic of China: Administrative Atlas,* 1971 ed. (entry 541). Supplement with *China in Maps* (entry 531) for historical maps, and *National Basic Intelligence Factbook* (entry 415) and *Reference Aids* (entry 435) for more current data.

533. *Map of China.* 26 × 40 in. Dist. by China Books & Periodicals. $3.95.

Wall map with separate glossary and pronunciation guide.

534. **Mongol Ascendancy to* A.D. *1100* (World History series). map, 162 × 112 cm (64 × 44 in) w/tchr's guide. Denoyer-Geppert, 1965. $48 on laminated paper w/spring roller.

Expansion during the Tang Empire and after. Includes a timeline.

535. **Mongol Ascendancy to* A.D. *1300.* (World History series). map, 162 × 112 cm (64 × 44 in), w/tchr's guide. Denoyer-Geppert, 1965. $48 on laminated paper w/spring roller.

Mongol conquests under Kublai Khan. Includes a timeline and insets of supplemental data.

536. *Onorato, Michael P. *Historical Atlas of the Far East in Modern Times.* Chicago, Ill.: Denoyer-Geppert, 1967. illus. maps. 32pp. $5.40 pap.

Growth of colonial empires from 1500 on. Includes detachable blank outline maps, study questions.

537. *Peoples of China.* map, 37½ × 30½ in, color, scale: 1 in＝113 mi. National Geographic, 1980. $3 pap. Also available as double-sided map with *People's Republic of China* (entry 538). $4 pap.

Colorful presentation of China's ethnic groups. Pinyin Romanization.

538. *People's Republic of China.* map, 37½ × 30½ in, color, scale: 1 in＝95 mi. National Geographic, 1980. $3 pap. Also available as double-sided map with *Peoples of China* (entry 537). $4 pap.

Pinyin transliteration is employed.

539. *The People's Republic of China* (Breasted-Huth-Harding series). map, 112 × 81 cm (44 × 32 in). Denoyer-Geppert, 1972. $39 on laminated paper w/spring roller.

Movement and expansion of Communist influence from early 1930s to 1949 expulsion of Nationalists, areas of border conflict, territories claimed by China.

Taiwan, Island Province of the Republic of China: Tourist Map. See entry 580.

540. U.S. Central Intelligence Agency. *China,* map, 32 × 22 in, color, scale: 1: 10,000,000. Washington, D.C.: Superintendent of Documents, 1980. $2.25. Pr Ex 3.10/4:C44/5. S/N 041-015-00134-5.

This folded map, suitable for wall display, shows physical features, transportation networks, and urban areas. There are smaller maps in the margins showing precipitation, agriculture, fuels, power, minerals and metals, industry, ethnolinguistic groups, and population. Insets depict the outlines of China superimposed on those of the United States and a view of the globe from China's perspective.

541. *U.S. Central Intelligence Agency. *People's Republic of China: Administrative Atlas.* Washington, D.C.: Superintendent of Documents, 1976. illus. maps. tables. 68pp. $3.45 pap. PrEx 3.10/4:C 44/3. S/N 041-015-00076-4.

The 1971 edition of this work was the basis for the Rand-McNally *An Illustrated Atlas of China* (entry 532).

Part 5
Professional Resources

Books and ERIC Documents

This section annotates curriculum guides, resource units, teacher's sourcebooks, directories, and bibliographies. Additional ones may be found in the descriptions of outreach centers under the heading "Sources" in this part. The most important of the latter are cross-referenced here, as are booklets noted in earlier sections that are also available as ERIC documents.

542. American Association of Teachers of Chinese. *Audiovisual Materials for Chinese Studies.* 1974. 178pp. ED 139 706.

A comprehensive compilation of some 750 programs of all types released from 1946 to 1974, on many topics, including Taiwan.

543. *Area Studies: China.* Chelmsford, Mass.: Chelmsford Public Schools, 1972. 62pp. ED 090 098. Gr. 4–6.

Starting with a "brainstorming" session to assess students' existing knowledge, this unit proceeds to the consideration of three "phases"—geographic, historic, and humanistic. Though its suggestions for teaching materials are dated, its structure is well thought-out and can be adapted to more current data and media.

Asia in American Textbooks. See entry 579.

Asia in American Textbooks: An Evaluation. See entry 579.

544. *Asian Americans: An Annotated Bibliography for Public Libraries.* Chicago, Ill.: American Library Association, 1977. 47pp. $2.50 pap.

Thirty adult and seventeen children's books about Chinese Americans are evaluated by the Asian American Librarians' Caucus.

545. Association for Asian Studies. *Mid-Atlantic Directory to Resources for Asian Studies,* ed. by Archie R. Crouch. Washington, D.C.: Mid-Atlantic Region, Association for Asian Studies, 1980. Dist. by AAS Secretariat. 145pp. $4.50 pap.

The services of more than three hundred information sources in five states and the District of Columbia are carefully annotated (including telephone numbers), but there is no subject index. The arrangement is by type of source—organizations; ethnic organizations; foreign embassies, consulates, etc.; chambers of commerce; colleges and universities; libraries; museums; bookstores; publishers. Section II, Curriculum Development and Services, lists state education departments, publications, and individual districts that have prepared materials with Asian emphases. Similar statewide or regional guides are available for Connecticut (entry 565), Minnesota (entry 576), Missouri (entry 577), the San Francisco Bay Area (entry 561), the Seattle area (entry 591), Texas (entry 587), and Chicago (entry 569).

546. Association of Chinese Teachers. *Facts and Figures about Chinese-Americans.* 1977. illus. maps. tables. 6pp. ED 155 253.

Among the valuable features of this brief guide are maps showing where in China immigrants originated and the distribution of Chinese Americans as of the 1970 census, charts of their economic status, of immigration patterns, and a parallel chronology of events in China, events in the United States, and events in Chinese–American history.

Bay Area Resources on China. See entry 561.

547. Buttlar, Lois, and Wynar, Lubomyr. *Building Ethnic Collections: An Annotated Guide for School Media Centers and Public Libraries.* Littleton, Colo.: Libraries Unlimited, 1977. 434pp. $22.50.

Thirty-eight books and fifteen audiovisual titles about Chinese Americans that were in print in 1976 are briefly annotated. It is updated in part by *Ethnic Film and Filmstrip Guide* (entry 558).

A Children's Palace. See entry 570.

China Update. See entry 576.

Chinese Literature. See entry 579.

Demystifying the Chinese Language. See entry 561.

548. Fersh, Seymour. *Asia: Teaching About/Learning From.* New York: Teahers College Press, 1978. 180pp. $8.25 pap.

"The contribution that Asian studies can make to American students will be revealed, not only by their increased awareness and understanding of Asian peoples and cultures, but also by their complementary insights into themselves and all humankind." This general approach to the objectives of studying Asian topics, to perceptions and perspectives, classroom activities, and sources and resources is by a former Education Director of The Asia Society (entry 579). Regrettably, there is no index.

Focus on Asian Studies. See entries 579 and 586.

Friendship First, Competition Second. See entry 568.

549. Hotchkiss, Jeanette. *African-Asian Reading Guide for Children and Young Adults.* Metuchen, N.J.: Scarecrow, 1976. 281pp. $10.

Among the books noted are thirty-two nonfiction, fifty-seven fiction titles, twenty-four biographies, and eighteen folklore titles concerning China, Taiwan, Hong Kong, and Tibet.

550. Howe, Christopher, ed. *Studying China: A Sourcebook for Teachers In Schools and Colleges.* London: Extramural Division, School of Oriental and African Studies, University of London, 1979. 177pp.

Contributions by the editor and other experts cover Chinese history before 1919, social institutions, art and archaeology, China's modern revolution, geography, economy, foreign relations since 1949, and life in China. Each chapter abstracts essential data and suggests topics for discussion and further work. Additional readings refer mainly to English publications. There is no index.

Intercom. See entry 581.

551. Kelly, Colleen A., comp. *Asian Studies: Catalogue of Asian Resources in Connecticut.* Storrs, Ct.: University of Connecticut, School of Education, World Education Project, 1980. illus. 94pp. $3.50 pap.

A bit of a *Whole Earth Catalogue,* this mimeographed directory supplies names and addresses of relevant colleges, universities, state education departments, consulates, information centers, museums, galleries, restaurants, food shops, specialty shops, martial arts instruction, resource persons, and lists of films available from rental libraries in the state. It includes many out-of-state addresses as well. Since it has no index, considerable browsing is required.

552. Kenworthy, Leonard S. *Studying China in Elementary and Secon-*

dary Schools. World Affairs Guides. New York: Teachers College, 1975. 68pp. $3.50 pap.

Kenworthy has been calling for an international dimension to social studies instruction in United States schools longer than most. This is his persuasive argument for paying attention to China, and a jargon-free prescription of how to do it. He dismisses the "China as the enemy," "China-as-a-quaint-country," and "China-as-basically similar" approaches, opting instead for studying China as a unique country and culture. The bulk of the booklet expands on the major concepts recommended for emphasis (see also Introduction, p. 00) and offers over fifty suggested activities. There is no index.

The Magic of Chinese Music. See entry 568.

553. *Mainland China—Abacus and the Hopes.* Westminster, Md.: Carroll County Public Schools, 1973. 28pp. ED 109 028. Gr. 8.

A Learning Activity Package for independent study of rural China prior to 1949. Student objectives, readings, activities, self-tests, and evaluation are directed at learning patterns of land ownership, comparing lives of landowners with those of peasants, and understanding the concept of extended family. Transparency masters and answers are in the attached teacher's guide.

Misty Mountains and Mountain Movers: Using Art and Literature in Teaching about Old and New China. See entry 575.

Misunderstanding China. See entry 561.

554. New York (State). Education Department. Bureau of General Education Curriculum Development. *Teaching About the People's Republic of China.* Albany, N.Y.: 1977. 2 vols. ED 116 984-5. Gr. 9 up.

Designed to update the state's ninth-grade social studies curriculum to take into account normalization of U.S.–China relations, and to supply classroom materials for mini-courses, this guide stresses student analysis of documents and evidence, and understanding of perception and points of view. Teaching modules deal with China since the Opium Wars, Chinese revolutionary arts (picture books, papercuts, opera, songs, posters), economic life, sex roles, marriage and the family, and education. The dissenter in the People's Republic is also considered. There is no index.

Oracle Bones and Mandarin Tones. See entry 575.

Parker. *What Can We Learn from the Schools of China.* See entry 382.

People of Hong Kong: Building Bridges of Understanding. See entry 589.

555. Posner, Arlene, and deKeijzer, Arne J., ed. *China: A Resource and Curriculum Guide.* 2nd ed. Chicago, Ill.: University of Chicago Press, 1976. 317pp. $15; $3.95 pap.

Three essays on teaching about China introduce this thoughtful and authoritative guide to some 275 books, one hundred films, fifty periodicals, and thirty filmstrips for secondary grades. See also remarks in Introduction, page xix.

Shao Nian Gong. A Children's Palace. See entry 570.

556. Smith, Gary R., and Otero, George G., Jr. *Images of China.* Denver, Colo.: East Asian Studies Center, Center for Teaching International Relations, University of Denver, 1977. Dist. by School Social Studies Service. 82pp. $9.35. ED 127 262. Gr. 5–12.

This is a "unit about finding out and checking out stereotypic images students may have about China and the Chinese," with stated objectives, twenty-five activities, and a post-test.

The Sounds of Silk and Bamboo: Chinese Music. See entry 563.

Teaching About China. See entry 568.

U.S. Office of Education. *National College Entrance Examination in the People's Republic of China.* See entry 439.

Where Is the Flowery Kingdom? See entry 586.

557. Womack, Nancy. *A Comparative Study of Taoism and American Transcendentalism: A Humanities Teaching Unit.* 1974. 24pp. ED 103 887. Gr. 12 up.

These lesson plans are for a fourteen-day unit comparing the writings of

Lao Tzu, Emerson, Thoreau, and Whitman. Reading selections are included.

558. Wynar, Lubomyr, and Buttlar, Lois. *Ethnic Film and Filmstrip Guide for Libraries and Media Centers.* Littleton, Colo.: Libraries Unlimited, 1980. 277pp. $25.

This supplement to *Building Ethnic Collections* (entry 547) annotates thirty-seven titles pertaining to Chinese Americans.

Sources

Here are noted information centers and academic outreach programs that are continuing sources of instructional materials, resource guides, regional directories, and other aids for the professional. Their services are described and representative publications annotated.

Arrangement in this section is by name of state or province, with appropriate cross references for organizations having more than one office.

The best way to obtain information from any of these sources is to follow the suggestions contained in The Asia Society's *Opening Doors: Contemporary Japan* (1979), reprinted here by permission:

> When requesting information, (1) be specific: What is the topic your class is studying (not just ["China"]); with how many students will the information be used; at what grade level; in what subject class? (2) If, as a class exercise, you have all the students write letters, DON'T SEND THEM; let the class select the ONE letter that best indicates needs and interests and countersign the letter. These offices have neither staff nor funds with which to reply to floods of student requests. (3) Allow plenty of lead time; don't ask for materials by return mail . . . .Agencies are interested in helping teachers, but have other, higher order responsibilities. (4) Despite pressure of school routine, don't neglect the opportunity to establish good will for the future by writing a note of thanks for materials received.

Arizona

559. University of Arizona, Department of Oriental Studies, East Asia Center, Tucson, AZ 85721 (602-626-5463; 2393). Ruth Patzman, Outreach Coordinator.

The outreach program publishes a newsletter for teachers, organizes workshops, provides speakers and community programs, and maintains an extensive resource center, from which teachers may borrow. Its holdings extend to books, films, photographs, curriculum packages, texts, study kits, and other materials on both the People's Republic and the Republic of China (Taiwan). A nineteen-page catalog, topically arranged, is available.

British Columbia

560. University of British Columbia, China Resources Project, Buchanan Building 374, Vancouver, BC V6T 1W5 (604-228-3881).

Publishes the *China Resources Bulletin*.

California

561. Bay Area China Education Project, Lou Henry Hoover Bldg, Stanford University, Stanford, CA 94305 (415-497-1115). David Grossman, Project Director; Leslie Moonshine, Project Coordinator.

BAYCEP is one of four projects that make up the Stanford Program on International and Cross-Cultural Education (SPICE). It "brings together resources offered by the university and local school districts" towards the dual objective of encouraging the greater use of materials on China in schools and improving the content and method of presenting available materials. Its services consist of workshops, consultation, the development of curriculum materials, and the evaluation of existing materials. Among its publications are

Demystifying the Chinese Language (1980, illus., 69pp., $5 pap., Gr. 5–8, also ED 201 175), discovery exercises to learn the origins of communication, characteristics of the Chinese written language and calligraphy of Chinese dialects and language reform. Stories in rebus form reinforce the learning of specific characters.

The Rabbit in the Moon: Folktales from China and Japan (1979, illus., 72pp., $3 pap., Gr. 4 up), a comparative folktale unit of four tales from China and four from Japan, which concludes with students creating their own folktale.

*All in the Family: China Old and New (kit, 7 slides w/10-page tchr's guide, $5 pap., Gr. 7–12), which explores traditional and modern family relationships.

*Chinese Calligraphy ($1 pap., Gr. 7–12), which gives step-by-step instructions.

*Misunderstanding China (1973, 9pp., Gr. 10–12, also ED 092

421), a teacher's guide to accompany the film by the same title (entry 501) and extend its exploration of stereotyping.

Bay Area Resources on China (1974, 39pp., $3.50 pap., ED 092 469), which gives institutions, libraries, museums, and print and nonprint media.

Units being developed for distribution beginning in 1981 are

Heelotia: A Cross Cultural Simulation Game ($3, Gr. 6–12). "Through this simulated cultural exchange, students gain firsthand experience in the formation of stereotypes and perceptions/misperceptions."

Education in the People's Republic of China (Gr. 7–12). Inquire for price.

Family Life in Rural China (Gr. 6–8). Inquire for price.

Earlier materials that have become dated due to recent policy changes are withdrawn pending revision.

562. China Books & Periodicals, Inc., 2929 24th St, San Francisco, CA 94110 (415-282-2994).

Through its retail stores here, in Chicago (174 W Randolph St, Chicago, IL 60601; 312-782-6004), and in New York (125 Fifth Ave, New York, NY 10003; 212-677-2650), and by mail, this distributor handles both books and periodicals from the Peoples Republic and books from commercial publishers elsewhere. The aim is completeness. A good deal of the material from the Foreign Languages Press in Beijing is heavily laden with political jargon, providing primary sources for a study of communication in the People's Republic. Books with considerable objective content are noted elsewhere in this guide (for example, entries 172 and 386). The China Books & Periodicals catalog (free) should be checked for titles from United States publishers—and even some government publications—listed elsewhere in this volume, in addition to those where the stores are noted as distributor.

563. Chinese Culture Foundation, 750 Kearny Street, San Francisco, CA 94108 (415-957-1146).

The Foundation publishes teacher's resource books on many aspects of Chinese culture, for example, *The Sounds of Silk and Bamboo: Chinese Music* (1976, 29pp., ED 178 665).

Chinese Information Service, 300 Montgomery, San Francisco, CA 94111 (415-362-7680). See entry 580.

Global Perspectives in Education, Hotel Claremont Office Park, Oakland/Berkeley, CA 94705 (415-430-9976). See entry 581.

564. US-China Peoples Friendship Association, 635 S Westlake, Rm 202, Los Angeles, CA 90057 (213-483-5810).

The goal of the Association, which also maintains an office in New York (302 Fifth Ave, New York, NY 10001; 212-736-7355), is "to build active and lasting friendship based on mutual understanding," through the Center for Teaching About China (entry 568), other educational activities, and publications. The tone is almost totally admiring. Selected publications are *Opium and China ($.25); Freedom Railway, by Martin Bailey ($.40), an account of the building of a railroad between Tanzania and Zambia, with Chinese help; and US-China Review (6/yr., $6). Though the text is starry-eyed, They All Look So Healthy! An Introduction to Health Care in the People's Republic of China (1978, 32pp., $.50) does contain a fair amount of factual data, black-and-white photographs of medical, surgical, and sanitation practices, and an eye exercise chart (also available separately as a 17 inch × 22 inch poster, $1).

Connecticut

565. Yale University, Council on East Asian Studies, 85 Trumbull St, Box 13A, New Haven, CT 06520 (203-436-0627). Constance R. O'Connell, Outreach Director (203-432-4029).

The Outreach Program serves Connecticut and New England, with a $5 fee charged for loan of materials out-of-state. It maintains a speakers bureau and an East Asian Resource Center, runs workshops for teachers, and publishes a newsletter, Go East, and *East Asia: The Yale Outreach Community Catalogue. The latter describes the holdings of the Resource Center and other resources and services at Yale for teachers. Among the materials available are slide sets from the Palace Museum in Taipei, Taiwan, on various subjects, including calligraphy and writing materials, and slide sets entitled *Taiwan Folk Customs, *Lung-shan Temple, *China in 1906, *Little Sisters of the Grasslands, *Chinese and American Stamps/Women in Stamps, and *China Trade Porcelain.

District of Columbia

566. Asia Society, China Council, 1785 Massachusetts Ave, NW, Washington, DC 20036 (202-387-6500). Robert B. Oxnam, Program Director; Terry E. Lautz, Richard Bush, Program Associates.

Established in 1975, the Council "brings the insights of diverse specialists [of varying viewpoints] on Chinese affairs to audiences." It "defines 'China' broadly to include traditional Chinese civilization and all its contemporary manifestations." The briefing of journalists is a major activity, as is the development of books and audiovisual resources (see entries 410, 497, 498). Affiliated regional councils (see pp. 182–184) serve as resource and programming centers.

Chinese Information Service, 4301 Connecticut Ave, NW, Washington, DC 20008 (202-686-1638). See entry 580.

Hawaii

567. University of Hawaii at Manoa, East Asian Language and Area Center, Moore Hall 315, 1890 East-West Rd, Honolulu, HI 96822 (808-948-8406). Fred C. Hung, Director.

The Center conducts several teacher workshops each year, maintains a resource center, publishes a newsletter, and helps develop curriculum materials.

Illinois

568. The Center for Teaching About China, 407 S Dearborn, Chicago, IL 60605 (312-663-9608). Mary Kay Hobbs, Director.

Established by the US–China Peoples Friendship Association (entry 564), the Center distributes both its own teaching materials and publications of its parent organization, and many other publications and audiovisuals annotated elsewhere in this guide. A free sixteen-page catalog is available. Its quarterly newsletter, Teaching About China ($2), carries feature articles on various aspects of life in contemporary China, teaching suggestions, and announcements. The Center also sponsors "friendship schools" (letters and other exchanges between American and Chinese schools).

Among its publications are: *Teacher's Introduction to the People's Republic of China–Basic Packet ($3.50), a selection of articles, pamphlets, and journals for teacher background; *The People's Republic of China—A Teaching Packet for the Primary Grades ($6), a four-week unit with instructional objectives, lesson plans, and worksheets; *Friendship First, Competition Second—Sports and Recreation in China (1979, $5), articles, stories, and the four-minute exercise program (see also entries 231 and 242);and *Art and Culture in China Today (1979, $5, Gr. 5

up), materials and projects for both traditional and newer art forms. Among inexpensive reprints of articles, activity sheets, and the like are *Understanding Christianity in China* ($.60); *Eye Exercises from the People's Republic of China; Who Came In First?*, a story on the theme of "friendship first, competition second," and many others. Filmstrips, slides, and films are also available. *The Magic of Chinese Music* (1974, 76pp., $2.50 pap.) is a teaching guide originally published by the San Francisco School District, and also available as ED 123 156.

China Books & Periodicals, 174 W Randolph St, Chicago, IL 60601 (312-782-6004). See entry 562.

Chinese Information Service, 20 N Clark, 19th Fl. Chicago, IL 60602 (312-263-4669). See entry 580.

569. University of Chicago, The Center for Far Eastern Studies, Chicago East Asian Resource and Education Center, Kelly Hall 403, 5848 University Avenue, Chicago, IL 60637 (312-753-2632). Althea K. Nagai, Outreach Coordinator.

CHEAREC maintains a resource center, sponsors public lectures, teacher workshops, and a speakers bureau, and publishes *Resources on China and Japan: A Guide for Chicago Area Teachers*, which is sent to all Chicago area high school social studies departments. It describes organizations, government and official agencies, libraries, bookstores, Asian resource centers in the Chicago public schools, places to visit, courses, and Chicago theaters showing films from the East Asian countries. In addition, there are annotated listings of published resource guides, regional and national East Asia Centers, sources for free and rental films, and publishers. An index separates China and Japan materials.

570. University of Illinois, Center for Asian Studies, 1208 W California Ave, Urbana, IL 61801 (217-333-4850; 0451). Peter Schran, Acting Director.

The Center maintains a free-loan classroom materials collection and publishes *Shao Nian Gong—A Children's Palace: Ideas for Teaching About China*, by Michele Shoresman and Roberta Gumport (rev. ed., 1980, illus., 152pp., $8.50 pap., Gr. 4-9). The pages of this loose-leaf source book are readily removed for duplication or transparency-projection. They introduce a potpourri of activities relating to Chinese culture and society. Most of the activities are original, some are reprints of BAYCEP (entry 561) and Foreign Languages Press publications. They include the Broken Squares Game, an agriculture game, eye exercises, the four-minute physical fitness plan, tangrams, other crafts, recipes, and cooking directions, learning materials on geography, inventions, use of an abacus, and much else.

Indiana

571. Indiana University, Department of East Asian Languages and Cultures, East Asian Studies Center, Goodbody Hall, Bloomington, IN 47405 (812-337-3838; 1992). Linda S. Wojtan, East Asian Outreach Coordinator.

The Outreach Program conducts workshops for teachers and teacher centers, lectures and demonstrations in schools, and film series in public libraries, and publishes a newsletter that advises readers of teaching resources, study tours, courses, exhibitions, pen pals, and the like. The Center provides guides to films and other resources and some free-loan materials.

Massachusetts

572. Children's Museum, Attn: Kit Rentals, 300 Congress St, Boston, MA 02210 (617-426-6500).

"Schools, community groups and Museum members" in the Boston area may rent kits. *Echoes of China (1979, $40/3-week rental; $20/2-week rental of individual kits, Gr. 5–8) is a comprehensive Chinese culture curriculum consisting of artifacts, graphic materials, audiovisual aids, activity instructions and supplies, a student guide, and a teacher's guide with structured lesson plans for each unit. It was developed in collaboration with the Ethnic Heritage Studies Committee of the Greater Boston Chinese Cultural Association. The separate units are
> Jia, Chinese–American families, which presents historical perspectives, traditional family values, and contemporary issues through stories and role play.
> China and Her Land, an examination of the diversity of China's topography, climate, and resources.
> Travels with Marco Polo: Life in 13th Century China, a look, through costumes, painting, and stories, at medieval China as Marco Polo saw it.
> Fine and Folk Arts of China, background and instructions for calligraphy, painting techniques, papercuts, book-making, and personal seals.

Chinese Celebrations, which presents what events are celebrated, how, and the values, traditions, and stories behind them.

Chinese Architecture, which describes how the Chinese design their homes, combining family values with ancient environmental principles, artistic symbolism, and economic good sense.

Chinese Games, which gives directions for To Catch a Thief, Tangram, Go, Go-Bang, and Chinese Chess, from the simple to the complex.

Japanese and Chinese Calligraphy ($10/2-week rental) is an activity kit containing instructions, equipment, graphic materials, supplies, and books. The exhibit kit *Traditional China* ($10/2-week rental) contains artifacts, books, pictures, and a guide.

573. Five College Center for East Asian Studies, Churchill House, 97 Spring St, Amherst, MA 01002 (413-253-9397). Carol Angus, Outreach Coordinator.

Amherst College, Hampshire College, Mount Holyoke College, Smith College, and the University of Massachusetts are the institutions affiliated with the Center. Its outreach program serves as liaison to nearby schools and communities by sponsoring workshops and courses, supplying speakers, maintaining a resource collection, and offering expertise in curriculum development. The Center publishes a monthly newsletter and a catalog of locally available audiovisual materials and teaching units.

574. The Museum of the American China Trade, 215 Adams St, Milton, MA 02186 (617-696-1815).

The museum maintains exhibits and an archival collection, and sponsors classes and other special programs. Among its holdings are Chinese art objects and other articles brought back by the traders, as well as porcelain and furniture manufactured solely for export, and paintings and photographs of nineteenth-century China. See also Beers's *China in Old Photographs, 1860–1910* (entry 152).

Michigan

575. University of Michigan, Project on East Asian Studies in Education (PEASE)—China, Rm 108, Lane Hall, Ann Arbor, MI 48109 (313-764-5109). Carrie Waara, China Program Coordinator.

In addition to developing adult education programs for college and university students and for business and community groups, the Project maintains a resource library for the use of elementary and secondary school teachers, and evaluates curriculum materials. Its publications include a list of holdings of its resource library, other resource guides, the semi-annual newsletter *East Asia Review*, and many learning packages for loan or purchase, including

Chinese Festivals and Customs (24 slides, color, w/tchr's guide, 1980. Gr. 2 up), which covers Ancestor Remembrance Day, customs relating to marriage, birth, death, etc., in addition to the New Year's and Dragon Boat Festivals.

From Canton to Yenan: Lessons on China's Geography (51 slides, color, w/tchr's guide, $19, Gr. 5 up).

Misty Mountains and Mountain Movers: Using Art and Literature in Teaching About Old and New China (29 slides, color, w/tchr's guide, $15, Gr. 9 up), The unit seeks to elucidate how Confucianism and Taoism were reflected in the art and literature of Old China, and Maoism in the art and literature of the New. Extensive selections of prose and poetry are provided, while the slides picture traditional and contemporary paintings. Five slides depicting filial piety, with story summaries, are of special interest.

Oracle Bones and Mandarin Tones: Demystifying the Chinese Language (28pp. $2.80), mimeographed exercises to discover and practice Chinese characters.

Three Views: Will the Real China Please Stand Up? (20pp., $2) The three are the traditional Chinese, the People's Republic of China, and the United States views of key events in Chinese history. This unit includes roleplaying and other exercises.

Minnesota

576. Midwest China Center, 308 Gullixson Hall, 2375 Como Ave W, St. Paul, MN 55108. P. Richard Bohr, Executive Director; Sally S. Hart, Outreach Coordinator. 612-641-3233; 3238.

China Update (3/yr. $3) consists chiefly of instructions for classroom activities on aspects of life in China, and is geared to both elementary and secondary instruction. Quotes from current newspapers and periodicals, and from books, are added features and are topically arranged, and there is also a calendar of the Center's programs. This may be the only "outreach" newsletter concerned exclusively with China, and containing materials immediately usable in the classroom. The Center also distributes *Exploring the People's Republic of China: Curriculum Activities*, prepared by the Minnesota State Education Department (1980, $5; portions also available separately) and the *Minnesota Guide to Resources on East Asia* ($1.50).

Missouri

577. University of Missouri, Center for International Studies, Asia Resource Center, 8001 Natural Bridge Rd, St. Louis, MO 63121. (314-553-5801). Katherine C. Pierson, Coordinator.

As a service to teachers and community, the Asia Resource Center conducts educational programs, trains teachers, offers consultation on curriculum development, and maintains a small library of teaching aids. It publishes the *Missouri Guide to Resources on Asia* (1977, illus., 52pp., $2.50 pap.), a collaborative project with the Missouri China Council. It is an attractively designed directory of resource centers, civic and educational organizations, audiovisual resources and libraries, travel programs, restaurants and specialty shops, places to visit, and courses and speakers, all within the state. These are supplemented by a separate section noting sources and resources available in the region or nationally. An index helps in locating resources by type (e.g., field trips, libraries, teaching aids) but not by subject.

New York

578. A.R.T.S. (Art Resources for Teachers and Students), 32 Market St, New York, NY 10002 (212-962-8231).

The artists and other residents of New York's Chinatown associated in this organization publish a small list of distinctive and strikingly handsome booklets dealing with Chinese (also Puerto Rican) culture. Among them:

Chinese Cultural Activities (1977, illus., 2 vols., $1.25 ea., Gr. K-6), which gives instructions for making a Chinese dragon and paper lanterns, suggestions for a New Year's parade, bilingual words and music for folksongs, and scripts for several plays, including two bilingual.

Chinese Culture (1973-76, illus., 5 vols., 1 cassette, $8.50; $1.25 ea book; $3.50 cassette. Gr. 2-7). Individual books, illustrated with brilliant blockprints on colored papers, are *Chinese Children's Games* (active group games requiring no equipment), *Chinese Lanterns—Two Methods, Chinese Folk Songs* (lyrics in Chinese, English, and romanized Mandarin; score; instrumental arrangement on cassettte), *Chinese New Year,* and *Children of the Yellow River: A Legendary History of the Chinese People* (legends and creation myths).

*Chinese Women in History and Legend. (2 vols., $1 ea, Gr. 5 up; bilingual text).
*A Pictorial History of Chinatown, NYC (1980, $5; 80 historical photos and text).

579. Asia Society. Education Department. 725 Park Ave, New York, NY 10021 (212-288-6400). Timothy Plummer, Director; Susan L. Rhodes, Program Associate.

The purpose of the Society is "to increase American understanding and appreciation of current Asian realities . . . and to educate Americans about the traditional cultures and civilizations of Asia." The Education Department publishes Focus on Asian Studies (3/yr., $5/yr., $2 single issues). Formerly issued by the Service Center for Teachers of Asian Studies at Ohio University (see entry 586), Focus is a must for anyone in elementary or secondary education concerned with teaching about Asian topics. Past issues of approximately sixty-four pages each reported on the activities of Outreach programs around the country, reviewed books and other resources, listed materials available from various sources, and carried announcements of courses and other matters of interest to teachers.

The Society has cooperated in the publication of resource guides and materials annotated elsewhere. Its important studies Asia in American Textbooks (1976, 37pp., ED 127 232) and Asia in American Textbooks: An Evaluation (1976, 342pp., ED 124 439) analyzed over three hundred social studies texts for Asian content. "Textbook Evaluation Guidelines" and "Materials Evaluation" (both reprinted in the Appendix, pp. 173-182) resulted from these studies, now out of print.

Other publications include *Sources for Slides on Asia (n.d. 9pp. $1.60 pap.) and Chinese Literature (1977, 10pp., ED 148 913), a survey with comparisons to Western literature and a two-page bibliography. The Performing Arts Department at the address listed above offers school and community programs, among them *Aspects of Peking Opera, demonstrations of dance and mime technique; inquire for the fee. Among audiovisual media issued by this Department are *Asian Dance and Drama: East Asia (300 slides, w/guide, 1981, $510, Gr. 7 up); *Chinese, Korean and Japanese Dance (16mm, 30 min, color, 1965, $300 sale, $35 rental, Gr. 7 up); *Chinese Shadow Plays (¾" videocassette, 30 min, black-and-white, n.d., $100 sale, $40 rental, Gr. 7 up); and *Hu Hung-Yen Aspects of Chinese Opera (¾" videocassette, 30 min, color, n.d., $200 sale, $40 rental, Gr. 9 up. The China Council is represented here; its headquarters are in Washington, D.C. (See entry 566).

China Books & Periodicals, 125 Fifth Ave, New York, NY 10003 (212-677-2650). See entry 562.

580. Chinese Information Service, Coordination Council for North American Affairs, 159 Lexington Ave, New York, NY 10016 (212-725-4950).

The official agency of the Republic of China (Taiwan) maintains offices here and in Washington (4301 Connecticut Ave, NW, Washington, DC 20008; 202-686-1638); Chicago (20 N Clark, 19th Fl, Chicago, IL 60602; 312-263-4669); Houston (1520 Texas Ave, Houston, TX 77002; 713-626-7445), and San Francisco (604 Commercial, San Francisco, CA 94111; 415-362-7680). The agency publishes both objective data on that country and on Chinese culture, and its particular version of the 1949 revolution and the Communist regime.

Free and low-cost pamphlets and leaflets include, among others, *Chinese Festivals; Chinese History* (1975, illus., 51pp., $.25), which covers from pre-history to 1949; *Education in the Republic of China* (1980, illus., 36pp.); *The Founding of the Republic of China* (1980); *Mass Media—Republic of China* (1978, 14pp.); *My Country: Questions and Answers about the Republic of China on Taiwan* (1980, 74pp.); *National Flag and National Anthem* (1979); *Needles of Healing* (1973, 16pp.); *A Profile in Slides of the Republic of China* (80 photographs and captions); *Republic of China* (1979, illus., 32pp.) *Taiwan, Island Province of the Republic of China: Tourist Map* (21 in. × 28 in., road map); and *3,500 Years of Chinese Books* (illus., 12pp.).

Its *China and the Chinese* series consists of leaflets entitled *Bronzes, Ceramics, Chinese Calligraphy, Chinese Music, Chinese Painting, Name Chops, Opera, Origins of Kung Fu,* and *Silk.*

A list of some fifty free-loan films and slide sets is available on request.

581. Global Perspectives in Education, Inc., 218 East 18th St, New York, NY 10003 (212-475-0850). Martha Crum.

Its Center for Global Perspectives is "an educational development, research, and consulting agency working . . . to increase public awareness and knowledge about our global society and its problems of conflict and social change. It publishes *Intercom* (4/yr., $8), each issue of which is devoted to a single topic, among them

Global Perspectives through Asian Experience, Edited by Betty Bullard and Loretta Ryan (*Intercom* #89, 1978, illus., maps, 32pp., $1.75 pap., Gr. 7–12), which provides suggested teaching activities aimed at having students learn to locate Asia in relation to the rest of the world, compare different ways of representing the world in maps, define ethnocentrism, compare writing systems, and achieve other well-stated objectives. It was prepared in cooperation with the Asia Society (entry 579).

Universals of Culture, edited by Alice Ann Cleaveland, Jean Craven, and Marianne Danfelser (*Intercom* #92/93, 1979, illus., 72pp., $5 pap., Gr. 7–12), which gives teacher background, suggested activities and readings for units introducing anthropological concepts such as material culture, language and nonverbal communication, kinship systems, sex roles, conflict and warfare, formal and informal education, etc.

Global Perspectives also maintains the West Coast Office (Hotel Claremont Office Park, Oakland/Berkeley, CA 94705; 415-430-9976).

582. Information Center on Children's Cultures, 331 E 38th St, New York, NY 10016 (212-686-5522). Melinda Greenblatt, Director.

A service of the United States Committee for UNICEF, the Center maintains a comprehensive collection of books and other materials that illustrate the way children live in all the countries in which UNICEF is active. It welcomes inquiries from teachers and students and answers them with a bibliography on the country or subject requested, information about further services, and announcements of publications available from it and from its parent organization. It offers mini-units and information sheets on cross-cultural topics such as food, clothing, family, and schooling.

Among its publications are the *Wall Calendar* (annual, $2 pap.), which gives dates for the holidays of all the world's religions, and national holidays, with illustrations by children depicting festival observances from various countries; *The Rooster's Horns* (see entry 94); *The Terrible Nung Gwama* (see entry 95); and *Chinese New Year: Teacher's Handbook,* which provides background information, lesson plans, stories, and Chinese zodiac charts.

583. New York University, Asian Studies Curriculum Center. 635 East Bldg, Washington Square, New York, NY 10003 (212-598-2785).

Teachers are invited to visit, by appointment, the Center's collection of books, pictorial materials, and artifacts, which may also be borrowed for classroom use. Filmstrip and slide-tape sets, prepared by graduate students, may be purchased or rented. These include a set of black-and-white slides, *China in 1906;* material on communes, on Chinese language, and on social and political values; and slides for *Little Sisters of the Grasslands* (see entries 79, 141).

US-China Peoples Friendship Association, 302 Fifth Ave, New York, NY 10001 (212-736-7355). See entry 564.

Ohio

584. Oberlin College, East Asian Studies Center, King 141, Oberlin, OH 44074 (216-775-8313). Bobbie Carlson, Outreach Coordinator.

The Center issues a newsletter with information about teaching resources, and a films and video rental catalog. It sponsors classes, workships, demonstrations, and activity programs. Filmstrips, slides on Chinese writing, books, and magazines may be borrowed by teachers in the surrounding area.

585. Ohio State University, East Asian Studies Program, School and Community Outreach Program on Asia, 308 Dulles Hall, 230 West 17th Ave, Columbus, OH 43210 (614-422-9660; 3838). Leslie Bedford, Coordinator.

SCOPA conducts teacher workshops, sponsors adult education courses, visits schools, helps teachers develop study units, maintains a free-loan resource library, and publishes a newsletter, *East Asia News*.

586. Ohio State University, Service Center for Teachers of Asian Studies, Association for Asian Studies, 29 W Woodruff Ave, Columbus, OH 43210. Dr. Franklin R. Buchanan, Director.

With Dr. Buchanan's retirement in 1980, publication of *Focus on Asian Studies* was taken over by the Asia Society (entry 579). The Center's earlier Service Center Papers are no longer distributed, but some are available through ERIC, among them *Where Is the Flowery Kingdom? Inquiry Exercises for Elementary Students*, by James Hantula (1974, 42pp., ED 100 748, Gr. 4-6). The twenty exercises, with titles such as "How the Chinese got their name," "Is the Chinese way of life like the American way of life?" and "When I think of China," make it an excellent tool for creating awareness.

Texas

Chinese Information Service, 1520 Texas Ave, Houston, TX 77002 (713-626-7445). See entry 580.

587. The Institute of Texan Cultures of the University of Texas at San Antonio, Box 1226, San Antonio, TX 78294 (512-326-7651).

Among the Institutes's publications are *The Chinese Texans* (1978, $2 pap.) and *The Chinese Texans: A Personal History Book* (1977, $2 pap.). It maintains permanent exhibits at its museum headquarters, sponsors traveling exhibits, and has extensive archival collections.

588. University of Texas, Center for Asian Studies, Texas Program for Educational Resources on Asia (TEXPERA), Austin, TX 78712 (512-471-5811). Louise Flippin, Program Coordinator; Sandra Martin, Program Secretary.

Issues of the quarterly newsletter (typically twelve to sixteen pages) carry news of Asian programs and events, available free-loan materials, additions to the library, and feature stories. Listings of articles about Asia in current periodicals is a unique feature. TEXPERA also issues many other free materials, including bibliographies, textbook evaluations, and *TEXPERA Guide to Asian Studies Resources in Texas*, *Chinese Language and Literature*, *The Taiwan Issue in US–China Normalization Negotioations*, *The "Four Modernizations"*, *The Conflict between China and Vietnam*, *Pronouncing the Chinese Language*, *Pulling Together a Curriculum Unit on China*, *The Chinese in Texas*.

Utah

589. Brigham Young University, Center for International and Area Studies, Box 61, Provo, UT 84602. Deborah L. Coon, Coordinator of Special Projects.

Following the motto "When in Rome, do as the Romans," the Center publishes a series of four-page *Culturgrams* ($.25 each) that instruct prospective travelers in the prevailing customs and courtesies (greetings, eating, gestures, etc.), life-styles, and elementary data relating to population, language, holidays, history, government, climate, education, and the economy. There are separate sheets for *China (People's Republic)*, *Hong Kong* and *Republic of China (Taiwan)*.

People of Hong Kong: Building Bridges of Understanding (1977, illus., 24pp., ED 144 347, Gr. 11 up) gives a brief introduction filled with data on history, government, economy, and education, then launches into a more chatty discourse on how to communicate and get to know the people of Hong Kong, and postulates problem situations, with self-tests, involving such themes as "face" and family relationships. Other cultural themes are also explained.

Virginia

590. University of Virginia, East Asian Language and Area Center, 1644 Oxford Road, Charlottesville, VA 22903 (804-295-1808). Mary H. Israel, Outreach Coordinator.

The Center sponsors lectures and language courses, maintains a collection of resources, and publishes a newsletter.

Washington

591. University of Washington, School of International Studies, East Asia Resource` Center, Seattle, WA 98195 (206-543-1921). Michael Robinson, Coordinator.

The Center maintains a resource library and publishes a newsletter and the periodically updated *Resource Guide for East Asia (3rd ed., 1977). Written and multimedia materials are available for free-loan ($5 fee for films) in the Northwest. New units for 1981–82 include the kit *Women in China* (filmstrip and study guides) and a slide-tape presentation, *Agriculture in China*. There are also workshops, school programs, curriculum planning, and a speakers bureau.

Art Museums

The following museums publish catalogs, books, slides, booklets, or card sets relating to the arts of China.

California

592. Asian Art Museum of San Francisco, Golden Gate Park, San Francisco, CA 94118 (film, slides)

Connecticut

593. New Haven Colony Historical Society, 114 Whitney Ave, New Haven, CT 06510 (China trade porcelain)

594. Wadsworth Atheneum, 600 Main St, Hartford, CT 06103

District of Columbia

595. Freer Gallery of Art, 12th & Jefferson Dr, SW, Washington, DC 20560

596. National Gallery of Art, Extension Service, Washington, DC 20565

Kansas

597. Spencer Museum of Art, University of Kansas, Lawrence, KS 66045

Kentucky

598. Speed Art Museum, 2035 S Third St, Louisville, KY 40208

Michigan

599. Detroit Institute of Arts, 5200 Woodward Ave, Detroit, MI 48202

600. University of Michigan Museum of Art, 525 S State Rd, Ann Arbor, MI 48109 (calligraphy)

Minnesota

601. The Minneapolis Institute of Arts, 2400 Third Ave S, Minneapolis, MN 55404 (textiles)

Missouri

602. Nelson Gallery of Art, 4525 Oak St, Kansas City, MO 64111

603. St. Louis Art Museum, Forest Park, St. Louis, MO 63110 (slides)

New York

604. Metropolitan Museum of Art, Fifth Ave & 82nd St, New York, NY 10028 (see also entry 247)

Ohio

605. The Cleveland Museum of Art, 11150 East Boulevard, Cleveland, OH 44106 (slides showing painting and decorative arts)

Ontario

606. Royal Ontario Museum, 100 Queen's Park, Toronto, Ontario M5S 2C6

Texas

607. University of Texas Art Museum, Austin, TX 78712 (excavations)

Washington

608. Seattle Art Museum, Volunteer Park, Seattle, WA 98112

Appendixes

A Curriculum for International Education

Reprinted with the permission of The Asia Society, 725 Park Ave, New York, NY 10021.

What shapes the learning experience? More than anything else, the attitudes of teachers and students about *why* we should learn what we learn. These attitudes determine the commitment we make to teaching and learning certain information and skills and our overall success. What about international education? Do we think it's important? necessary? Or just nice if there is time left over from other subjects? We can, perhaps think of a number of reasons why intercultural education is valuable and good;[1] we can also see, from a recent study,[2] that only 15 percent of the American high school students surveyed believed world survival to be a primary purpose of global education.

The materials presented here—and our purpose in presenting them—is based on the belief that intercultural education is in fact crucial to that survival. Through the mass media, other sophisticated technologies, and increasing cross-cultural "traffic," international education is happening. To avoid misconceptions and distortions, we believe schools must place intercultural education in a framework that will enable students to realize the necessity for and experience the joy and growth of acquiring a world view. These materials are an attempt to contribute to that framework.

The traditional approaches to the study of cultures (memorizing names, dates, and places; impromptu "discussions" of current world issues; transcultural themes; and speculation on the future) do not really help students acquire this broader outlook. Far more effective, it seems to us, is looking at the universal aspects of human life and then at how different peoples have chosen to solve the problems we all face. It is important, then, to consider the similarity of human needs, and the importance of differences, change, interdependence, and conflict.

The Similarity of Human Needs

The human connection between others and us must be clarified. International education should be a study of people that also includes a consideration of us—our patterns, our experiences, our problems, and our solutions to those problems. To this end, students should be made aware that all people strive to satisfy certain needs:

1. Physiological needs: Dependence upon such elements as a supply of food, water, and air has dominated the efforts and energies of people for most of human history.
2. Physical security: The avoidance of pain and disease, the quest for safety, protective security, and freedom from fear are clustered together in this second category.
3. Awareness of the environment: It is not possible to feel secure without being aware of the setting in which one exists and its possible impact upon the self.
4. Affiliation (connecting with others): The striving for a sense of belonging or identity is a fundamental force in the lives of all people.
5. Self-esteem: The need for status, wealth, and prestige is often logically linked to striving for achievement.
6. Self-fulfillment: The need to create, produce, respond esthetically; to pursue a way of life that is physically, intellectually, and spiritually rewarding is also a common human need.
7. Moral needs: While the moral response varies significantly from culture to culture, there is one cross-cultural common denominator: the motivation to help others satisfy, individually or collectively, some aspect of their life needs.

Students can be made aware that peoples of other cultures have developed certain strategies and institutions in an attempt to satisfy comparable human needs. It is obviously true that the existing patterns and customs of a culture greatly affect the present behavior of any people, but over an extended period of time, the needs of a people and the ways in which these needs are met determine and shape the form and the characteristics of that culture. What students can see is that knowledge, beliefs, art, morals, laws, customs, and other skills and habits are results of attempts to satisfy common needs.

Coping with Differences

Societies demonstrate diversity in a great number of areas. There are differences in family structure ranging from extended to nuclear forms, of which ours is an example. Patterns of loyalty among family members can vary. In certain Pacific island cultures, the greatest loyalty is among brothers and sisters; this is not so in most of the world. The concept of time, or at least punctuality, differs from culture to culture. Western cultures often think of time in a linear fashion, so that a past, present, and future are possible. A traditional Navajo conceives of only the immediate moment. In one form of Zen, time is an infinite pool in which an act causes waves or ripples that eventually subside: a place where there is no past, no present, no future.

An assumption behind the Western idea that people are rational beings, freely capable of logical problem solving, is not accepted by many Asian cultures. In the Taoist view, for example, a person is neither a force nor a rational being. Truth is something to be recognized and accepted in a moment of intuitive insight (enlightenment). There are differences in the reward of ownership. To some, an object is worthwhile because of its value; to others, it is prized because of its effect on personal relationships.

Perceptual differences affect assumptions about life. To move students as much as possible to a position where social perceptions can be shared, they can study both how other peoples view themselves and their reality and how other people view us and our reality. At another and probably more important level, students can learn that they also view the world from a specific, culturally conditioned frame of reference; that is, they too have a culturally defined perspective. Students can be given opportunities to consider cultural values at levels deeper than those afforded by the typical "tourist" view: they can be encouraged to see situations through other eyes and to deal with them using a different set of values. They can also try to find out *why* unique behavioral patterns have developed. By examining the causes of behavior, not only can "strange" ways of acting be rendered "unstrange," but the positive and negative consequences of behavior can be clarified.

Change

As a factor in the global system, change is a reality that is potentially both productive and dangerous. New medical discoveries, food technology, new energy processes, information retrieval techniques, communication systems, and problem-solving systems appear promising. Yet new weaponry, insecticides, pollution, atomic wastes, increasing populations, diminishing fuel sources, and urban crime seem threatening. Students need to learn not only that change is inevitable, but that its consequences can be both good and bad. Classroom programs can help students to grasp more than the fact of change; they can prepare students to cope effectively with the forces of change that threaten the earth.

Interdependence

Crop failures, political changes, new lending rates, money devaluations, wars, threats of war, strikes, investment decisions, and trade agreements all have global significance. Late rains in the Ukraine can cause an

American wheat sale to the Soviet Union which, in turn, can affect the price of bread in England. A change in leadership or policy in Libya can directly contribute to oil company executives in Los Angeles losing their positions, farmers paying more for fertilizers in Japan, canceled oil tanker contracts in Spain, and political unrest in India. For a variety of reasons—including the need for food, natural resources, manufactured goods, or financing—one country can be seriously affected by developments in another.

This is a major historical shift. Students need to extend their awareness of connections with other countries beyond the level of knowing where certain natural resources and manufactured products come from. The world marketplace is a complex network and a delicate balance exists among the nations of the globe. Students can be helped to understand the conditions that cause events and to discover the complexity of the causes.

Conflict Management

When negotiations to end the Korean conflict were getting under way in the 1950s, an argument developed over the date for the first meeting. The UN/US command proposed a date, and the Chinese turned it down. Headlines in US newspapers read, "Communists Stall Negotiations," and the stories suggested that this was a Communist phenomenon. The Chinese were not interested in real negotiations, just what one would expect of Communists. The truth was actually quite different. The date proposed by the U.S. was the equivalent in Chinese eyes of proposing to start on Friday the 13th—an unlucky day. As Chinese (not as Communists), they were irritated by the proposal. A date was finally agreed on and the negotiations began, but the incident underscores how difficult cross-cultural communication is and how vital cultural learning has become.

Interactions among societies are dominated and shaped by three forces: exchange (trade agreements, diplomatic bargaining, treaties, alliances, etc.), threats (warnings, forceful statements, military movements, etc.), and integration (cultural exchange, declarations of friendship and respect, cooperative ventures, etc.). Although exchange and integration do play major roles, more and more the international system seems to be shaped by threats, usually given credibility by the power to use military force or to deny access to natural resources. It is an awesome fact of our time that nearly a quarter of a trillion dollars is spent each year to maintain the credibility of threats (estimated to equal the total income of the poorest half of the world). Roughly 0.3 percent of this amount is spent on such activities as the United Nations and the International Labour Organizations. In this context too, students can learn that as voting citizens they play a role in the management of global conflicts, and that the more they know about the rest of the world, the better the decisions they will make.

Materials Evaluation

This form is reprinted here by permission of the Project on Asian Studies in Education, University of Michigan, Ann Arbor.

TITLE, AUTHOR, PUBLISHER, DATE_____

CONTENT SYNOPSIS: _____

_____

I.   *Format and Illustrations*
   A. How does the written text initially impress you (i.e. simple/ confusing layout; current/outdated; easy to use/cumbersome)?

   _____

   B. Describe briefly your impressions of the illustrations (i.e. relationship of pictures to captions; projection of stereotypes, invites inquiry, fosters empathy).

   _____

II.   *Content*
   A. What is the dominant approach (i.e. chronological, thematic, discipline/field, fictional)?

   _____

   B. Given the intended focus of this material, are the topics/ themes treated in depth or in a superficial way? Are there any serious omissions/misrepresentations (i.e. only reference to Taoism is as a religion of superstition that didn't become as popular as Confucianism)?

   _____

III.   *Methodology*
   A. What is the *stated* instructional approach (i.e. concept oriented, skills oriented, comparative study, inquiry method, humanistic or values clarification)?

   _____

B. How is material/information presented (i.e. paragraphs of information followed by questions to test comprehension; case studies with questions on "why," underlying values etc.)?

C. Is there any discrepancy between the stated approach and how the material is presented? Explain.

IV. *Underlying Assumptions*
A. Is there a clear statement of the underlying assumptions in the design of this material or is that left to inference? Explain.

B. What approach is used? Check one or more.
_____Western-centered approach (i.e. accomplishments are measured by Western standards; social and cultural forces are presented as "problems"; the culture is presented as exotic, alien)
_____Asia-centered approach (i.e. culture and/or political developments are presented as rational in own cultural value system/historical context?
_____Eclectic approach (i.e. several possible approaches/ interpretations given)
_____Factual approach (information is presented as data with implied objectivity)
_____Humanistic approach (i.e. the people and their cultural traditions are at the center)

C. What concepts are treated as being of positive or negative value? (i.e. individualism = positive   conformity = negative   nationalism = negative   global interdependence = positive)

D. What is the tone? Give examples (i.e. use of value laden words; clear context and connection between text and illustration; implied racial or ethnic superiority)

V. *Cultural Traditions*
A. Does the material sensitize the learner to the people involved

(their feelings, thought patterns, behaviors)?

_____

B. What about the material does/doesn't contribute to this (i.e. use of literature, music, visual arts, personal accounts, documents, maps, tables)?

_____

C. What new insights does this material potentially offer?

_____

VI. _Use of Material_
   A. What is the stated (or implied) use of this material? Check one or more.

Content Level:	Reading Level:
____introductory material	____early elementary
____comprehensive overall	____elementary
____supplementary material	____junior high
____comprehensive treatment of given subject (be specific)	____high school
	____adult

   B. Is this material suitable for this intended use/level? Be specific.

_____

   C. What other uses could be made of this material?
      ____text, illustrations useful for certain aspects
         Be specific: _____
      ____useful in comparing/contrasting with other approaches
         Be specific: _____
      ____other
         Be specific: _____
      ____not useful, given limitations/drawbacks

VII. _Evaluator_
   A. What information/context should a reader of this evaluation have regarding you (i.e. academic, teaching, travel, living experience)?

_____

Textbook Evaluation Guidelines

Reprinted with the permission of The Asia Society, 725 Park Ave, New York, NY 10021, from Asia in American Textbooks, *pp. 31–33 (Asia Society, 1976).*

I. Format

Describe format and its implications briefly. Appraise text, including cover design, as if you were thumbing through the book with intent to purchase. Does it look like a "real" book or a textbook? What size is the print? Does the book invite you to read on? Why? If not, why not? If you were a student would you want to read it?

II. Disciplines

What are the specific disciplines? Describe weight given to each approach (historical, anthropological, sociological, economic, humanistic, etc.). Is the approach chronological, expository, interpretive, case-study, primary source, or other? Is the primary purpose of the book to introduce Asia or to introduce a discipline?

III. Topics

What are the specific topics covered in the Asian material (e.g., Long March, land reform)? Are there glaring omissions (e.g., the Opium War in treatment of European involvement with China)? Which topics are emphasized? What are the general topics dealt with in world history material? How does coverage of Asia compare with coverage of other regions?

IV. Accuracy and Authenticity

Evaluate accuracy in terms of factual information, use of foreign terms, and sources. Evaluate authenticity. If the material is not authentic, give examples. For instance, if the text relates in the author's own words "A Day in the Life of Beero," is the day an authentic one for an Indian child? Are names and places authentic? Identify and give examples from the text and teacher's guide as follows:
   1. Factual inaccuracies and inauthenticity.
   2. Inauthenticity through invented case studies. Are the names accurate?

3. Inaccuracy in the use of foreign terms (e.g., Mt. Fujiyama, hara-kiri).
4. Inaccuracy in the definition of foreign terms.
5. Inaccuracy through the misspelling of foreign terms.
6. Inaccuracy through the use of out-of-date material.
7. Inaccuracy as the result of omission or a fragmented or superficial treatment of a topic, resulting in distortion.
8. Inaccurate sources used in bibliography.
9. Inaccurate pronunciations in the pronunciation guide.
10. Are authors and consultants qualified in Asian background? Total number of consultants:____; number with Asian specialization:____.
11. How would you rate the overall accuracy/authenticity level of this book? 1) poor 2) fair 3) good 4) excellent

V. Use of Foreign Terms

Please list foreign terms (common words) used in each text by country. Is there a pronunciation guide? Where is the pronunciation guide?

VI. Assumptions and Approaches

Listed below are various approaches and assumptions that occur in textbooks. They may be found in the text, the illustrations, or the end-of-chapter questions.

1. Developmental approaches:
   (a) Does the text emphasize change and growth or persistence and continuity in a culture?
   (b) Is there an assumption that all societies follow a developmental or evolutionary pattern? Does this imply the superiority of the West?
   (c) Are large, powerful societies emphasized to the neglect of the small?
   (d) If comparisons between Asian countries and Western countries are made, how are they made?
   (e) If comparisons are made, is there an effort to compare the "likes"? Are they valid?
   (f) Are the accomplishments of Asian cultures measured by Western standards?
   (g) Are differences between Asian and Western countries explained in such a way that there is an emphasis on what the Asian cultures do not have?

(h) Is Asia seen as a stage for Western history?

(i) Are foreigners always helping or intervening to the extent that the people of the area seem to have little initiative or influence?

(j) Are differences between Asian and Western countries explained in such a way that Asian social and cultural forces are seen as "problems"?

(k) Are terms like "modernization" and "Westernization" used? How are they used and defined?

(l) Is the term "Westernization" used interchangeably with "modernization"?

(m) Is there a dichotomy assumed between tradition and modernity in the text?

(n) Is there a definition of human, societal, or a civilization's worth in economic terms?

(o) Is there an overemphasis on the poverty of a country or area?

(p) Is the study of Asia justified in terms of strategic importance to the U.S.?

(q) What assumptions are made about the relationship between technology and change? Are both the advantages and limitations of technology explored?

(r) Is an effort made to see development issues from Asian perspectives? (See Asia-centered approach below.)

2. Asian superiority approach:
   Are Asian cultures presented as superior to the Western (e.g., more spiritual, exotic, artistic)?

3. Asian inscrutability approach:
   Is Asia presented as mysterious and inscrutable?

4. Asia-centered approach:
   (a) Is the culture presented as rational within its own context and cultural value system?

   (b) Does the text help students develop empathy for other cultures? If so, how?

   (c) Is the culture viewed within an Asian historical context?

   (d) Are there attempts to get beyond the exotic or alien nature of some social customs?

5. Eclectic approach: Is a conscious effort made to present different possible approaches in the text?

VII. General Considerations Concerning Assumptions

1. Does the author recognize his or her assumptions?

2. Is the text consistent in its assumptions?

3. What values or aims does the text promote? Does the text carry this out successfully (e.g., interdependency, Asia as part of the entire world system, futuristic thinking, prevention of war and preservation of peace, restoration of ecological balance, expanded social justice, sharing of world resources)?
4. Are the text's assumptions and values as they apply to different Asian countries consistent? For example, are five-year plans seen as totalitarian in China and progressive in Indonesia?
5. What assumptions are made about the organization of societies and historical change (e.g., organismic, cyclical, diffusionist, historical, geographic, or economic determinist)?
6. Is an effort made to portray both the Great and Little Traditions? (Great Tradition is considered to be classical philosophy, religion, and literature. Little Tradition is considered to be folk myths and practice.)
7. Is there an effort to present a balanced view of topics?
8. Is there a conscious effort to portray pluralism in a society when it exists?

VIII. Humanistic and Human Interest Materials

Humanistic materials include literature (poetry, fiction, diaries, letters, drama, etc.) art, music, philosophy, religion. Human interest materials include such things as letters to the editor of the *Asahi Shimbun* from a Japanese woman, or matrimonial ads in an Indian newspaper.

1. To what extent does the text take a humanistic approach? Are people (men and women) at the center? To what extent does the text include Asian humanistic sources or voices as opposed to outside observers? (e.g., Lu Hsun vs. Pearl S. Buck)
2. Even if the humanities are not introduced as a specific discipline, which humanistic traditions are represented? (e.g., religion, philosophy, literature, music, visual arts, performing arts)
3. How are humanistic/human interest materials used? Give examples.
   (a) Is a humanistic language, style, or tone used?
   (b) Are humanistic materials included to give extra information about an area (i.e., to indicate an area has an art or a literature as well as an economic policy)?
   (c) Are humanistic materials (especially literature) used to increase student understanding of social science concepts (e.g., social change)?
   (d) Are humanistic materials included to increase student appreciation of Asia's cultural heritage?

(e) Are humanistic materials included to illustrate cultural values?

(f) Is humanistic material presented so that students are given direct contact with other peoples and their values and can empathize with them? (Do not confuse creating sympathy with the plight of others with empathy.)

(g) Does humanistic material balance Western observers' interpretations of situations under study? For instance, are Japanese impressions of Perry included in word and picture along with Perry's impressions of the Japanese?

4. Do end-of-chapter questions encourage empathy? When possible, check desired responses in the teacher's guide to see what is expected. Do the end-of-chapter questions encourage ethnocentricity?

5. What about questions that follow humanities material? Are they done sensitively to foster empathy? (Debates that encourage students to decide the value of retaining different cultural practices do not always foster empathy. Nor will everyone empathize with the same material.)

6. Are writings (poetry, journals, quotations, etc.) by Asians set off in a different format or treated as an integral part of the text? If set off, does the design enhance the statement or does it look like an afterthought or something to be skipped over?

7. What Asian humanistic/human interest sources can you recommend be included as source readings either in the body of the text or in the teacher's or student's bibliography?

IX. Style and Tone

1. Are value-laden, ethnocentric, and/or charged words and terminology used (e.g., Red China, Far East, progress, development)?

2. Are cliches used (e.g., "dawn of civilization", "cradle of civilization", "emerging giant")?

3. Is there a we-they tone?

4. Is there a condescending, moralistic, or patronizing tone?

5. Is there a "brotherhood of man" approach that denies differences?

6. Is the treatment of any given topic at such a high level of abstraction that students would have difficulty understanding the material?

7. Is there evidence of racist and/or sexist attitudes on the part of the author (e.g., "white man's burden" or "little brown brother" approach)?

X. Format and Illustrations

1. Do the illustrations "extend" and enhance the text, adding to its meaning, or are they purely decorative?

2. Analyze type, number, and date of illustrations (charts, cartoons, photographs, etc.). Is there a balanced variety? Are art objects, historical paintings, and documents also represented?
3. Are different groups within a society portrayed?
4. Do pictures project stereotypes (e.g., poverty, aggresive behavior, women in subservient or "supporting" roles, "quaint" Asian scenes, modern technology)?
5. If color reproduction is used, is the quality good? What about black and white illustrations?
6. If applicable, what kind of first impressions about Asia does the cover convey? The frontispiece?

XI. Credits

What types of credits are given for illustrations and photos? Do they appear on the same page or in another part of the book? Are dimensions given for art work? Names of artists? Period? Museum? Collection? Are dates given for maps and illustrations?

XII. Source Readings

1. Are source readings in body of text credited? If so, does the credit appear in footnote form on the same page? What kind of information is in the footnote? Does it indicate whether the reading is a direct quote or adapted from another work? Are the translator and source credited?
2. List Asian source readings within text.
3. Are the translations in contemporary language or are they dated?

XIII. Bibliography

Is there a bibliography listing further Asian sources? Are sources listed in the student's book as well as in the teacher's manual? Please list sources. If there is a distinction between student and teacher sources, please make two separate lists. Indicate which sources are humanistic or human interest.

XIV. Supporting Materials

1. Is there an accurate pronunciation guide?
2. Is there a glossary of foreign terms?
3. Is there an index?
4. Is there a teacher's guide?
5. Does the teacher's guide promote the same values and rest on the same assumptions as the student text?

6. Does the teacher's guide make a conscious effort to avoid ethnocentrism? Does it succeed in this?
7. Does the teacher's guide assist in carrying out the objectives of the text? Is the teacher's guide useful?
8. Is the teacher's guide realistic about what can be achieved through the student text?
9. Are humanistic materials made available through the teacher's guide? Are these intended to be shared with the student? Could they have been presented directly to the student?

Directory of Regional China Councils

The following China Councils of The Asia Society focus primarily on adult audiences. Several publish regional resource guides, in addition to those annotated above (entries 545 and others). These addresses of China Council directors and coordinators are printed here by permission of the China Council of The Asia Society, Washington, D.C.

Arizona

Paul Leung (Director)
College of Education
Education Bldg, Rm 428
University of Arizona
Tucson, AZ 85721
Tel: 602-626-1860

Ruth Patzman (Coordinator)
Department of Oriental Studies
University of Arizona
Franklin Bldg, Rm 404
Tucson, AZ 85721
Tel: 602-626-2393

Colorado

Dr. Noel Miner (Director)
725 Gilpin
Boulder, CO 80303
Tel: 303-492-7655

Ms. Alice Renouf (Coordinator)
Office of International Education
University of Colorado
Boulder, CO 80309
Tel: 303-492-7741

Georgia

Professor Everett Keach (Director)
Global Education Program
Department of Social Science
   Education
University of Georgia
Athens, GA 30602
Tel: 404-542-7265

Ms. Nancy E. Pruitt (Coordinator)
Global Education Program
Department of Social Science
   Education
University of Georgia
Athens, GA 30602
Tel: 404-542-7265

Michigan

Professor Warren Cohen (Director)
Department of History
Michigan State University
East Lansing, MI 48824
Tel: 517-355-7507

Ms. Lillian Kumata (Coordinator)
Asian Studies Center
Michigan State University
East Lansing, MI 48824
Tel: 517-353-1680

Minnesota

Mr. Frederick B. Wells (Director)
President, Asian Imports
830 Baker Bldg
Minneapolis, MN 55402
Tel: 612-333-4740

Dr. Richard Bohr (Coordinator)
Midwest China Study Resource
   Center
308 Gullixson Hall
2375 Como Ave W
St. Paul, MN 55108
Tel: 612-641-3238

Missouri

Mr. Michael Witunski (Director)
McDonnell Douglas Corporation
P.O. Box 516
St. Louis, MO 63166
Tel: 314-232-5595

Professor Joel Glassman
   (Coordinator)
Department of Political Science
University of Missouri–St. Louis
8001 Natural Bridge Rd
St. Louis, MO 63121
Tel: 314-553-5521

Ms. Katherine Pierson (Coordinator)
Center for International Studies
University of Missouri–St. Louis
8001 Natural Bridge Rd
St. Louis, MO 63121
Tel: 314-553-5753

North Carolina

Professor Lawrence D. Kessler
   (Director)
Office of International Programs
403 Hamilton Hall 070A
University of North Carolina
   at Chapel Hill
Chapel Hill, NC 27514
Tel: 919-933-5091; 933-3094

Ms. Louisa Kilgroe (Coordinator)
Office of International Programs
403 Hamilton Hall 070A
University of North Carolina
   at Chapel Hill
Chapel Hill, NC 27514
Tel: 919-933-5091

Northwest

Donald Jenkins (Director)
Portland Art Museum
1219 SW Park
Portland, OR 97205
Tel: 503-226-2811

William Campbell (Director)
Attorney
Lindsay, Hart, Weigler
111 SW Columbia, Suite 700
Portland, OR 97201
Tel: 503-226-1191

Ms. Jane Larson (Coordinator)
World Affairs Council of Oregon
1912 SW Sixth Ave, Rm 252
Portland, OR 97201
Tel: 503-229-3049

Seattle Branch

Elizabeth Parry (Director)
School of International Studies
University of Washington
Seattle, WA 98195
Tel: 206-543-0840

William G. Crowell (Coordinator)
East Asia Resource Center
School of International Studies
University of Washington
Seattle, WA 98195
Tel: 206-543-1921

Ohio

Ms. Helen Sandfort (Director)
275 E Dunedin
Columbus, OH 43209
Tel: 614-263-7927

Ms. Sara Mazak (Coordinator)
Department of International Studies
308 Dulles Hall
Ohio State University
Columbus, OH 43210
Tel: 614-422-3838

Southern New England

Dr. John Bryan Starr (Director)
The Yale–China Association
905A Yale Station
New Haven, CT 06520
Tel: 203-436-4422

Ms. Nancy Levenburg (Coordinator)
The Yale–China Association
905A Yale Station
New Haven, CT 06520
Tel: 203-436-4422

Texas

Professor Edward Rhoads (Director)
Center for Asian Studies
Speech Building 310
The University of Texas at Austin
Austin, TX 78712
Tel: 512-471-5236

Mr. James Rice (Coordinator)
Center for Asian Studies
Speech Building 310
The University of Texas at Austin
Austin, TX 78712
Tel: 512-471-5811

Wisconsin

David D. Buck (Director)
Department of History
The University of Wisconsin
   at Milwaukee
Milwaukee, WI 53201
Tel: 414-963-4361

Douglas McLain, Jr. (Coordinator)
Institute of World Affairs
668 Bolton Hall
The University of Wisconsin
   at Milwaukee
Milwaukee, WI 53201
Tel: 414-963-4252

Comparative Chronology of Pre-Modern China

This chronology is issued by the National Committee on US–China Relations, Inc., New York, New York, and is reprinted here by permission.

China	Western & Other
PRIMITIVE SOCIETY (c.600,000–4,000 B.C.) Lantian Man (c.600,000 B.C.)	

	Neanderthal Man (c.200,000 B.C.)
	Domesticated animals
	    (c.9,000–7,500 B.C.)
	Pottery and farming in Mesopotamia
	    (c.7000–6000 B.C.)
	Writing, wheeled vehicles,
	    pottery wheel, sailboat,
	    animal-drawn plough in
	    Sumer (c.3300 B.C.)

Agriculture (c.2700 B.C.) Pottery	Great Pyramids (c.2500 B.C.)
XIA DYNASTY (c.2205–c.1766 B.C.) Domestication of Animals Silk	Stonehenge (c.2000–1400 B.C.)

SHANG DYNASTY
    (c.1766–1122 B.C.)
Trade, cowrie shells as medium
    of exchange
White incised pottery
Carved ivory and jade
Bronze vessels and weapons
Written language
Ancestor worship
	Hammurabi (c.1750 B.C.)
	Aryan invasions, the Vedas
	    (c.1500–1000 B.C.)
	Syrian alphabet (c.1500 B.C.)
	Beginning of Iron Age
	    (c.1200 B.C.)

ZHOU DYNASTY (c.1122–249 B.C.) Spring and Autumn Period (770–481 B.C.)	King Solomon (c.950 B.C.) Homer (?8th Century) Rome founded (?753 B.C.) Buddha (c.560–480 B.C.) Pythagoras (c.525 B.C.)
Iron Age (c.500 B.C.) Metallic coins	

Warring States Period
(403–221 B.C.)
Rise of merchant class, growth
of cities
Philosophy:
Confucius (c.551–479 B.C.)
Laozi (?5th Century B.C.)
Mencius (c.386–312 B.C.)
Zhuangzi (?4th Century B.C.)

Philosophy:
Aristotle (c.384–322 B.C.)
Alexander the Great
(336–323 B.C.)
Hannibal crosses the Alps
(218 B.C.)

QIN DYNASTY (221–207 B.C.)
Emperor Qin Shi Huangdi
Standardization of weights
and measures
Large irrigation projects
Great Wall begun

HAN DYNASTY (206 B.C.–220 A.D.)
Conquest of Korea
Alchemy
Compass
Paper
Introduction to Buddhism
Civil service examinations
Five Classics

Roman aqueducts (c.145 B.C.)
Julius Caesar (c.104–44 B.C.)
Glass-blowing (c.55 B.C.)
Jesus Christ (24 B.C.–30 A.D.)
2nd Destruction of Temple of
Jerusalem (70 A.D.)
Destruction of Pompeii (79 A.D.)

THREE KINGDOMS PERIODS
(220–265 A.D.)
Decline of Confuciansim
Rise of Taoism, Buddhism

JIN DYNASTY (265–420 A.D.)
Barbarian invasions from North

Partition of Roman Empire (285 A.D.)
Visigoths sack Rome (400 A.D.)

SOUTHERN AND NORTHERN
DYNASTIES
(386–581 A.D.)
Unstable period, numerous
kingdoms

Barbarians overrun West (c.440 A.D.)
Justinian's law code (334 A.D.)
Silkworms introduced to Europe
(532 A.D.)
Mohammed (570–632 A.D.)

SUI DYNASTY (590–618 A.D.)
Construction of Grand Central
Block printing

Height of Byzantine, Persian, Arab
civilizations (600 A.D.)

TANG DYNASTY (618–907 A.D.)
Conquest of central Asia and Korea
Cultural flowering: dance; music;
   three-colored pottery; poets
   Li Bo and Du Fu
Gunpowder

Arab invasions of Egypt, Spain,
   Indus Valley (636–711 A.D.)
Spread of Buddhism to Nepal, Tibet
   (700–800 A.D.)
Charlemagne (768–814 A.D.)

FIVE DYNASTIES (907–960 A.D.)
Warlordism
Footbinding
Printing of Confucian classics

SONG DYNASTY (960–1279 A.D.)
Flowering of painting and pottery
Paper currency
Movable type
Neo-Confuciansim

Leif Ericson (1000 A.D.)
Norman conquest of England
   (1066 A.D.)
Crusades (1095–1270 A.D.)
Paper manufactured in Europe
   (c. 1150 A.D.)
Magna Carta (1215 A.D.)
Thomas Aquinas (1225–1274 A.D.)

YUAN (MONGOL) DYNASTY
   (1271–1368 A.D.)
Genghis and Kublai Kahn
Marco Polo
Great road construction
Flowering of classical opera
   and drama
Blue and white porcelain

Papacy moves to Avignon (1308 A.D.)
Gunpowder introduced to Europe
   (1313 A.D.)
Dante (1265–1321 A.D.)
Hundred Years War (1337 A.D.)
Outbreak of Black Death (1347 A.D.)

MING DYNASTY (1386–1644 A.D.)
Commercial expansion
Jesuit missionaries
Finest porcelain

Printing in Europe (1400 A.D.)
Leonardo Da Vinci (1452–1519 A.D.)
Columbus discovers America
   (1492 A.D.)
Martin Luther (1483–1546 A.D.)
Vasco DaGama discovers route to
   India around Cape of Good
   Hope (1498 A.D.)
British defeat Spanish Armada
   (1588 A.D.)

QING (MANCHU) DYNASTY
   (1644–1911 A.D.)

Isaac Newton (1642–1727)
American Revolution (1776–1781)
Napoleonic Wars (1804–1814)

Opium War (1840)
Taiping Rebellion (1850–1864)
Introduction of industry;
   railroads
Impact of Western culture
Christianity

Marx and Engels, *Communist
   Manifesto* (1848)
Telephone (1878)

Table of Variant Spellings

Pinyin	Wade–Giles
Nanjing	Nanking
Beijing	Peking
Xian	Sian
Suzhou	Soochow
Yangzi	Yangtze
Yanan	Yenan
Xinjiang	Sinkiang
Xianggang	Hongkong
Guomindong	Kuomintang
Chiang Ching	Jiang Qing
Deng Xiaoping	Teng Hsiao-p'ing
Hua Guofeng	Hua Kuo-feng
Lin Biao	Lin Piao
Mao Zedong	Mao Tse-tung
Zhao Ziyang	Chao Tzu-yang
Ye Jianying	Yeh Chien-ying
Zhou Enlai	Chou En-lai
Lao Tzu	Lao Tse
Qin	Ch'in
Shigh Huang Di	Shih Huang Ti
Zi Xi	Tzu Hsi

Directory of Suppliers

Directory of Suppliers

ATC Publications
Box 1276
Kankakee, IL 60901

Abelard
10 E 53rd St
New York, NY 10022

Abrams
110 E 59th St
New York, NY 10022

Addison-Wesley Publishing Co.
Jacob Way
Reading, MA 01867

Allyn & Bacon, Inc.
Rockleigh, NJ 07647

American Heritage Publishing Co.
10 Rockefeller Plaza
New York, NY 10020

American Historical Association
400 "A" St, SE
Washington, DC 20003

American Library Association
50 E Huron St
Chicago, IL 60611

American Map Co.
1926 Broadway
New York, NY 10023

Anchor Press—Doubleday
501 Franklin Ave
Garden City, NY 11530

Annals of the American Academy of
Political and Social Science
3937 Chestnut St
Philadelphia, PA 19104

A.R.T.S. Art Resources for Teachers
and Students
32 Market St
New York, NY 10002

Asia Society
725 Park Ave
New York, NY 10021

Asia Society—Washington Center
1785 Massachusetts Ave, NW
Washington, DC 20036

Asian Art Museum of San Francisco
Golden Gate Park
San Francisco, CA 94118

Association Films
866 Third Ave
New York, NY 10022

Association for Asian Studies
1 Lane Hall
University of Michigan
Ann Arbor, MI 48109

Atheneum Books
597 Fifth Ave
New York, NY 10017

Atlantis Productions
1252 La Granada Dr
Thousand Oaks, CA 91360

Avon Books
959 Eighth Ave
New York, NY 10019

BAYCEP-Bay Area China Education
Project
Lou Henry Hoover Building
Stanford University
Stanford, CA 94305

BFA Educational Media
2211 Michigan Ave
Santa Monica, CA 90406

A.S. Barnes & Co.
Forsgate Dr
Cranbury, NJ 08512

Bantam Books Inc.
666 Fifth Ave
New York, NY 10019

Barron's
113 Crossways Park Dr
Woodbury, NY 11797

Basic Books
10 E 53rd St
New York, NY 10022

Bay Area China Education Project
Lou Henry Hoover Building
Stanford University
Stanford, CA 94305

Bellerophon
36 Anacapa Street
Santa Barbara, CA 93101

Benefic Press
1900 N Narragansett
Chicago, IL 60639

Bobbs-Merrill Co.
4300 W 62nd St
Indianapolis, IN 46268

Bradbury Press Inc.
2 Overhill Rd
Scarsdale, NY 10583

**Brigham Young University
Center for International and
  Area Studies
Provo, UT 84602**

CBS News
Dolores Sura
524 W 57th St
New York, NY 10019

CMS Records
14 Warren St
New York, NY 10017

Caedmon Records Inc.
1995 Broadway
New York, NY 10023

Cambridge Documentary Films
Box 385
Cambridge, MA 02139

Cambridge University Press
32 E 57th St
New York, NY 10022

Cardinal Publishers
Box 207
Davis, CA 95616

Carroll County Public Schools
Westminster, MD 21156

Celestial Arts
231 Adrian Rd
Millbrae, CA 94030

Center for Teaching About China
407 S Dearborn
Chicago, IL 60605

Centron Educational Films
1621 W 9th St
Lawrence, KS 66044

Childrens Book and Music Center
2500 Santa Monica Blvd
Santa Monica, CA 90404

Children's Museum
300 Congress St
Boston, MA 02210

Childrens Press
1224 W Van Buren St
Chicago, IL 60607

China Books and Periodicals Inc.
2929 24th St
San Frnacisco, CA 94110
and
174 W Randolph St
Chicago, IL 60601
and
125 Fifth Ave
New York, NY 10003

China Council of The Asia Society
1785 Massachusetts Ave, NW
Washington, DC 20036

Chinese Culture Foundation
750 Kearny St
San Francisco, CA 94108

Chinese for Affirmative Action
121 Waverly Pl
San Francisco, CA 94108

Chinese Information Service
159 Lexington Ave
New York, NY 10016

Churchill Films
662 N Robertson Blvd
Los Angeles, CA 90069

Cinema Perspectives
200 Park Ave S
New York, NY 10003

Charles W. Clark Co. Inc.
168 Express Dr S
Brentwood, NY 11717

Clearvue
6666 N Oliphant Ave
Chicago, IL 60631

Cleveland Museum of Art
11150 East Blvd
Cleveland, OH 44106

Cloudburst Press
2116 Western Ave
Seattle, WA 91821

Kenneth E. Clouse
333 Quail Hollow Rd
Felton, CA 95018

Collier/Macmillan
866 Third Ave
New York, NY 10022

Columbia University Press
562 W 113th St
New York, NY 10025

Conflict Games
Box 432
Normal, IL 61761

Congressional Quarterly Inc.
1414 22nd Ave, NW
Washington, DC 20037

Contemporary Books Inc.
180 N Michigan
Chicago, IL 60601

Continental Press
520 E Bainbridge St
Elizabethtown, PA 17022

David C. Cook Publishers
850 N Grove Ave
Elgin, IL 60120

Coward, McCann, and Geoghagen,
    Inc.
200 Madison Ave
New York, NY 10016

Criterion Books/Harper & Row
10 E 53rd St
New York, NY 10022

Thomas Y. Crowell
10 E 53rd St
New York, NY 10016

Crown Publishers
One Park Ave
New York, NY 10016

Crystal Productions
107 Pacific Ave
Aspen, CO 81611

Current Affairs
Box 426
Ridgefield, CT 06877

Current History
4225 Main St
Philadelphia, PA 19127

DaCapo Press
227 W 17th St
New York, NY 10011

John Day. Co.
10 E 53rd St
New York, NY 10022

Delacorte Press
One Dag Hammarskjold Plaza
New York, NY 10017

Denoyer-Geppert
5235 Ravenswood Ave
Chicago, IL 60640

Detroit Institute of Arts
5200 Woodward Ave
Detroit, MI 48202

Dharma Publishing
5856 Doyle St
Emeryville, CA 94608

Dial Press
One Dag Hammarskjold Plaza
New York, NY 10017

Dodd, Mead and Co.
79 Madison Ave
New York, NY 110016

Dorrance & Co.
Cricket Terrace Center
Ardmore, PA 19003

Doubleday and Co., Inc.
501 Franklin Ave
Garden City, NY 11530

Dover Publications Inc.
180 Varick St
New York, NY 10014

E.P. Dutton & Co., Inc.
201 Park Ave S
New York, NY 10003

ERIC Document Reproduction
  Service
Box 190
Arlington, VA 22210

Editorial Research Reports
1414 22nd St, NW
Washington, DC 20037

Educational Activities
Box 392
Freeport, NY 11520

Educational Design
47 W 13th St
New York, NY 10011

Elsevier–Nelson
2 Park Ave
New York, NY 10016

Empire State College
State University of New York
Saratoga Springs, NY 12866

Encore Visual Education
1235 S Victory Blvd
Burbank, CA 91502

Encyclopedia Britannica Educational
  Corp.
425 N Michigan Ave
Chicago, IL 60611

Eurasia Press
55 W 42nd St
New York, NY 10036

Facts on File
119 W 57th St
New York, NY 10019

Farrar, Straus & Giroux
19 Union Square W
New York, NY 10003

Fawcett Book Group
1515 Broadway
New York, NY 10036

Feminist Press
Box 334
Old Westbury, NY 11568

Fideler Social Studies
31 Ottawa Ave NW
Grand Rapids, MI 49503

Film Images
1034 Lake St
Oak Park, IL 60301

Filmakers Library
133 E 58th St
New York, NY 10022

Filmfair Communications
10900 Ventura Blvd
Studio City, CA 91604

Films Inc.
733 Green Bay Rd
Wilmette, IL 60091

Five College Center for East Asian
  Studies
Churchill House
97 Spring St
Amherst, MA 01002

Folkways Records
43 W 61st St
New York, NY 10023

Foreign Policy Association
205 Lexington Ave
New York, NY 10016

Four Winds Press
50 W 44th St
New York, NY 10036

Free Press
866 Third Ave
New York, NY 10022

Freer Gallery of Art
12th & Jefferson Drive, SW
Washington, DC 20560

GEM Publications
Gary E. McCuen
411 Mallalieu Dr
Hudson, WI 54016

GNP Great Plains National Instruc-
tional Television Library
Box 80669
Lincoln, NE 68501

Garrard Publishing Co.
1607 N Market St
Champaign, IL 61820

Global Perspectives in Education,
Inc.
218 E 18th St
New York, NY 10003

David Godine
306 Dartmouth St
Boston, MA 02116

Golden Press
1220 Mound Ave
Racine, WI 53404

Great Eastern Book Co.
Box 271
Boulder, CO 80306

Great Plains National Instructional
Television Library
Box 80669
Lincoln, NE 68501

Greenhaven Press
577 Shorevieew Park Rd
St. Paul, MN 55112

Grove Press
196 W Houston St
New York, NY 10014

Guidance Associates
Box 3000
Communications Park
Mt. Kisco, NY 10549

Hammond Map Co.
515 Valley St
Maplewood, NJ 07040

Harcourt, Brace, Jovanovich
757 Third Ave
New York, NY 10017

Harper & Row
10 East 53rd St
New York, NY 10022

Harvard University Pres:
79 Garden St
Cambridge, MA 02138

Harvard University Press
Audiovisual Division
79 Garden St
Cambridge, MA 02138

Hastings House
10 E 40th St
New York, NY 10016

Hawthorn (Dutton)
2 Park Ave
New York, NY 10016

Heinemann Educational Books Inc.
4 Front St
Exeter, NH 03833

Hill and Wang
19 Union Square
New York, NY 10003

Holt, Rinehart and Winston
383 Madison Ave
New York, NY 10017

Houghton Mifflin Co.
2 Park St
Boston, MA 02107

Hubbard Scientific
1946 Raymond Dr
Northbrook, IL 60062

Indiana University
Department of East Asian Languages
and Cultures
East Asian Studies Center
Goodbody Hall
Bloomington, IN 47405

Indiana University Press
Tenth & Morton Sts
Bloomington, IN 47405

Information Center on
Children's Cultures
331 E 38th St
New York, NY 10016

Institute of Texan Cultures
Box 1226
San Antonio, TX 78294

International Film Bureau
332 S Michigan Ave
Chicago, IL 60604

International Film Foundation
200 W 72nd St
New York, NY 10023

Island Heritage
324 Kamani St
Honolulu, HI 96813

January Productions
124 Rea Ave
Hawthorne, NJ 07506

Journal of General Education
Pennsylvania State University Press
University Park, PA 16802

Karol Media
625 From Rd
Paramus, NJ 07652

Kendall/Hunt Publishing Co.
131 S Locust St
Dubuque, IA 52001

Alfred A. Knopf, Inc.
201 E 50th St
New York, NY 10022

Kodansha International
10 E 53rd St
New York, NY 10022

Robert E. Krieger Publications
Box 542
Huntington, NY 11743

LCA Learning Corporation of
America
1350 Ave of the Americas
New York, NY 10019

Learning Resources in International
Studies
60 E 42nd St
New York, NY 10017

Lerner Publications
241 First Ave N
Minneapolis, MN 55401

Libraries Unlimited
Box 263
Littleton, CO 80160

J.B. Lippincott Co.
East Washington Square
Philadelphia, PA 19105

Little, Brown and Co.
34 Beacon St
Boston, MA 02106

Littlefield, Adams & Co.
81 Adams Dr
Totowa, NJ 07512

Longman Inc.
19 W 44th St
New York, NY 10036

Lothrop, Lee and Shepard
105 Madison Ave
New York, NY 10016

MIT Press
28 Carleton St
Cambridge, MA 02142

Gary E. McCuen
GEM Publications
411 Mallalieu Dr
Hudson, WI 54016

McDougal, Littell & Company
Box 1667 C
Evanston, IL 60204

McGill University Press
1020 Pine Ave W
Montreal, Quebec H3A 1A2, Canada

McGraw-Hill
1221 Ave of the Americas
New York, NY 10020

McIntrye Visual Publications Inc.
716 Center St
Lewiston, NY 14092

David McKay Company
2 Park Ave
New York, NY 10016

MacLean Hunter Learning Resources
708 Third Ave
New York, NY 10017

Macmillan Films Inc.
34 Macquesten Parkway S
Mt. Vernon, NY 10550

Macmillan Publishing Company
866 Third Ave
New York, NY 10022

Macrae Smith
Routes 54 & Old 147
Turbotville, PA 17772

Marshfilm
Box 8082
Shawnee Mission, KS 66208

Mass Communications, Inc.
23 White Birch Rd
Weston, CT 06883

Media Guild
118 South Acacia, Box 881
Solana Beach, CA 92075

Mentor Books (New American
   Library)
120 Woodbine St
Bergenfield, NJ 07621

Merit Audio Visual
7 W 81st St
New York, NY 10024

Merrill
1300 Alum Creek Dr
Columbus, OH 43216

Julian Messner
1230 Ave of the Americas
New York, NY 10020

Metropolitan Museum of Art
Fifth Ave & 82nd St
New York, NY 10028

Midwest China Center
308 Gullixson Hall
2375 Como Ave W
St. Paul, MN 55108

Miller–Brody Productions
342 Madison Ave
New York, NY 10017

Minneapolis Institute of Arts
2400 Third Ave S
Minneapolis, MN 55404

Monthly Review
62 W 14th St
New York, NY 10011

William Morrow & Co.
105 Madison Ave
New York, NY 10016

Multi-Media Productions
Box 5097
Stanford, CA 94305

Museum of the American China
   Trade
215 Adams St
Milton, MA 02186

National Assessment and Dissemi-
   nation Center
49 Washington Ave
Cambridge, MA 02140

National Committee on US-China
   Relations
777 United Nations Plaza
New York, NY 10017

National Film Board of Canada
1251 Ave of the Americas
New York, NY 10020

National Gallery of Art
Washington, DC 20565

National Geographic Educational
   Services
Washington, DC 20036

National Public Radio
2025 M St, NW
Washington, DC 20036

Thomas Nelson
Box 946
Nashville, TN 37203

Nelson Gallery of Art
4525 Oak St
Kansas City, MO 64111

New American Library
120 Woodbine St
Bergenfield, NJ 07621

New Directions
80 Eighth Ave
New York, NY 10011

New Haven Colony Historical
   Society
114 Whitney Ave
New Haven, CT 06510

New York Graphic Society
140 Greenwich Ave
Greenwich CT 06830

New York State Education
  Department
Bureau of General Education
  Curriculum Development
Albany, NY 12234

New York University
Asian Studies Curriculum Center
635 East Building
Washington Square
New York, NY 10003

New York University Press
113-15 University Place
New York, NY 10003

Newsweek
444 Madison Ave
New York, NY 10022

North Carolina State University
Office of Publications
School of Education
Box 5096, Poe Hall
Raleigh, NC 27650

W.W. Norton Co.
500 Fifth Ave
New York, NY 10036

Nystrom
3333 N Elson Avenue
Chicago, IL 60618

Oberlin College
East Asian Studies Center
Oberlin, OH 44074

Oceana Publications
Dobbs Ferry, NY 10522

Ohio State University
East Asian Studies Program
308 Dulles Hall
230 W 17th Ave
Columbus, OH 43210

Ohio State University
Service Center for Teachers of Asian
  Studies
29 W Woodruff Ave
Columbus, OH 43210

Outdoor Pictures
Box 277
Anacortes, WA 98221

Overseas Development Council
1717 Massachusetts Ave, NW
Washington, DC 20036

Oxford see Sadlier/Oxford

PBS Video
475 L'Enfant Plaza, SW
Washington, DC 20024

Pacific Books
Box 558
Palo Alto, CA 94302

Pantheon
201 E 50th St
New York, NY 10022

Parents Magazine Press
52 Vanderbilt Ave
New York, NY 10017

Pathfinder Press
410 West St
New York, NY 10014

Penguin Books
625 Madison Ave
New York, NY 10022

Peter Pauper Press
135 W 50th St
New York, NY 10020

Phi Delta Kappa
Eighth St & Union Ave
Bloomington, IN 47401

Philomel Books
200 Madison Ave
New York, NY 10016

Pictura Films
111 Eighth Ave
New York, NY 10011

Prentice-Hall
Englewood Cliffs, NJ 07632

Prentice-Hall Developmental Learning
  Centers
Box 655
West Paterson, NJ 07424

Prentice-Hall Media
150 White Plains Rd
Tarrytown, NY 10591

Presidio Press
Box 978
Edison, NJ 08817

G.P. Putnam
200 Madison Ave
New York, NY 10016

Pyramid Films
Box 1048
Santa Monica, CA 90406

Q-Ed Productions Inc.
Box 4029
Westlake Village, CA 91359

Rand, McNally
Box 7600
Chicago, IL 60680

Random House
201 E 50th St
New York, NY 10022

Rowman & Littlefield
81 Adams Dr
Totowa, NJ 07511

Royal Ontario Museum
100 Queen's Park
Toronto, Ontario M5S 2C6, Canada

Running Press
38 S 19th St
Philadelphia, PA 19103

SRA Science Research Associates
155 N Wacker Dr
Chicago, IL 60606

Sadlier/Oxford
11 Park Place
New York, NY 10007

St. Louis Art Museum
Forest Park
St. Louis, MO 63110

St. Martin's Press
Box 5352
New York, NY 10163

Scarecrow Press
52 Liberty St
Metuchen, NJ 08840

Schocken Books
200 Madison Ave
New York, NY 10016

Scholastic
50 W 44th St
New York, NY 10036

Scholastic Book Services
904 Sylvan Ave
Englewood Cliffs, NJ 07632

Science Research Associates
155 N Wacker Dr
Chicago, IL 60606

Charles Scribner's Sons
597 Fifth Ave
New York, NY 10017

Seabolm Design
Route 1, Box 2188
Lopez Island, WA 98261

Seabury Press
Somers, CT 06071

Seattle Art Museum
Volunteer Park
Seattle, WA 98112

M.E. Sharpe
901 N Broadway
White Plains, NY 10603

Silver–Burdett
250 James St
Morristown, NJ 07960

Simile II
Box 910
Del Mar, CA 92014

Sino Publishing Co.
745 Fifth Ave
New York, NY 10051

Social Education
3615 Wisconsin Ave, NW
Washington, DC 20016

Social Studies School Service
10,000 Culver Blvd
Culver City, CA 90230

Speed Art Museum
2035 S Third St
Louisville, KY 40208

Spencer Museum of Art
University of Kansas
Lawrence, KS 66045

Spoken Arts, Inc.
310 North Ave
New Rochelle, NY 10801

Stanford University Press
Stanford, CA 94305

Sterling Publishing Co.
2 Park Ave
New York, NY 10016

Stryker-Post Publications, Inc.
888 17th St, NW
Washington, DC 20006

Teachers College Press
1234 Amsterdam Ave
New York, NY 10027

Theory Into Practice
College of Education
Ohio State University
149 Arps Hall, 1945 N High St
Columbus, OH 43210

Time-Life Books
777 Duke St
Alexandria, VA 22314

Time-Life Films
100 Eisenhower Dr
Paramus, NJ 07652

Charles E. Tuttle Co.
26-28 S Main St
Rutland, VT 05701

United Learning
6633 W Howard St
Chicago, IL 60648

United Nations
Information Centre
New York, NY 10017

US-China Peoples Friendship
  Association
635 S Westlake
Los Angeles, CA 90057
  and
41 Union Square W
New York, NY 10003

US Committe for UNICEF
331 E 38th St
New York, NY 10016

U.S. Government
  Bureau of Mines
  Washington, DC 20240

  Congress. House
  Washington, DC 20515

  Congress. Senate
  Washington, DC 20510

  Department of Agriculture
  Washington, DC 20250

  Department of Defense
  Washington, DC 20301

  Department of Education
  Washington, DC 20202

  Department of State
  Washington, DC 20520

  Library of Congress
  Washington, DC 20540

  National Defense University
  Research Directorate
  Washington, DC 20319

  National Institutes of Health
  Bethesda, MD 20014

  Senate
  Washington, DC 20510

  The Smithsonian Institution
  Washington, DC 20560

  Superintendent of Documents
  Washington, DC 20402

University of Arizona
Department of Oriental Studies
  East Asia Center
Tucson, AZ 85721

University of British Columbia
China Resources Project
Buchanan Building 374
Vancouver, British Columbia
  V6R 1W5 Canada

University of California
Extension Media Center
Berkeley, CA 94720

University of California Press
2223 Fulton St
Berkeley, CA 94720

University of Chicago
East Asian Resource and Education
  Center
Kelly Hall 403, 5848 University Ave
Chicago, IL 60637

University of Chicago Press
5801 Ellis Ave
Chicago, IL 60637

University of Connecticut
School of Education
Storrs, CT 06268

University of Hawaii
East Asian Language and Area Center
Moore Hall 315, 1890 East-West Rd
Honolulu, HI 96822

University of Illinois
Center for Asian Studies
1208 W California Ave
Urbana, IL 61801

University of London
School of Oriental and African
  Studies
Market St
London, WC7E 7HP, England

University of Michigan
Museum of Art
525 S State Rd
Ann Arbor, MI 48109

University of Michigan
Project on East Asian Studies in
  Education–China
Room 108, Lane Hall
Ann Arbor, MI 48109

University of Missouri
Asia Resource Center
8001 Natural Bridge Rd
St. Louis, MO 63121

University of Texas
Center for Asian Studies
Texas Program for Educational
  Resources on Asia
Austin, TX 78712

University of Texas
Institute of Texan Cultures
Box 1226
San Antonio, TX 78294

University of Virginia
East Asian Language and Area Center
1644 Oxford Rd
Charlottesville, VA 22903

University of Washington
School of International Studies
East Asia Resource Center
Seattle, WA 98195

Van Nostrand Reinhold Co.
135 W 50th St
New York, NY 10020

Vanguard Press
424 Madison Ave
New York, NY 10017

Ventura County Superintendent
  of Schools
535 E Main St
Ventura, CA 93009

Viking Press
625 Madison Ave
New York, NY 10022

Vintage (Random House)
201 East 50th St
New York, NY 10022

Visual Education Corporation
14 Washington Rd
Princeton, NJ 08540

WNET/TV
356 W 58th St
New York, NY 10019

Wadsworth Atheneum
600 Main St
Hartford, CT 06103

J. Weston Walch
Box 658
Portland, ME 04104

Henry Z. Walck
2 Park Ave
New York, NY 10016

Washington Square Press
1230 Ave of the Americas
New York, NY 10020

Watson-Guptill
1515 Broadway
New York, NY 10036

Franklin Watts
730 Fifth Ave
New York, NY 10019

Weatherhill
Salem, MA 01970

Westminster Press
925 Chestnut St
Philadelphia, PA 19107

Westview Press
5500 Central Ave
Boulder, CO 80301

Albert Whitman & Co.
560 W Lake St
Chicago, IL 60606

H.W. Wilson Co.
950 University Ave
Bronx, NY 10452

Worldmark Press
242 E 50th St
New York, NY 10022

Yale Divinity School
Visual Education Service
409 Prospect St
New Haven, CT 06511

Yale University
Council on East Asian Studies
85 Trumbull St
New Haven, CT 06520

Young People's Specials
140 W Ninth St
Cincinnati, OH 45202

Indexes

Author and Name Index

Title Index

This index includes series titles. The references are to entry, not page numbers. The following abbreviations are used to indicate nonbook formats: au (audiorecording), f (film), fs (filmstrip), per (periodical), sl (slide), sp (study print), tr (transparency), vr (videorecording).

Institution Index

This index lists the organizations found throughout the book, and includes permutations of their names. The references are to entry, not page, numbers.

Subject Index

Note: All of the references are to entry, not page, numbers. "China" refers to the
entire course of Chinese life or portions of it prior to 1949. "PRC" refers to works
dealing with the post 1949 period only. "Taiwan" is used to refer to both the
island and to the Republic of China, its government since 1949.

Formats other than print are indicated in parentheses after the entry number.
These include audiorecordings (au), films (f), filmstrips (fs), kits, maps (m),
periodicals (per), slides (sl), study prints (sp), transparencies (tr), and videore-
cordings (vr).

The historical period covered is indicated when warranted. In addition, works
falling into one or more of the categories noted below are so designated in italics:

annuals
anthologies
art reproductions
autobiographies
bibliographies
biographies
case studies
Chinese viewpoints
chronological tables
collected biographies
collections
coloring books
compared with
critical studies
directories
documents
dramatizations
encyclopedias
excerpts
exhibitions
fictional treatment
for bilingual education teachers
general works and textbooks
guidebooks

historical maps
historical treatment
illustrations
interviews
laws
legends
manuals
nonnarrated films
PRC viewpoints
papercut illustrations
personal observations
photographs
profiles
programmed texts
readings
reproductions
statistics
Taiwan viewpoints
teaching materials
teaching units
textbooks
texts with commentaries
writings
yearbooks

This index follows the style and structure of PRECIS (PREserved Context Index System), slightly modified in the interest of brevity and typography.